To Christine

with gratitude

for

help in the

tradition

THE HEAVENLY WITCH

By the same author

Betwixt Heaven and Charing Cross: A Documentary History of Saint
Martin-in-the-Fields
Westminster Abbey—Its Links with the Famous
Dick Shepherd, A Biography

THE HEAVENLY WITCH

The Story of The Maréchale

by

Carolyn Scott

HAMISH HAMILTON LONDON

First published in Great Britain 1981
by Hamish Hamilton Ltd
Garden House 57–59 Long Acre London WC2E 9JZ

Copyright © 1981 by Carolyn Scott

British Library Cataloguing in Publication Data

Scott, Carolyn
   The heavenly witch.
   1. Booth, Catherine
   2. Salvation Army – Biography
   267'.15'0924   BX9743.B6

   ISBN 0–241–10412–2

Photoset, printed and bound
in Great Britain by
Redwood Burn Limited
Trowbridge & Esher

'Aimez toujours et malgré tout. It requires a broken heart to love as Christ loved.'
                                        La Maréchale

For José and Noel

LIST OF ILLUSTRATIONS

Between pages 118 and 119

1. William Booth
2. Catherine Booth
3. Kate Booth in 1881
4. The Maréchale with her first group of officers
5. The trial at Boudry, 1883, by Paul Bouvier
6. La Maréchale in 1890
7. La Maréchale with two of her children
8. Arthur and Catherine Booth-Clibborn, 1887

Between pages 150 and 151

9. Cartoon published in *John Bull*, 1905
10. Family portrait
11. The Maréchale in 1913
12. Arthur Booth-Clibborn
13. The Maréchale with her twenty-fifth grandchild
14. At the Metropolitan Hall, Dublin, 1924
15. Arthur and Catherine at Margate

ACKNOWLEDGEMENTS

My deep gratitude to the many friends and relatives of the Maré-chale for their loving and generous help and co-operation, and especially to Theodore Booth-Clibborn, her son. Also to Colonel Clarke, Editor-in-Chief of the Salvation Army, and his staff, for their interest, patience, and enthusiasm, to Ruth Lees-Jones, Robert Booth, George Brown, Jean and Leslie Slide.

PROLOGUE

When the Maréchale was in her nineties she began to wear pink.
'I have worn navy all my life,' she said. 'Now I shall wear pink.'
And she wore it with the delight and the charm of a child, sport-
ing riotous pink silk bonnets that made people look at her and
smile.

If the weather was warm enough, she walked in the garden of
her Devon cottage among the rockeries and flower-beds. Often,
under her breath, she sang songs of victory:

   '*Aimez toujours et malgré tout,*
   Aimez toujours!'

Whatever happens, never stop loving. Sometimes she sat in
the kitchen and wept. 'I am doing so little for the Lord,' she said.
The rest of the time she spent in bed, writing. If anyone tried to
indulge her, she was indignant: 'I am a warrior!'

Seventy years earlier, in 1881, the Salvation Army sent its first
soldiers to France: three young girls wearing navy uniforms
with crimson ribbons round their bonnets. Captain Kate Booth,
the General's eldest daughter, was twenty-two years old, with
long fair hair and blue eyes. Neither of her lieutenants could
speak French. One played the guitar. Years later, Kate's most
vivid memory was of her mother's tears 'dropping on my felt
boots as she laced them up.'

There were three farewell meetings in London, and women
with red armbands and men in red jerseys thronged the galleries
and stood in the aisles to cheer. Catherine Booth, the General's
wife, presented her daughter with the colours to take to France:
it was the first Army flag, and Catherine had embroidered it
herself, red for the saving blood, blue for holiness, and the
golden star of the Spirit.

'Carry it into the slums and alleys and preach under its
shadow wherever there are lost and perishing souls,' she said.
'Charge on the hosts of hell and see whether they will not turn
and flee.' Kate called Christianity, heroism. Within a week she

was to be ridiculed, sworn at, jeered at, and pelted with stones and mud. Later she was to be put in gaol.

'Some friends think it does not cost us what it would cost them to give up their children for such work,' said her mother. 'They do not know us. I do not think any mother could have felt more the difficulties and dangers connected with this work than I have. But I have offered her for France. The Lord will take care of her, though I feel that she has gone from me for ever.'

Kate's father saw them off at Victoria station. 'You have remarkable instincts,' he said to her. 'Follow them, and you will never go wrong.'

'You have a chance the angels in heaven covet,' wrote her brother.

In France, Kate engaged a French teacher for five francs an hour and dismissed him because he was not colloquial enough. Then with nothing but a Bible and a dictionary, she began to preach. At first they called her La Capitaine, but soon she became famous throughout Paris as the Field-Marshal, or La Maréchale.

'Our precious one has gone,' wrote Mrs Booth to a friend. 'Satan says it will kill her, or that she will come back a helpless invalid for life. The doctor told me this, and Satan has repeated it night and day ever since. I can only say "Lord, I have given her to Thee".'

Fields and trees swept away from the bow window of the cottage bedroom, beyond the bluebell wood, 1400 feet down to the Devon sea. Everything in the room was blue, and much of her time was spent there, receiving visitors like royalty and writing letters in big, exuberant handwriting, filling all the space and writing round the margin.

As she grew older, her letters corresponded more exactly with those she used to write a long time ago when she was young. 'Dear Comrade,' they began, and ended, 'Yours in love and fire, La Maréchale'.

CHAPTER 1

William Booth is described with exasperated admiration as a God-infested man: inevitably those born to him became infested too. Kate was born on 18 September 1858, the first girl after two boys, with her father's profile and her mother's eyes.

'You are not in this world for yourself,' said her mother. 'You have been sent for others. The world is waiting for you.

'The most important matter for a parent to settle in her own mind,' she said, 'is to whom this child belongs. Is it mine, or is it the Lord's?' The answer, at the birth of each of her children, was given gladly and without hesitation. The struggle began not before the glorious presentation at the altar, but afterwards, when it became evident that the Lord had taken her at her word. Illogically for a woman so full of common sense, whose life was one long willing sacrifice, realisation of the inevitable provoked unjustified dismay, and the cry 'Let this cup pass from me!'

Just before Kate was born, Catherine began to pray aloud in the little Bethesda Chapel at Gateshead where William was minister. Praying was not a woman's task, and people came especially to see and hear her, like watching a side-show at a fair. She also started house to house visiting, climbing the long, steep Gateshead hills to dingy back parlours where she was confronted with grotesque caricatures of her own meagre but blissful existence.

'I remember finding a woman lying on a heap of rags,' she said later. 'She had just given birth to twins and there was nobody to look after her. By her side was a crust of bread and a small lump of lard. I was soon busy trying to make her a little more comfortable. The babies, I washed in a broken pie dish.'

William called his wife God's love gift to him, more precious to his sight day by day. Catherine called William 'a stranger who drew around him the finest tendrils of my heart.' Foolishness irked her, but inequality, poverty, exploitation and despair, left her kneeling in tears, praying with her arms round

1

William's neck.

'I never look at a little child but I feel unutterable things,' she told him. 'What influences will gather round it in its life's pilgrimage? What friends will aid it? What foes try to ruin it?'

When Kate was born, her parents were both twenty-nine years old. Catherine, with dark hair and sparkling eyes, was the older by two months, neat, quiet and indomitable, the practical, analytical mind behind her husband's impulsive, creative spirit. William was unknown: dramatic, depressive, with his black beard, long Jewish nose, and burning eyes, a Methodist minister of the New Connexion, ardent and out on a limb, at loggerheads with his colleagues, suffering a final term on the circuit in the belief that he was then to be returned to the itinerant revival work that he loved.

They were neither aristocrats like Shaftesbury nor visionaries like Blake. William's father had been an opportunist builder who died in debt; William began work at thirteen as a pawnbroker's apprentice. Before he met Catherine, he had been expelled from his local Methodist chapel for revivalist preaching. Catherine had been expelled for supporting Reformers in their bid for a return to primitive Methodism. Both were on fire with a faith kindled much like Wesley's, on the mean altars of their hearts, where it burned stubbornly and chaotically with ever bright undying blaze. Earnest proclaimers of love divine all loves excelling, they proved the quality of God's love by exhibiting an excess of their own – for each other and for those around them.

Conscientious, direct, and clear as a bell when it came to following the course where duty lay, Catherine called herself 'One of the most timid and bashful disciples the Lord Jesus ever had,' her head constantly challenging conventions which her heart held dear. When Kate was two, Catherine began, almost involuntarily, to preach. In the past she had excused herself 'because of the babies': suddenly she saw the real stumbling-block to be her own timidity, and she set herself the quiet resolution to preach 'or die in the attempt'.

William watched his wife's new achievement with pride and astonishment. Newspapers condemned her as unseemly, immodest, and vulgar, all of which hurt her badly but left her unrepentant. When William was ill, she took over his engagements and confounded the Methodist Conference, which referred stuffily to the 'perambulations of the male and female'. It also turned a resolutely deaf ear to William's pleas, at the end of his term in Gateshead, to return to itinerant evangelism, offering him instead a renewal of the Newcastle Circuit.

Catherine was prepared to go to the workhouse if necessary. 'Does securing our bread and cheese make that right which would otherwise be wrong?' she asked. 'I cannot believe it would be right to spend another year plodding round this wreck of a circuit preaching to twenty or thirty people when he might be preaching to thousands.

'God has promised to feed and clothe us and I am willing to trust Him.'

William was more cautious, pacing miles each day without coming to any conclusion, depressed and unsure of himself, fretting over the future of 'my precious children'. In the end, 'on their knees', they decided to resign, and Catherine felt happier than she had done for months. There were now four children, and she and William were giving up home and income to trust in God as truly, she said, as Abraham did when he left his native land: 'And like Abraham, we have no idea what God is going to do with us.'

They went first to the Mumfords, Catherine's parents in Brixton, the children sent cheaply by the long sea route, with all the gaiety of a summer adventure. 'Katie is a little gem,' rejoiced Catherine. 'She looks so well and jaunts about like a little queen. Everybody falls in love with her, but she has the facility of keeping them at arm's length!' Later, and with hindsight, she made a more serious assessment. 'I am convinced,' she said, 'that the Spirit of God works on little children long before grown-up people think they are able to understand. From the earliest dawnings of reason, Katie was favoured with the fashioning of the Holy Spirit.'

It was a fashioning augmented by Catherine's quiet but dogmatic tenacity. 'There is a way of speaking to and handling an infant compatible with the utmost love and tenderness, which teaches it that mother is not to be trifled with,' she was to write later. 'Although she loves and caresses, she is to be obeyed.

'Suppose that your son of six months old is in a fractious mood and indisposed to take his morning nap. Take him, lay him down with a firm hand, saying in a firm voice, "Baby must lie still and go to sleep", putting your hand on him at the same time to prevent him rising in the cot or turning over after you have spoken . . . He will perhaps become boisterous and resist you. If so, you must persevere. You must, on no account, give up – no, not if you stop till night.

'But you say, "It is hard". Not half so hard as the other way for when the child finds out that the mother is not to be got over, he will yield as a matter of course.

'I have proved it, I think, with some as strong-willed children as ever came into the world. I conquered them at six and ten months old, and seldom had to contend with any direct opposition after.'

Fortuitously, like a second honeymoon, William and Catherine were offered a preaching engagement together, taking a short series of revival campaigns from an insignificant little Cornish chapel at Hayle. The short series became fourteen months, with fishermen rowing through choppy seas and villagers tramping miles across the hills, and Catherine wrote to the children, William Bramwell, Ballington, Kate and baby Emma, about the fields and the lanes and the kites flying on the moors. Long absences from London were off-set by a constant closeness in spirit and erratic visitations with all the clamour of joyful family reunions, encouraging in Kate the freedom and independence of security. On her third birthday, Catherine wrote to Bramwell with instructions:

'This is Katie's birthday, dear little girl. It is just three years today since the Lord sent her to us. I wish I could give her a birthday kiss, but I am so far away. You must give her one for me – a real bumper one, right on her sweet little cheek, and tell her how much her Mama loves her, and that she must be a very good little girl.

'When you get here,' she added, making arrangements for them to come and stay, 'Papa and I will take you with us on the cliffs and show you the great and beautiful sea . . .'

When the children came at last, 'digging mountains' on the beach and 'running into the waves and back', Kate went to one of her father's meetings and never forgot it. She sat high up in the gallery of the packed hall watching him far down below with his long face and unruly black hair, leading the singing and beating time enthusiastically with his rolled umbrella:

'Let the winds blow high or let the winds blow low,
It's a pleasant sail to Canaan, Hallelujah!'

Instead of going back to live with the Mumfords, the family remained together, travelling from place to place and enduring what Catherine called the torture of always treading on other people's carpets and using other people's furniture. Only the nursery remained ostensibly the same so that the children felt at home, nursery carpet rolled up and taken wherever they went, a crate of toys, a menagerie of white mice, rabbits, birds, dogs and cats, and some plain nursery furniture.

'There is one God and His apostle is John Wesley,' William had been known to say. Now he claimed that seven thousand people had found salvation during the Cornish revival and it was said that there had been nothing like it since Wesley. Ironically, wherever they went, Methodist chapel doors were now closed to them, provoking a new style of campaign, more far-reaching and radical than ever before.

In Cardiff, they preached in music halls and circuses. In Walsall, meetings featured converted boxers, gamblers, and poachers, and Catherine led the prototype of a Salvation Army march, linking arms with labourers and leading them to the chapel. She and William were working apart again, making ends meet on meagre support, with only zeal to keep them going. Catherine made the children's clothes, mending and turning and making winter frocks and flannel petticoats. Necessities became luxuries: 'I regret having my shawl,' she wrote to her parents. 'We cannot afford it.'

William was less stringent in his attitude to saving, more cavalier when it came to reality. 'What folly in you to do without a fire,' he wrote from Sheffield. 'It is not in these little things that our cash goes, but even if it were, surely you can afford a bit of fire while you are at home? I am going to study economy with all my might.

'I want no company but yours,' he ended wistfully, watching a young couple turn into the doorway opposite his lodgings. 'I should like to see you today; to hold you in my arms and look at you, right through your eyes into your heart, and then press you to my heart and hold you there and cover you with kisses.'

Catherine was more down to earth. 'I don't like this mode of living at all,' she wrote tersely to her parents. She was staying in Birmingham with the children while William spent five days away each week preaching. 'I sometimes feel as though I had taken a path which is too hard for me.' She liked a goal – a cause to fight, evil to attack, a point to be made with clarity and driven home – but for a time it seemed as if there was no goal, only treading dark waters and a constant questioning as to what the will of the Lord could be.

In February 1865, with William wondering dispiritedly whether to give up and go into business, Catherine came south again to take a series of campaigns in Rotherhithe. On the strength of their success, the entire family moved to London, 'hoping, trusting, and walking on the waters. Faith says "Well, is not that enough?"' commented Catherine. 'The Lord help us to feel it so.'

At first William stayed up north, preaching in Ripon, while Catherine and the children settled into a cheap house in Hammersmith. They were almost wholly dependent on Catherine's earnings, and she arranged to speak in Bermondsey, relying for her income on the financial results of the meetings and on the sale of pamphlets she had written. Bramwell described her with small feet, dark passionate eyes, and a short temper with what she called the dear Lord's idiot children.

'In dress, nothing could be neater,' said an onlooker. 'A plain black straw bonnet, slightly relieved by a pair of dark violet strings. A black velvet loose-fitting jacket with tight sleeves, and a black silk dress. A prepossessing countenance, with at first an exceedingly quiet manner, enlists the sympathies and rivets the attention of the audience. Her delivery is calm, precise, and clear, without the least approach to formality or tediousness.'

It was 1865, the London of Dickens and Dr Barnardo, of child labour, gin palaces and twopenny cans of gin. When William arrived, he took the place of a minister who had fallen ill, and on the way home to Hammersmith he walked through Whitechapel and the time for treading water was at an end.

'Here were the masses,' he said. 'And here was the devil.' Undertaking a week's service for the East London Special Service Committee, he continued instead for six weeks, preaching in the market place on Mile End Waste, surrounded by boxing, gambling and dog fights, and then continuing in a tent on an old Quaker burial ground because police had forbidden meetings in the parks. Services were lit by naptha lamps strung on a rope, and as William waited to preach for the first time, he watched a boy threading them. 'One of these days,' he told himself, 'they will be stringing lights like that round the world.'

It was a strong and yet intangible force that drew him: a sudden, unquestioning certainty. 'I found my heart strongly and strangely drawn out on behalf of the million people living within a mile of the tent, ninety out of every hundred of whom never heard the sound of the preacher's voice from year to year,' he said.

'"Here is a sphere!" was being whispered continually in my inward ear by an inward voice, and I was continually haunted with a desire to offer myself as an apostle for East London.'

Night after night he came home in the early hours of the morning with bandages round his head where he had been cut by the stones that were thrown at him, and the children became used to noticing his eyes fill with tears as he told them what he had seen: tenement buildings where whole families lived in half a passageway divided by a curtain wall; men with no work dying of drink and disillusion; women fighting, twelve-year old thieves and prostitutes, and children scouring the sewers for food. One night he came home more thoughtful than usual, and Catherine was sitting waiting for him by the fire.

'Oh Kate,' he said to her, 'as I passed the gin palaces tonight I seemed to hear a voice sounding in my ears: "Where can you go and find heathen such as these?" I feel I ought at every cost to stop and preach to these East End multitudes.'

Catherine was silent. 'The devil whispered, "this means another new departure, another start in life,"' she admitted later. Then she said, 'Well, if you feel you ought to stay, we have trusted in the Lord once for our support, and we can trust Him again.'

It was the end of July, with six children and another on the way. By November, they had moved to a house in Hackney. Refusing offers of financial help because of strings attached stipulating how and where they worked, William began what he called a Christian Revival Association. He was prepared for anything.

'We have no very definite plans,' he said. 'I have seen multitudes of my fellow creatures not only without God and hope, but sunk in the most desperate forms of wickedness and misery. These crowds have a fascination for me. It is evident that if they are to be reached, extraordinary means must be employed. We propose, God helping us, to devote our time and energy to this.' William's passion for his new work consumed the entire family. It was impossible to be near him and not become involved. There is a picture of Kate at five years old, with long corkscrew curls and grave eyes. God was already real to her, indignant, amused, angry, tender as a mother, his black beard shaking like her father's when he laughed.

'I think her experience from the age of five would justify the conclusion that her heart was in great measure renewed by the Spirit of God,' Catherine wrote later. 'She evinced great tenderness of conscience and extreme sensitiveness to reproof, so much so that frequently after what would generally be considered most insignificant childish faults, she would show the most passionate grief and an incapacity to enjoy anything until realising my full forgiveness and believing in her own heart that the Lord had forgiven her also.

'At about seven, it was evident that the Spirit of God was teaching her.'

When she was alone in bed at night, Kate studied her Bible long after she should have been asleep. She searched painstakingly for passages relevant to her own life, and if she could find none, she picked out a text, took it to her mother, and asked her to explain it and pray about it. They went visiting together, washing, cooking, encouraging, braving filth and chaos and disease, bringing to distress and misery the balm of a lucid, practical mind and a bleeding heart. Kate exhibited her parents' characteristics, direct and passionate in her emotions, indignant and difficult to deter.

'The Lord endowed her with a tremendous sense of justice,' explained her mother. 'Frequently she would experience a passion of indignation on witnessing acts of cruelty towards animals or wrong towards children or poor people in the streets. Many times I had the greatest difficulty to pacify her and throw her back on the goodness and mercy of God over-ruling these apparent contradictions and mysteries.'

For the first time she was meeting children unlike herself or her brothers and sisters: children with no loving security to cushion them, and no intimation of a loving God. 'I was once walking with my mother when a stone, thrown by a boy, narrowly missed hitting us,' she wrote later. 'Turning round sharply, my mother asked him, "Why did you do that?"

'"Because you are good and I am bad," he said.'

When Kate was eight years old, she shut herself away in her top attic room and 'dedicated herself to the Lord.' Maybe it was no more than play-acting: an impressionable and quixotic bid to right the world's wrong. Later, she was to say that it was then that her life really began.

The following year the Booths moved to Gore Road bounding the new green East End paradise of Victoria Park, with its trees and grass and lake. The house was noisy, a hostel and an office as well as a home, and Kate found herself caught up in the charm of it while at the same time longing to shut herself away in the quiet. Catherine believed that children thrived on happiness like plants growing towards the sun, but within Kate there was always a struggle: unruly self-will yearning to burn itself out in submission to the will of God; the inheritance of her father's fire and drama at war with the quiet inward tusslings of mind and spirit and conscience that required silence and solitude.

Walking in a favourite tree-lined alley through the park, she sensed someone walking beside her, and she told her mother it was like the men of old who walked through the burning fiery furnace with a fourth, like to the Son of God.

William was content at last. Secure in having found a vocation, albeit a vocation riddled with insecurity, he sang all over the house, fitting the words of hymns to popular tunes. Catherine tried, for his sake and not very successfully, to play the piano. The children were naturally musical, playing instruments and singing. Nursery games consisted of preaching, heckling, and dragging to the penitent bench: 'Give up the drink, brother!' Ballington preached to pillows, bashing them into submission, while his sisters watched spellbound with their dolls in their arms, 'Take the babies out of the theatre', being countered indignantly with 'Papa wouldn't have stopped. Papa would have gone on preaching!' Family walks were taken together in Epping Forest, singing and talking while William lay with his head on Catherine's lap as she sat against a tree,

9

moving her hands through his hair.

Catherine considered toys as necessary to children as food. The rocking horse which stood in the nursery had travelled with them wherever they went. Other toys were ingenious inventions of necessity: raisins and apples to count with, rice to weigh out on an old pair of scales, and Catherine's work basket to tidy while she mended. Clothes were plain. 'It would be the most glaring inconsistency if I were to deck out my children as the worldlings do,' Catherine said soberly. 'The seeds of vanity are too deeply sown in their young hearts for me to dare to cultivate it. It is a species of self-denial, I confess,' she conceded honestly, 'to abstain from making them as beautiful as they might be made to look.'

Kate had what she remembered later as 'one nice little dress'. It was navy blue and worn every day of the week with a clean collar and cuffs for Sundays. 'They're nice, but are they Christian?' summed up her attitude if ever Mrs Booth scraped up enough money to buy the girls new frocks.

'She was the most economical woman,' Bramwell wrote later of his mother. 'She not only patched our clothes, but made us proud of the patches. She used to patch my knickerbockers until I was almost an exhibition, and when I remonstrated "the boys will laugh at me" she would reply "Never mind, Willie, it will be good for your soul". Thus we were taught early to swim against the stream of outside opinion, custom, and respectability. We were, in every practical way that was available, taught to despise the world.'

Meals were prompt, Catherine carving and pouring out the tea, William opening his mail and falling on his knees in spontaneous thanksgiving when gifts of money fell out. The smell of freshly baked bread rose constantly from the big kitchen range, and meals were made into banquets: sometimes a joint of meat, more often no more than potatoes, with dried fruit which Catherine bought cheap in bulk and rice pudding with currants on special occasions. However small the rest of the meal, the rice pudding was always so large that no one could complain of being hungry while there was still some left in the bowl.

A chimney sweep, calling inadvertently during morning prayers at the breakfast table was invited to join in, and any of the children, expressing particular concern over a tramp, were encouraged to give him their pudding. Singing and praying and talk of salvation were part of daily life and as natural as eating and sleeping. To Catherine, religion was action, not words. 'Mother was intensely practical,' said Bramwell. 'Kneeling by her bed, she gave us wonderful counsel.'

Sunday was a day of joy, a large Noah's ark kept for lessons and used in every conceivable form to point a moral. One Sunday there was a noise of shouting and raucous laughter from the street outside, and when they ran to the window to look, they saw a boy who had drunk too much lurching along the road watched by a jeering crowd.

In a moment Noah was forgotten, and Catherine was down the stairs and out in the street beside him, castigating the onlookers and helping him into the house. Then after tea and prayers, she took him safely home. Kate admired her mother's fearlessness; her disregard for custom; her lack of pretence. 'Why is it that when speaking about religion, a stilted and unnatural style should be so commonly in vogue?' Catherine asked. 'The stirring tones, the flashing eyes, the eager gesture which emphasises conversation on every other important theme – why should these be banished?'

In 1868, William and Catherine decided to give the children the best Christmas they could manage. They saved a little and bought in extra food, and on Christmas morning, William played Fox and Mouse with the children, lying down like a dead weight on the floor while they tried to pull him up. Then he went out to preach, leaving them to cook the lunch.

When he came home again, he looked withdrawn, unhappy and tired out. 'We must never have another Christmas like this one,' he said. The next was spent boiling puddings and delivering them to the poor.

Within three years he had thirteen preaching stations and a People's Mission Hall in the old Whitechapel market, with classrooms, offices, and a public hall. Kate attended the Whitechapel meetings on Sundays, and a Children's Mission ran briefly in Bethnal Green, led by Bramwell, with two or three hundred attending. Although only initials are used, it is evident how many of the Booth children were involved from a report in November 1869. Testimonies were recorded from BB (12); CB (10) – 'a little girl'; EB (9); and WB (13).

The hymns they sang would appear to have been vastly unsuitable, waiting for angels to bear them o'er the river, but against a Victorian context of grief, guilt, constant impending disaster and sudden death, they brought comfort to the minds of many resigned and prematurely ageing toddlers. The Booths themselves were spared what William once referred to as dismal visits to the graveyard: the children had whooping cough, but escaped smallpox, Catherine suffered intermittent bouts of dysentery, and Kate contracted a weakness of the spine, but on the whole, illness was kept at bay by visits to cheap rented houses by the sea.

'My dear old Sis,' wrote Bramwell cheerily, in a letter pathetic for its adult concern and childish gaiety, 'you must take great care. Do not go out into the garden without something on; don't run about in the morning half-dressed without your shoes and stockings on; and get into bed at night as soon as you are undressed.

'This is a very nice place indeed: pretty good beach, some sand, some rock, and some stone and shingle. Emma goes with me and we dig together. We have been out this morning, but the tide was up and so we did not enjoy ourselves so much as usual. We are going out again, so I must conclude . . .'

Later, when Kate was staying by the sea with friends at Clifton, she had a tiny upper room in which she said she never felt alone. 'Above all, my darling girl,' Catherine wrote to her, 'keep close to Jesus. Run to Him in every difficulty. Tell Him all, just as you would me if you were at home.'

Invited to take the local Clifton Church of England Bible class for children, Kate talked constantly of sin and salvation, the theme on which her father's ministry centred and which brought such tears of shame and joy to the degenerate and down-trodden multitudes of Whitechapel. The Vicar, fascinated by her face, asked what she liked best in the Bible, and she said 'the Atonement'. She was eleven years old.

Travelling home on her twelfth birthday she begged her mother to begin a similar class at Gore Road, and soon she and Emma were holding kitchen meetings for the children they met in the Park. The Christianity they offered – that which they had seen and heard from their parents – sang of joy for the sinner and demanded sacrifice from the saved. 'It was when she was thirteen, after the reception of a more perfect understanding of all that was involved in a life of separation from the world, that she presented herself in the large hall at Whitechapel at one of my meetings as a seeker for the blessing of holiness,' recalled Catherine. 'On this occasion, I believe she made a full abandonment of herself to a life of cross-bearing, sacrifice, and suffering.'

Kate may have thought dimly in such terms – all her life she accepted hardship and sacrifice with grit and indifference. At the time, Catherine certainly did not. 'It is curious that although so largely engaged myself in public work,' she admitted later, 'I had so thoroughly imbibed the false idea in which I had been trained, looking upon my own experience as an exception, that I never once conceived the idea of my daughters being called to the same public service. I anticipated their working for God in quieter, more congenial ways.'

Bramwell was in weak health, evading preaching which exhausted him by running food shops supplying hot soup and three-course dinners for sixpence. Daunted by the impetus of the Booth bandwagon, the burden of which would inevitably fall on his shoulders, he recognised Kate's strength and eagerly urged her forward. When she was fourteen, she spoke with him for the first time on a Sunday morning at an open-air meeting for men outside the Leg of Mutton public house in Hackney. It was a reckless thing to do at a time when it was considered shocking for a woman to speak in public, let alone a child. Afterwards, Catherine tentatively agreed to allow her to address children's meetings.

'I was not present,' she wrote, 'but I received such a report of divine blessing that it began to dawn on me that God was calling my child to a path from which my mother's heart shrank, and I said "If it be possible, let this cup pass from me..."'

William was suffering from nervous dyspepsia, visiting hydros and eating vegetarian food. Intense and irritable with a constitution struggling to keep pace with the demands of the spirit, he was likened to John the Baptist in a Victorian wilderness of doubts and conflicts. While he was in Matlock in Derbyshire, he met a young man called Launcelot Railton, who introduced him to his brother, George.

Soon after Kate's birthday, George Scott Railton arrived at Gore Road for an interview. He was to stay for the next ten years:

13

among the most impressionable years of Kate's life.

Like William, he was dismissed by those who knew him as a likeable fanatic. Nine years older than Kate, he had grown up against a background of war – the Crimea, the American Civil War, the Franco-Prussian war, with its recent horrors during the siege of Paris, when thousands of communards had been massacred in a week. At a time when revolution was fashionable, Railton the soldier saint preached Christ the revolutionary and practised militant evangelism.

Tall and attractive with a pleasing voice, black hair, and a curling beard like William's – anyone without a beard looked, in Railton's words, 'a decided doggy bloke' – he had been orphaned at fifteen, roamed the docks converting Spanish sailors at sixteen, and travelled impetuously to take Christianity to Morocco when he was nineteen. Returning penniless, he pawned his overcoat and took work in a lead mine in Cornwall where he learned that the culture of God could, as he put it, 'fit a great rough fellow to sit down at the table of the King of Kings.'

He exerted the innocent, spellbinding charm of a man utterly unaware of his own foolishness in the eyes of others. Morocco had been his first crusade; the Christian Mission as it was now called, was the second, and it was to last, tortuously, all of his life. With his arrival, acting as general secretary to her father, Kate's home became busier and more frenetic than ever, and she likened it to a public house, with doorbells ringing, cables arriving, and cooks giving notice.

'I don't want a home like this,' she said. 'I want privacy.' Addressing a hall full of people or talking intimately with a few children, her heart took over and she forgot everything but the immensity of the message she was bound to convey, but at night in the silence, away from Railton's persuasion and her father's magnetism, there was nothing but cold fear of a life she had come to know only too well, a life of chaos and hardship, precarious, thankless, uncomfortable, and wholly unpredictable, and she had no peace until suddenly one day she gave in.

'All right, Lord,' she said. 'I'll give my life to you. I'll accept that my home may one day be the kind of home I don't like.'

Soon after that she went with her parents campaigning in Ryde on the Isle of Wight, and Bramwell persuaded her to speak in public again. When he told his mother what he had done,

Catherine was angry. Kate was nearly fifteen, tall, slim and striking, not very strong, but full of spirit and determination. When she spoke, it was as if another, stronger than herself, was speaking through her.

'You will have to settle this question with God, Mama,' Bramwell told Catherine. 'She is as surely called and inspired for this work as you are.'

It had been so easy when they were babies. 'The first important matter for a parent to settle in her own mind is this,' Catherine had taught confidently all those years ago: 'To whom does this child belong? Is it mine, or is it the Lord's?' And when Bramwell was born, the first of the family, she had said with such assurance and security, 'In all my ambitions for this child and for any that may follow, Thy Kingdom shall be first.' Now the words which had seemed so innocent and obvious at the time took on a new and ominous meaning. 'I held her back,' Catherine admitted later. 'I felt the same shrinking any mother might feel.'

After dinner that night, she went upstairs and shut herself in her room and prayed for a long time, and when she came down again, she had made her decision. 'I faced the question,' she said. 'I faced it alone with God, and I promised God that I would never hold any of my children back from what seemed to be His way for them.'

'From that hour,' said Bramwell, 'my sister's path was clear.'

CHAPTER 2

A little bit of Railton, commented William, lamenting his own anxious temperament, would do a world of good.

Railton was unquestionably eccentric, and appealing in his open contempt for the world. Like Saint Francis, with whom he was later to be compared, he would willingly have stripped naked if his notion of God had demanded it. It would hardly have been surprising if he had not seen in Kate, his emergent Sister Clare.

At twenty-three years old, he was indifferent to food, health and clothing. He worked far into the night and slept in the kitchen when he arrived home late. Sometimes he slept out on the street. He sang, and he played the castanets, an unexpected accomplishment he picked up in Morocco which earned him the nickname Bone Man. He saw the Christian Mission as an army, William as its general, and composed battle hymns with words like 'Christian, rouse thee, war is raging!'

He also accepted without question that male and female fought side by side equally in this war as soldiers of Christ, and he had little time for those who thought otherwise.

Surrounded by such giants of the spirit, dramatic, volatile, extravagant in their emotions and yet vigorous in self-denial and discipline, Kate's adolescent letters display an earnestness which is endearing rather than daunting; a composure riddled with strenuous self-criticism and vulnerability. A little bit of Railton was to do her the world of good too.

'How differently I look upon my fifteenth year to what I did my fourteenth,' she wrote to her mother in 1873. 'O Mama, in my heart I have a deeply depressed feeling. Such a sorrowful feeling. And it is just as if I were to remain in it.

'Mind you, I know I am saved, and that God has not forgotten me, but I am down in the dark. Do understand me, dear Mama. I know it will take such a long time to bring me up again. I can laugh and go on as if nothing was the matter, but when I am

16

alone or go to bed, there is deep down an intense longing: a longing to be fully His, and to know that I live moment by moment in Him. This must be beautiful.

'I want such a lot doing at me to get to such a state. I am trying to deny myself more; to be more quiet. Sometimes I feel I must give vent to my feelings, and I have done today by having a good cry. I could not help thinking of when I first came into this world as an innocent baby fifteen long years ago, and how many times I have grieved you and made you angry with me. You will never know how much I love you and dear Papa.

'This is very private, is it not? Do not show it to anybody except Papa. I have told you something I would not tell anybody else. I do love you, and I want to tell you more. With much love from your own Catherine Booth.'

Outwardly confident, she toured London speaking in Poplar, Stratford, Hammersmith. Inwardly, she felt condemned – at times humiliated – by what she saw as her own petty failings, and she examined herself mercilessly, pinning her hopes on a text she had found, like a distant promise of perfection: 'The Lord whom ye seek shall suddenly come to his temple . . .'

In these dark, brooding years of doubt, not in God but in herself, Kate was unconsciously mirroring her own mother's development. As a child of twelve, Catherine had endured what she was later to describe as a fearful conflict of soul, when 'the billows of the Almighty seemed to go over me.' She, too, examined her childhood conscience rigorously and learned to read the Bible as if it were a personal document. At fifteen, she had impatiently rejected all theological theories but those which were consistent with her own instincts of right and wrong.

'I am more and more having an opinion of my own,' Kate wrote to her. 'And I think I agree with you on everything.'

Haunted by the onus to do well, she began taking missions lasting three weeks or a month, with Bramwell in the unaccustomed position of chaperon, accompanying her all over the country insisting that she rather than he was the born preacher. Until now the reluctant head of the Booth children, he unquestioningly, and with a certain relief, handed over the lead to Kate, who possessed the dual advantages of a child's directness and a woman's perception, singing to audiences of thousands, preaching, cajoling, exhorting, berating, and afterwards, sharing their agony of soul, sobbing side by side with them as they recited their sins.

'How often I got up in my girlhood missionary days more tired than when I went to bed,' she was to remember later, ordering comfy beds for her Training Homes. 'There was always beautiful furniture in the rooms – but a terribly old, hard bed.'

Catherine viewed success with suspicion. 'I did not forget your birthday,' she wrote when Kate was sixteen. 'I think I gave you to God more fully than ever before. I laid you on His altar for Him to glorify Himself in you in any way He sees best. You must say Amen to the contract, and then it will be sealed in Heaven.

'I rejoice that the Lord is so gracious as to condescend to draw you after Himself,' she went on. 'I can truly say that it delights me more than any earthly good possibly could. But while I rejoice, I trouble.

'I know that many are thus drawn who never give themselves fully to God. It is in the yielding ourselves up to be led by the Spirit in everything, that the peace and victory come.

'This requires us to crucify nature. When inclination, or temper, or pride, or desire, would lead us one way, and conscience and the Spirit, another, we must follow conscience and the Spirit. This is walking in the light.

'Fourteen years ago, you were learning to walk, and in the process, you had many a tumble. Now you can not only walk yourself, but teach others. So, spiritually, if you will only let God lead you, He will perfect that which is lacking in you and bring you to the stature of a woman.

'Praise Him that you feel you are His child, though but a babe. It is a great thing to be a child of God at all.'

Kate was sixteen, her mouth determined, her eyes penetrating, already betraying a depth of vision and experience. The bones of her face were well-shaped, fine and serene but firm. Her long fair hair she wore tied back or put up under her bonnet. Her voice, speaking or singing, was pure and clear, cutting the air like a knife. Her gaze was unfaltering, shrewd but compassionate, as if she had infinite faith in the potential of the human spirit, while being under no illusions as to its frailty. It was at this time that Bramwell left a description of the effect her preaching had on the toughest audience. 'People were greatly prejudiced until they saw and felt for themselves that God was with her,' he said.

18

A noisy crowd of jeering locals collected outside a north country theatre where she was due to speak. As soon as the doors opened, they pushed in and filled the galleries, sitting with their hats on and their feet up, smoking, spitting, swearing and shouting. The service began, and the noise continued. 'Then my sister rose,' wrote Bramwell, 'and standing before the little table just behind the footlights, commenced to sing with such feeling as it is impossible to describe:

'"The rocks and the moutains will all flee away,
And you will need a hiding place that day –
Oh, may we be ready."

'There was an instantaneous silence over the whole house. After singing two or three stanzas, she stopped and announced her text: "Let me die the death of the righteous and let my last end be like His". While she did so, nearly every head was uncovered. In moments, the 1400 or 1500 present were completely absorbed in her subject. For forty minutes her clear young voice rang through the building. No one stirred, and when she called for volunteers to begin the new life, a man rose up in the midst of the throng in the gallery and exclaimed, "I'll make one!" There were thirty others that night.'

Railton began talking of a worldwide war of salvation, and Bramwell said he would rather be a successful talker for God than be Queen Victoria. 'So would you,' he told Kate. 'Then why not? Papa and Mama will both consent, I am sure. I can manage them. Will you go in for preaching? YES. Hit or miss. Go in!'

The eight Booth children – three boys, Bramwell, Ballington and Herbert, and five girls, Kate, Emma, Eva, Marian and Lucy – were tutored at home and forbidden to read fiction, since Catherine had much the same sentiments as Saint Francis, who climbed onto the roof of the library his brothers had built and began to dismantle it tile by tile. So far as she was concerned, schooling upset God's order, and nothing was more important in bringing up children than being 'beforehand with the devil'. Schools, she said, were all alike, 'being at more pains to make youth clever than to make them good; cultivating the intellect at the expense of the heart.' There was nothing more important, she felt, than to serve God and to serve man. Any form of education which appeared to ignore these two cardinal aims seemed to her unequivocal mind 'one-sided, unphilosophical, and irrel-igious'.

Bramwell had been sent to school and the other boys had ambushed him and swung him against the trunk of a tree to beat the salvation out of him, and he had never fully recovered. Ballington went to school for a term, and, according to Catherine, 'came home and ridiculed the name of Jesus'. Herbert's preparatory school she dismissed as run by 'lazy or over-taxed' mistresses. 'A school,' she said, 'is a little world where all the elements of unrenewed human nature are at work with as great variety, subtlety and power as in the world outside.'

By the time Kate was seventeen, she had read about the bright stars of the military stage, Napoleon, Garibaldi, Bismarck, and had studied their strategy and their psychology, which she admired. She had become good at French, and instinctively wanted to learn more French and German too: she had no idea why, unless it was the first step towards Railton's glorious worldwide battle ground. In order to learn more, nothing would dissuade her from going to school, and as a result, she encountered the full force of Catherine's logical, biting, and distinctly dogmatic opposition.

'I dare not think of it,' wrote her mother. 'You will say "You don't want me to learn any more". Yes I do, a great deal more. I would like you to learn to put your thoughts together forcibly and well, to think logically and clearly, to speak powerfully with good but simple language, to write legibly – which will have more to do with your usefulness than two languages.'

A headmistress offered to take Kate free of charge, and Catherine went to inspect the school, returning predictably horrified at what she had seen. However Kate had not only her mother's name, but her mother's persevering nature, which eventually wrung reluctant assent, promptly postponed for a term or two. Capitulation made Catherine uncharacteristically irritable and sarcastic.

'I have written at least three times that you might go to school,' she said crossly. 'I did not think it needful to say it again. For the first time in my life, I consent to a step (on so important a matter) on which my judgement is not satisfied. We shall see how it ends.

'I see that you are all set on the fruit that is to make you wise.

Eat it, my child, and God grant that it may not turn bitter in your belly.

'Your Papa is dead against the school – he says it will ruin you. But it is of no use us talking, because you think you know better than we do. You think also that we do not understand you. How I wish I did not so well as I do. One of the greatest writers on mental philosophy says self-knowledge is the most difficult of all knowledge to attain, but then he did not know you, or he might have altered his opinion.

'You think you know yourself perfectly, and that we are all either mistaken or prejudiced or unkind or foolish. You think we do not rightly value education and are too indifferent to it, whereas we have denied ourselves common necessities of life to give you the best in our power. Being so many of you, even if I had sent you to schools, they could only have been common schools. If I had my life to come over again, I should be still more particular.'

In her own childhood, Catherine had revelled in school from the time she was twelve years old, but her words held an unaccustomed harshness, and Kate found herself caught between being true to herself – which had lately become especially important – and loyal to her parents, which had been important for as long as she could remember. Catherine, when crossed, was awe-inspiring, her tirades the harder to resist, since they were never delivered without love and concern as their basis.

'My dearest Katie, I have not changed about the school,' she wrote more gently a couple of days later. 'I do not think your desire to learn sinful, if it be subordinated and rendered helpful to your serving God. Your letter seemed as though education was first in your mind, and righteousness and the Spirit only thrown in as an adjunct.

'I do not want to misjudge you or to think one unjust thought of you. I never loved you so deeply – not when you were my baby girl, as pure and beautiful as a snowdrop. But oh, I do so want you and all my children to live supremely for God. I do so deeply deplore my own failure, compared with what my life might have been, that I feel as though I could die to save any of you from making a mistake. I see as I never saw before, that all God wants is for us to be honest and wholehearted with Him, and I want you to begin life by being so.

21

'You see the whole question with me is not whether you shall have some more teaching, but whether this is of the right kind. Perhaps if we pray and wait a bit . . .'

In 1876, Kate spoke on the platform with her father at his annual conference, held in the People's Hall in Whitechapel, and she was described as 'a fragile, lady-like girl of seventeen, half woman, half child, a characteristic product of the Christian Mission, whose words fell on the crowd like summer rain.' William called her his Blucher because she always made victory out of defeat. 'Our trump card,' he said. 'When all else fails, put on Katie.'

'My dearest Katie,' wrote her mother, 'how I thank God for the way He is blessing you. Keep low at His feet and He will bless you more.'

At the conference, the decision was made to appoint women evangelists. 'Miss Booth,' recorded the Minutes, 'was reserved for general evangelistic tours.' William was ill again from overwork, suffering from gastric fever, drinking nothing but rice water and experiencing alternate moods of elation and depression. Catherine became ill after nursing him, and took Kate with her to Deal to convalesce. Kate's back was troubling her, nagging and tedious.

'I don't know what to do about her,' Catherine wrote anxiously to Bramwell. 'She is so poorly. I think twelve months away from the work in some country place would help.'

Before anything could be settled, a smallpox epidemic hit London. Lucy contracted it and recovered, but the Booth's nanny died. Railton, visiting the nanny in hospital, came near to death, or, as he chose to call it, 'promotion from the infantry of the earth to the cavalry of the skies.' While he was ill, he worked, and before he was really better, his boots had to be hidden to stop him leaving to attend the mission station. Instead, he left in his carpet slippers with a scarf across his face to hide the sores.

Catherine sent Kate and Emma away to the seaside and communicated constantly with them regarding their health. 'I am more than ever satisfied that indigestion aggravates every other malady,' she wrote, sending them daily letters urging them to eat the right things, drink the right things, and to love one another and get well. 'Do you get fish and eggs? Try Cadbury's cocoa essence for a drink. Watch what you find agrees with you and stick to it. I am certain that both tea and coffee are bad for you – one cup of tea in an afternoon is all you ought to take.'

At a time when it was not easy to keep well, Catherine energetically resorted to blackmail: 'Remember,' she said, 'you have gone at all this expense on purpose to get good, and your mother is doing without many things. I don't mind in the least – nay, I shall enjoy doing it, if you get good, but if you go and defeat my purpose, I shall be bitterly grieved.'

Inexhaustible herself, she was an exhausting mother. Kate was strong-willed and yet conscientious, in the strange position of being able to move thousands to a new life, while her own life was still in the hands of her parents – and especially in the firm hands of tenacious little Mrs Booth. Perhaps it was this incongruity in her life which drove her, as much as any desire for further education, to persist in her request to be sent away to school, and yet when taxed on her mother's strictness later in life, she replied indignantly, 'Strict! Yes, she was strict. But you'd do anything for her because you wanted to please her!'

Returning to London, Kate began her work as a travelling evangelist for her father's Mission. In Hammersmith, 'Miss Kate Booth spent a Sabbath with us, preaching twice with great acceptance.'

In Poplar, 'Mr Bramwell and Miss C. Booth were with us. On Sunday, one sister's face was cut with a stone, and heavy stones fell upon some, but we endure as seeing Him who is invisible.'

In Portsmouth, 'Miss Booth preached in the music hall to upwards of three thousand people and all felt it good to be there.'

In Limehouse, 'We had dear Miss Booth and her brother and a blessed day!'

In Whitechapel, 'An earnest appeal was made by Miss Booth.'

In Middlesbrough, 'Miss Booth visited us for five days and it will not soon be forgotten by those present. It was a grand sight to see a large hall filled to the door while hundreds went away.'

In Leeds, 'Miss Booth in the circus. A glorious month. Hard-hearted sinners broken down. Christ has been bringing to His fold rich and poor, young and old.'

In King's Lynn, 'the town has had a royal visit from the Lord of Lords and King of Kings. There has been a great awakening and trembling and turning to the Lord.'

23

And in Whitby, the proprietor of the main hall had large posters advertising a troupe of "Arctic skaters", but cancelled their appearance because 'it was no use coming as all the town was being evangelised.'

'Her control of an audience was extraordinary, both in its charming naturalness and its intense reality,' wrote a fellow officer at the time. 'Her youth, her appearance, her girlish simplicity, her tender and yet impressive voice and manner combined with the songs she sang and the truths she proclaimed to give her complete mastery of the minds and hearts of her hearers.

'Although extremely nervous, her intense realisation of the value of each opportunity lifted her entirely above any personal fear, and gave a remarkable presence of mind, as well as a wonderful sense of power over the people. Often, when in the early part of a meeting before she rose to speak, some unruly disturbers made it extremely doubtful whether there would be anything like good order, I have seen her rise, and fixing her eyes upon the culprits, literally quell them into silence and attention in her first dozen sentences, and in as many more, entirely secure their sympathy.

'The doubters and the backsliders seemed her special care, and her great success in helping seeking ones into the light and faith seems attributable largely to her uncompromising thoroughness and her capacity to enter into the struggle and darkness and agony of the particular soul with whom she was dealing. How often have I seen both weeping over a past lost life, until her faith seemed to bear the doubting one out of the storm of fears and fightings, over the bar and into the harbour of trust and assurance.'

The Whitechapel Mission was still without an official name, but by June 1877, the annual conference was called a Council of War. Handbills announced "War on Whitby", where William was called General for the first time, and women enlisted in the Hallelujah Army. When William and Kate went to take campaigns in Stockton, a cornet led the procession.

Beneath her joy, Catherine was still haunted by the fear that Kate might forget to give God the glory. 'William is utterly amazed at Katie,' she wrote to a friend. 'He had no idea she could preach as she does. He says she is a born leader and will, if she keeps right, see thousands saved.

'Dear friend, join me in praying that she may be kept humble and simple, and that all the Lord has given her may be used only for Him.'

But even Catherine was not immune. Listening to her daughter after not having heard her for a long time, she wrote, 'I was astonished at the advance she had made. It was sweet, tender, forcible, divine. I could only adore and weep. She looked like an angel and the people were melted and spell-bound like children.'

'How I thank God for raising you up,' wrote General Booth. 'Go on, my beloved Blucher, and you will win more battles for the Lord.'

Kate walked beside him at the head of a Salvation procession, and he watched her with pride. 'You shall wear a crown by and by, my lass,' he said.

'He bids me tell you that you are his second self,' Emma wrote, and in looks and manner, it was becoming so, for at eighteen years old, Kate was tall and striking, with her father's long nose and straight blue eyes.

The following year, she went at last to school in Penzance. It was run by a religious woman, but such slight assurance could not prevent Catherine's spate of customary advice.

On school work: 'Are you sure it is wise to absent yourself from many of the lessons in school? You may not know as thoroughly as you should, some things which younger children may know who have been more regularly taught. Geography, for instance. Perhaps you can do a little Euclid – worth all the German in the world for mental improvement. You want mental discipline and method to learn to systematise your thoughts.'

On health: 'It troubles me to hear that your back is so bad. Nothing but lying down in the day will save it. You might try a compress worn at night and the back washed over with cold water in the morning and a bit of flannel worn down it. There is no accounting for the benefit of warmth to the spine.

'I hope you are not wearing your stays at all tight . . .'

And the old fear that school was the breeding-ground of the devil: 'I see that God has given you a rare gift of influencing others for good, and I tremble lest the abuse of it should sink you in hell. It is dangerous for you to mingle with the wordly, the gay,

25

the ambitious, and I see that my responsibility is very great in allowing you to do so.

'Oh my dear child, my heart is full of tenderness towards you. I would give all I have to make you see as I see. To make you know yourself and realise that your besetment is to be ambitious and vain of superior attainments. Do not think I do not sympathise with you: I believe it was my own snare when I was young. Will you go to the Lord and ask Him to search your heart as with a lighted candle? Will you be willing to know the worst of yourself and put away this desire to be learned and wise and great, as an end, and only desire anything in order that you may be holy and useful?'

Once the petty panickings were over, Catherine's letters were needle-sharp and heart-searching, guaranteed either to provoke dismay or defiant determination. Kate had her way at last, and she settled down to learn in her own independent manner, but her mother's criticism and questioning at times left her despondent, alienated and unsure, with her confidence badly shaken.

'My very dear Katie,' wrote Catherine reassuringly, 'you know how I always answer Papa when he asks me if I love him! It seems such a superfluous question. I feel much the same to you. However, if it is a comfort to you to be told it, I snatch a moment this busy morning to tell you.

'Yes, a thousand times more than you know.

'I am sorry my letter discouraged you, but why should it? Supposing that you are in yourself of a restless and discontented nature, are we bound always to remain what we were at the beginning? By watchfulness on our part, and discipline and succour on His, what may we not become? It is not of nature's tree the fruit of the Spirit springs. It is of the tree of the Lord's own right-hand planting.

'Remember, He who reveals the need can supply it. Let nothing frighten you or lure you from your trust. This is all the difference between a conqueror and a coward.'

Kate returned from school to what was probably one of the most exciting periods in the history of the Salvation Army. Preparing the Annual Report of the Christian Mission, William called it a volunteer army. Railton had called it a holy war, an earthquake to the root of convention. Bramwell was twenty-two

26

years old, stronger and less nervous, beginning to relish his position as the General's eldest son, and wondering whether he had been mistaken to relinquish it so gladly. 'Volunteer!' he exclaimed. 'I'm no volunteer! I'm a regular or nothing.' At which William deleted the word 'volunteer' and inserted 'Salvation'.

All over the country, in the big cities where there was obvious degredation and exploitation, and in the country and provincial towns, riddled with hierarchical class structures and superstition, the Army began to make inroads, its officers becoming notorious for being mobbed and stoned and put in gaol for petty offences. More often than not, the adversaries of the Army were the rich and conventional, and clergy, reluctant to see their wealth and spiritual dominance whittled away.

Sergeants and captains were culled for the Army from the ranks of reformed drunks, thieves and murderers, for 'You may send the gospel through a leaden trump as well as through a golden one; as well through a poor man who cannot read as through a bishop,' asserted Catherine. 'He may not be able to put together two sentences of the Queen's English, but if he can say "I once was blind but now I see", he will do for the Salvation Army.'

'All is rush and drive,' she told Kate, 'with tribes of captains coming, cooking bad, and meals all irregular, no place for you!'

When she arrived, Kate enlisted as one of the first of the Salvation Army's women officers, and preached in a hall packed with more than three thousand people at Whitby. At home in Gore Road, she took tea to her father at midnight as he worked with Bramwell and Railton, singing hymns to them in her dressing-gown and making them stop and join in the choruses 'because a few minutes singing is more reviving than tea.' Much of the time she spent lying on her back in her attic room in extreme pain, until what Bramwell called 'being strung up from the ceiling and then set in cement' cured the threatened curvature, although for the rest of her life she was to suffer from a weak back, dictating letters lying down and fighting fatigue after long hours on her feet preaching and counselling.

Railton came and talked with her every day while she was ill: later she was to call him her spiritual mentor. He had about him the reckless zeal and abandon of the early church, taking literally the demands of Christ to go into all the world and preach the gospel to every creature. 'Men like us,' he had once said to Bramwell, 'without time for self, always at it . . .'

He was compiling a set of Rules and Regulations framing Salvation Army doctrines, many of them brought in at his own instigation – the abandonment of the sacraments which he considered too esoteric for simple people, and the elevation of women as well as men to the ranks of officers – and he talked of the days tramping through Morocco and Tunis waving a holiness flag until his money ran out and he worked his passage home.

William had confidence now to stand alone and to behave autocratically even, as befitted a General. Bramwell was eager to become his father's second in command. Railton spoke restlessly of moving on, taking up the Army flag and going abroad again, and Kate, praying through tears of frustration and pain, begged to be allowed to do the same.

'For hours together she would lie in great weakness and pain, almost unable to think or pray,' it was remembered later. 'People said it was awful, until they came and saw and felt for themselves that God was in it. Others thought, and said, and wrote, in loving unbelief, that she would die: that she was killing herself.'

'I feel I am with you in heart,' wrote Bramwell. 'My joy and sympathy is to an enormous extent in what others do and suffer and are, and so I look towards you often.'

In February 1880, Railton left for New York, 'happy as an angel' reported Catherine, who led the march down Fenchurch Street to the docks to see him off. Kate was preaching again, writing from Sheffield for the Army paper, the *War Cry*, of packed halls with doors locked and people turned away; of men and women in tears, 'grooving' – her own graphic word – out their hearts to God.

'I want to work for God and win souls,' Emma said ruefully, 'but I shall not be able to do it in the way Katie does . . .'

'If I were in your place,' wrote Catherine, 'young, no cares or anxieties, with such a start, such influence, such a prospect, I should not be able to contain myself for joy. Take the flag and hold it firmer and steadier and hoist it higher than ever your mother has done. Look onward, my child, into eternity, on and on and on. You are to live for ever. This is only the infancy of existence, the schooldays, the seed-time...'

In March, the General began receiving pleas from the French to send soldiers to France, and especially to Paris, which was called the city of the lost. In contrast, he and Kate went on a tour of the Trossachs, and captivated by the beauty of the scenery, Kate begged him to let her stay there for ever. 'Men are more interesting than scenery,' he replied.

'Pa and Bramwell,' according to Catherine, were exhausted; Catherine 'going on to the end' and living at what she called 'the utmost tension of every power'. 'It rejoices my heart to see the blessed results,' she said, 'but I suffer a crucifixion every time to see the blood and sweat it costs those dear to me... I don't think God requires *life* as a sacrifice?'

In June, the Booths celebrated their silver wedding, with meetings in Whitechapel where their children spoke and sang. 'People say, "They have put their children into the movement too,"' said Catherine. 'Yes, bless God, and if we had twenty, we would do so!' Railton, lodged in a cellar from which he brought out his own American copy of the *War Cry*, watched cars creeping over the Mississippi bridge and held a holiness meeting on the ice to beat a St Louis writ forbidding open-air meetings. Few people came to listen; those who did remarked that the British freaks dropped their aitches.

It is debatable whose decision it was that Kate should be the one to go with her two lieutenants to France. 'When I turned to consider who should go to France, she was the only one. I soon decided and she had no choice,' said the General, typically authoritarian. 'She rose to the opportunity, faced the new circumstances and strange land and language in the spirit of the martyrs, and set herself to prepare for the conflict.'

Kate's version is different: in those pioneering days, where would the Army have been without a streak of congenital egotism? 'An influential gentleman visited my father's home and begged him to send me to his country,' she said later. 'Neither the General nor I consented at once. Well do I remember the morning when I put my arms round his neck and said "I will go."'

Adelaide Cox and slight, fair-haired Florence Soper, Kate's teenage lieutenants, came to stay, with their new Army uni-

29

forms, bonnets trimmed with crimson ribbon lettered in gold. Together they spoke at farewell meetings in Clapton, arriving home late at night and talking into the early morning, crunching spring onions dipped in a plate of salt on the kitchen table. When the time came, they really did set out much like the martyrs of old, to waving hands and cheering and prophecies laden with doom.

'Take the flag, hold it firm, hoist it high . . .' The colours had changed hands, from mother to daughter. 'I can't bear the thought that you are gone,' wrote her sister Eva. 'You cannot know how much I felt your leaving,' wrote Herbert. 'The blow came so suddenly. You were gone. Only God and myself know how much I had lost in you. You have a chance that men of the past would have given their blood for, and that the very angels in heaven covet.'

Acquaintances condemned Catherine for sending her daughter to 'that wicked city'. 'You don't know Katie,' Catherine answered. 'Her innocence is her strength, and she knows the Lord.' The turmoil of her true feelings, she kept to herself.

'My darling girl,' she wrote. 'I cannot tell you what I felt after you left, but my heart found relief in pouring out its desires for you to the Lord. I have given you to Him for the salvation of the souls for whom He gave His Son. I am proud to have such a daughter to give to Him who gave Himself for me. Now let us hush our grief and look onward. The Lord bless you. My dear little Katie you shall ever be.'

CHAPTER 3

As Kate sailed for France, Railton was sailing home, his American mission a failure. He brought with him the hymn he had written standing in the snow on the steel bridge over the Mississippi:

'No place on earth I own,
No field, no house, be mine...'

Kate and her lieutenants rented the only rooms they could afford in Paris, on the seventh floor of a tenement building in the slums of the Rue Parmentier, occupied by prostitutes and rats. Their allowance from the Army was meagre, a stop-gap until they became self-supporting, and they lived on boiled potatoes and beans. 'From now on,' William told her, 'I am a General first and a father second.'

'Si le Roi m'avait donné Paris ...'

Before she had been there a month, working against an impenetrable wall of indifference, Kate called the place a very Sodom: 'a shrug of the shoulder and a contemptuous smile.' Instead of capitulating, she began, in her own idiom, to fight *'comme une tigre.'*

'When I went to France,' she wrote later, 'I said to Jesus, "I will suffer anything if You will give me the keys". And if I am asked what was the secret of our power in France, I answer: first, love; second, love; third, love. And if you ask how to get it, I answer: first, by sacrifice; second, by sacrifice; third, by sacrifice.

'Hours and hours we spent on our knees: you don't know the value of prayer until you are driven to bay.'

In March, a telegram was received from Paris at the London offices of the *War Cry*. 'Hall full,' it said. 'No disturbance stop wonderful attention comma power comma conviction stop people eager to hear stop full of praise to God.' Such blatant disregard for the truth of the situation was a measure of Kate's determination. She had been forced to repeat her address twice,

31

each time to astonished and stony silence.

Paris in the 1880s lived in the shadow of the Commune and the Folies Bergère. Absinth was the counterpart of London's gin; the evening, according to Baudelaire, was the criminal's friend. Radicals roamed the back streets still seeking revenge for the shameful terms of the Franco-Prussian peace and the violent Week of Blood that ended the Paris siege, when 17,000 were shot. Workers, nursing vociferous resentment towards the clergy and towards politicians who governed with ferocious ineptitude, had formed the Socialist Workers of France.

Nietzsche called Paris the only home in Europe for an artist, and attracted by turbulence, New Wave painters and musicians were flooding the city. Pissarro and Gauguin exhibited unconventional art at the *Salon des Refusés*. Saint-Saens lived in Paris, where he had founded the *Societé Nationale de Musique* for modern musicians; Fauré played the organ at the Madeleine; Rodin was scandalising France with the realism of his figures in bronze; Zola – 'the truth is on the march' – was writing short stories about drunkenness and prostitution; girls in black lace stockings danced the can-can at the Moulin Rouge where Manet painted backstage, and Toulouse-Lautrec was on his way to Montmartre where Renoir painted models in blue.

In 1880, a year before Kate's incongruous arrival on the scene, described later by the *Daily Telgraph* as 'a tall, thin, earnest-looking young lady,' Jesuits, Benedictines, and Carmelites had been expelled from France. Sellers of religion, whatever the brand, were not merely unpopular: they were hunted down and killed.

'A hall has been taken,' reported the *War Cry* with a naïveté which was scarcely credible. 'A deposit has been paid. The fittings ordered. There remains nothing to be done but for the officers to move to the front and take command.'

The hall, could they have seen it, was a filthy factory on the Rue d'Angoulême in the slums of Belleville. It held 600 people, but at first only the curious came: a handful of workers in blue blouses and clogs. Soon they were joined by refugees of all kinds, thieves, murderers and revolutionaries, who were more hungry for Bismarck's blood and iron than for the blood and fire of the Salvation Army. Young women alone in Paris were considered objects of entertainment, and this entertainment was more

32

novel than some. They gathered round to watch in open and often hostile astonishment as the girls knelt on the floor to pray. They mocked Kate's halting French, mimicked her schoolgirl accent and laughed at her uniform. New Testaments were torn up and used to light cigars.

Onlookers commented that well-bred English girls needed an elderly lady chaperone. 'Christ was our elderly lady,' said Kate. 'Christ was our sister, our mother, our brother.'

Forbidden by the police to distribute handbills advertising meetings, they paraded the streets wearing sandwich boards, and waited at six o'clock in the morning outside the stations as workers poured into the city. Soon, out of self-defence, they learned to pin on their bonnet strings instead of sewing them because men sitting drinking at café tables on the boulevards tried to strangle them from behind by catching the ends and pulling them tight. They visited the places where police only patrolled in pairs, the stench of the courtyards making them sick in the gutters when they came away, and in the evenings, Kate walked in the park, touching the trunks of the trees, pressing the palms of her hands against them and clinging to them because they were clean.

'God won't send you to purgatory: you have it here,' said a French baroness, horrified by what she saw. At home in England, Mrs Booth read about Paris in the newspapers and said that the state of society there made her shudder.

'How could you fear for a single moment that you would be any less near and dear to me on account of your brave going forth to a land of strangers to help me in the great purpose and struggle of my life?' wrote the General. 'My darling, you are nearer and dearer than ever.

'Go on in the face of difficulties, opposition, obstacles,' he encouraged her. 'Only go on. Something always happens to those who go on.'

At night, when they were exhausted and trying to sleep, Kate and her girls were woken by the violent fights which broke out between prostitutes and their clients. Kate, desperately wanting to help and finding her French inadequate, proved startlingly effective nonetheless, bursting through doors and dropping on her knees to pray. 'What scenes of anguish we witnessed there,' she wrote later. 'Once we were called down by the concierge to a girl who had shut every opening in the room and gassed herself. She could not face shame and sorrow alone. That same week, several girls were taken from the Seine.'

Often, though, the stairways rang with laughter, for Kate had an unquenchable sense of humour and a gift for seizing on the ridiculous. Preaching, as she always had done, without the aid of notes, working painstakingly from a dictionary and a Bible – 'If I begin with crutches I shall always need crutches,' she insisted, refusing an interpreter – there were inevitable ambiguities: a sermon preached on the efficacy of the water of life, oblivious to the fact that *eau de vie* meant brandy. Insisting that her lieutenants should speak French, she taught them a few phrases inviting listeners to the next meeting. When they began tentatively to use them, men asking cheekily for a date or a kiss were given the careful response: *'Oh oui, monsieur, demain soir à huit heures et demi.'*

Within the Army – in France they called themselves *L'Armée du Salut* – Kate was styled La Capitaine; the French called her one of the English freaks. *'Voyez La Capitaine Catherine et ses Catherinettes'* they laughed, as if she were a circus side show. She composed her own hymns with her own quaint phraseology, and sang them the same day, as her father and Railton had done, to popular tunes:

> *'Quand je suis souffrant*
> *Entendez mon cri . . .'*

A local policeman refused to go into the hall for 50,000 francs because he said half the cut-throats of Paris were there, and when Kate preached Jesus in the streets, she came back bruised and bleeding with derisive shouts of 'Jesuits!' ringing in her ears. Protestant priests condemned her, as her mother had been condemned, for being immodest, unwomanly, and heretical.

'Go home to your mother, Miss Booth,' one man told her after attending a meeting. 'The Salvation Army cannot succeed in France.'

'If I can't live for France, I can die for her,' retorted Kate, who, in spite of weak health and low spirits, was finding Christ most real, as she put it, in the presence of the devil.

'I never feel so much at home or in my right place as when the moral darkness is deepest,' she said. 'When I am most alone in a hard region with little help, I feel that it is then that my Lord needs me most, and when He can be most glorified.' As if she were a child again, she became aware of another beside her, 'the feet of the fourth, like to the Son of God', who never failed, she said, to keep an appointment. 'The people of the nineteenth century want apostles, not men and women with theories, and if you want to be an apostle, you must be familiar with God. You must be able to say 'I *am* what I say. I live and I'll die for God.'

Before long, it was being rumoured that the aim of the Salvation Army in Paris was not only to shelter dangerous criminals, but, since they spoke so much of Jesus, to bring back the hated Jesuits, and people began signing a petition.

'They shout "Jesuits!" but they have never seen Jesus,' said Kate, calling Paris a city sensitive to disinterested love, and religious machinery the hardest machinery in the world. 'Could they but see Jesus, they would receive Him gladly.

'The bridge to France lies in making the French people believe in me,' she said. 'Cold, dry sermons, exquisite solos, perfect tearless prayers – all leave souls as they found them. That is what the protestants do not understand. They preach the Bible. They write books. They offer. tracts. But that does not work. "Curse your Bible! Curse your books! Curse your tracts!" cry the French.

'France has not waited until now for religion, for preaching, for eloquence. Something more is needed. Only if Jesus is lifted up in flesh and blood, will He draw men to Him.

'This is the bridge to the masses who believe in nothing; who hate religion and cry "Down with Jesus Christ!" It is the priests' religion that has made them bitter. "Money to be baptised; money to be married; money to be buried!" I have heard them mutter, and what sympathy I feel with them as I listen to their angry cries against something they have never really seen or known. The face, the character, the life of Jesus, is to be seen in men and women.

'The conviction took shape in my mind,' she said later, 'that unless I could inspire faith in me, there was no hope. You may say this leads to fanaticism and all sorts of error, but Christ's primary means of saving the world is, after all, personality.

'I said "We will lay ourselves out for them. They shall know where we live. They can watch us day and night. They can see what we do, and judge us."

'These were the convictions with which I began the work in

Paris, and when I knew what I had to do, my mind was at rest.'

It was a spiritual, but hardly a physical rest. Every day and every evening far into the night was spent out in the streets, speaking in front of the theatres, taking meetings, visiting from house to house, and after standing all day there was the nagging pain in her back and sleepless nights to endure. Naïveté and a tough core of conviction enabled her to carry on, and her endurance was impressive, for it was taking longer than she had imagined possible to break through the blasé shell of sophistication, ignorance and wretchedness.

Unbelievably foolish, in the Paris of that time, was the sight of someone willing to weep over those who had no claim on her but the unshakable belief that they too were children of God and brothers and sisters in Christ; someone who had nothing to gain.

'I shall never forget those early meetings,' Kate said later. 'The rows of working people seated on rough straw-seated chairs listening intently and doing their best to sing from ragged, dirty hymn books.'

In April, she cabled home asking prayers 'to restore me to my usual health and strength,' and nineteen-year-old Herbert – Kate called him the poet of the movement – was sent out to help. He came with doubtful encouragement, betraying Catherine Booth's mounting lack of confidence in the venture.

'Lean back on God and don't worry: it is His affair,' she told him, shortly before he arrived. 'There are plenty of other countries to save beside France, and if God's time has not yet come, you cannot help it . . .'

Herbert, serious and eager, with his steel-rimmed pince-nez, told the story with all the meticulous detail of a war correspondent sending in a despatch. 'Half past eleven o'clock on Thursday morning, I was sitting reading at Nottingham when a telegram announced that I was to pack up and come to London by the next train,' he reported.

'Seven o'clock found me at Headquarters, and having received my orders, I left by the first train the next morning. After a journey lasting ten hours, I reached the French capital. After some little difficulty, the cab pulled up before what seemed to be a factory and what proved to be the *Salle du Salut,* the Hall of Salvation.

'I had no difficulty in finding out that it was the Salvation

Army, for although I could not understand what was being said, I could plainly feel how it was said.

'I entered the building, which is an oblong room, a small platform at one end, upon which sat Catherine Booth and her staff. I mounted and took a seat. The hall was three parts filled with some of the most awful, most degraded, most miserable people I have ever seen in my life.

'Women without bonnet and shawl. Little children with dirty pinafores and unwashed faces. Old men with unkempt hair and bony fingers over the end of which the nails protruded at least a quarter of an inch. Young men and women with ashy pale countenances, all sitting with eyes fixed on Miss Booth. Wherever she moved, their eyes followed her. She spoke and every mouth, eye, and ear, was opened to catch what she said.

'I had not been seated long when a hymn was started and they sang: *'Viens à Jésus'* – "Come to Jesus". And the singing went on: *"Il pardonne, Il pardonne maintenant"*. Then one of them prayed at the bench: *"Je Te servirai . . . je Te servirai".'*

Herbert left the hall in tears. Outside a hostile crowd jostled and shouted, waving their petition. A few days later, police closed down the hall, but before it closed, Herbert had received his first black eye for the Lord 'as an Army doorkeeper'.

While Kate made repeated requests to the Paris officials to re-open her hall, and cabled to England asking for official support, Herbert and Captain Stitt, a friend who had joined him from home, looked for a new hall.

'We scoured the neighbourhood for miles around,' he said. 'At last we hit on an old foundry in the Quai Valmy, opposite a canal famous for suicides, about two hundred yards from the poverty-stricken and irreligious quarter of the Place de la Villette.' Ideal in terms of Salvation work, 'after much manoeuvring, we got it.'

The hall had at one time formed part of the great Exhibition building of 1868. During the Paris Commune, it had been the scene of fighting between government troops trying to re-enter the city and revolutionaries who refused to lay down their arms. The walls still bore the marks of bullets. Herbert and his friend donned peasant blouses and bought pots of paint. It was a big hall – big enough to hold 1200 people, with a gallery at one end. 'And behold, it was very dirty,' added Herbert cheerfully. 'Iron girders stretched across supporting the roof, a great deal of which was glass. The gallery was supported by hundreds of iron rods. I shall not forget those girders and rods. Upon each had accumulated the filth of an age The whole place was floorless, shapeless, a depository of dirt, and Captain Stitt and I tackled it like a couple of gladiators.

'Cash was scarce. Hard work and a little self-denial, we thought, would accomplish the end more reasonably than letting out contracts. Accordingly, we set to work. We scrubbed and scraped off the muck and rust from every one of those girders and rods. We washed and painted them with paint we ourselves mixed. The building was ultimately turned into a hall which for beauty and cleanliness could not be beaten.

'It took us about six weeks. During that time, our diet was mostly spoiled grapes and fried potatoes . . .'

Kate thrived on Herbert's enthusiasm: when she was depressed, her family was the security from which she went forth fighting. His loyalty touched her, and his energy gave her strength. While he sat astride the girders, ridiculously proud of his handiwork, Kate went to England for a rest, and helped her parents persuade the Lord Mayor of London to add his name to those of the City Chamberlain and the Commissioner of the Metropolitan Police, in a message to the Paris authorities, vouching for the Army's good reputation.

'I wish some of our detractors could have been behind the door this morning when my precious daughter returned to Paris,' said Mrs Booth. 'If you could have seen the agony of nature we all endured, you might comprehend that it is not so easy a thing after all to send your child to a foreign land, to bear the responsibility and anxiety and toil of propagating a spiritual work with all the malice and spleen of the Pharisees arrayed against you.'

When the hall re-opened, the damage had been done. It had been re-opened with the permission of the police, and the Army's "dangerous" friends who so offended the neighbourhood stayed away. The second hall would not be finished for some time, and to Kate, it was like beginning all over again, only this time, it was even harder.

'Every evening we go forward to deal blow after blow on the enemy, who holds out hard and fast, seemingly determined to resist to the last,' wrote Kate. 'But we can hold out too. It is hard ground: far harder than you can imagine, or I expected. This is truly war. Intercede for Paris that God may have mercy and send a mighty tide of salvation. I live and breathe for this.

'We have some converts. Pray that these, our first French children, may be kept faithful to live and die in the carrying of blood and fire to thousands of their countrymen.

'It seems just now that we are cutting through difficulties and obstacles and the darkest midnight of unbelief and superstition, but light, joy and conquest, are on the other side . . .

'Yours, following hard after Him,' ended her letters to the *War Cry* at this time.

'We are going on, and nothing in the world can hinder us,' wrote Herbert, describing a Monday night meeting disrupted by boys with kettledrums, saucepan lids and whistles. 'We have the devil and two million of his best soldiers against us, but we are going on. Something wonderful must happen before long.'

'One may criticise, one may blame the proceedings of these evangelists, one may doubt their success and not believe in the solidity of the conversions wrought amidst such circumstances,' said *L'Espérance*, the organ of French youth and the only branch of the French press not to receive the Army with hostile or sarcastic criticism. 'But one cannot remain indifferent at the thought of the courage, the zeal, the attachment to the cross, the love for souls, the renunciation of the world, the contempt for routine and old ruts which the Salvation Army manifests.

'Are there many amongst the members of our unions burning with love for souls who would go and do such work in a strange country? No. We are too wise, too intelligent, too careful about the honour of the gospel in order not to compromise it and ourselves, and we prefer to hold our tongues and do nothing.

'We have need of the example of the Salvation Army. May it communicate something of its enthusiasm, of its ardour for the battle, and of its faith.'

At one of the first meetings after the re-opening of the hall, it was announced that since it was May, there would be an explanation of the Ascension into Heaven.

'I hear you are going up tonight,' said one man. 'I'm coming to see how you do it.'

'A good many came to see how we did it,' reported Herbert

later. 'And they found that the way we got into heaven was by getting heaven into our hearts, thus having a constant heaven on the way to heaven.'

'People may say what they will,' remarked "a stranger" who attended a meeting run by the people Paris called *'les evangelistes étranges'*, 'but one thing that strikes you is their entire consecration. Here are a few young women with weak and delicate health, who have left their families, their homes, and their comforts, in order to give themselves up to the work of God in the most miserable parts of Paris, and who are every day entreating men and women to come to Jesus. It humbles one to see it.'

Kate attended every evening meeting except those held on Saturdays, when she shut herself in her room to pray. Every Friday they prayed together for three hours early in the morning, and called it the most precious time in the week. Kate spent long hours lying flat writing letters asking for money and working on her French which still produced ripples of merriment.

'She would sing her choruses,' says her daughter, *'Aimez toujours et malgré tout, aimez toujours!* Go on loving whatever happens! The place was electric. The French were blowing kisses to each other. They loved it. *Aimez toujours!* They believed in love. They laughed, and she laughed with them.'

Radiant and increasingly confident, her mastery of French was becoming instinctive and colloquial enough to counsel, and to counter repartee.

'Go away! Pleasure is our God!'

'Yes. And God is my pleasure. That's why I've come.' The French who recognized God as a requisite of the state, a threat, a tyrant, had seldom been presented with a God who was in any way pleasurable.

Sometimes her audiences altered words to suit themselves and *'approchez-vous'* – 'Draw near' – became *'embrassez-vous'* as they kissed each other. 'Bear and believe was my rule,' she said. 'Don't be frightened if you are accosted by a man,' she told her women cadets. 'Answer clearly, sharply, and memorably.' Silent for a moment herself in the face of a request for a rendezvous, her silence was taken for acceptance.

'Where?' asked the man.

'Devant le trône de Dieu,' came the devestating reply.

'God is working,' reported Bramwell, who visited Paris and wept at what he saw.

Kate addressed her audience as citizens and comrades and studied the methods of the Roman Catholics, hearing confessions, dispensing occasionally with the penitent bench which was the mark of Salvationism in England, and introducing an after-meeting in a little loft above the hall which she called her Cure of Souls, where individuals could unburden their secret sorrows and fears. There was a camp bed and a table, a bottle with a candle stuck in it, a stove and a stool. A notice on the door advertised her presence between nine and five daily, and there was always a queue.

'Why don't you stop her?' asked a Protestant, when Kate encouraged a young woman to pray and she produced a crumpled picture of the Virgin Mary and a rosary and began to pray: 'Ave Maria...'

'Because God isn't as narrow as you are,' Kate replied. 'Our Lady would like it if you prayed to her Son,' she suggested gently to the woman. 'Because it was her Son who died on the cross for you.'

'But,' anxiously, 'I don't know any prayers to say to Him.'

'I do. Would you like me to pray for you?'

There was no room for haste. One man received a New Testament with delight. 'I had a book like this when I was young,' he said. 'The priest said I couldn't understand it and told me to burn it. When I didn't, he took it away from me and I stopped believing. Now you have given me another, I will read it and tell you what I think.'

Every day he read it sitting in the shade under the trees. When he had finished, he began all over again at the beginning. 'I do not quite understand yet,' he said. 'Leave me. I shall see for myself.'

After he had read it three or four times, his wife said he was as different as water from wine. 'Now I understand why God took my children,' he said at last. 'He wanted me. I shall see them again: He is keeping them safe.'

'If you only go on,' the General had said, 'something always happens...' By August, Kate was almost twenty-three years old, fighting her own impatience and the advice of everyone she knew to return home. She had been in Paris six months, and her meetings were still rowdy and disordered, occupied night after night in battling with men and women hostile to everything she held dear. Beauty afforded relief: the trees in the parks, beautiful Paris buildings and the river. In the Louvre she searched out one of her mother's favourite pictures which showed Christ on the cross. One of the women standing at the foot of the cross had her arms thrown round Jesus' feet.

'As I looked,' she said, 'the thought came to me that she could not have Jesus' feet without having His cross. So many want His joy, His peace, His blessing, but they do not want the nails, the blood, the scandal. They pray to be like Jesus, meek and lowly, gentle and holy, but they do not wish to be despised, hated, misrepresented, forsaken, howled after by the mob, and put to death as He was. They want His feet, but not His cross, and they miss both.'

More girls had joined her from England, surprised at what they found. Each night, those who wanted to pray and sing and testify were howled down by those who had found a hall in which to dance and sing and shout. One night, Kate tried a new approach. 'I will give you twenty minutes to dance in my hall,' she said, 'if you will give me twenty minutes to speak to you afterwards.'

A tall, dark man leaped to his feet. 'That's fair play, citizens,' he shouted. Then he stood and timed the dancing. After twenty minutes, he told them all to sit down and listen to Kate, who seized her opportunity and spoke for an hour and twenty minutes. For the first time, they listened to her in silence. When they had gone, the dark-faced man stayed behind. 'Thank you for helping me,' said Kate. 'Did you understand what I said?'

His face was hard, and it remained hard as he replied: 'I think you believe what you say.'

'Of course I do.'

'I wasn't sure before.' Then, almost involuntarily, his face relaxed. 'Have you time to listen?' he asked. At last Kate sensed a breakthrough. Determined not to betray her tension, she said 'Certainly.'

He spoke quietly, muttering, almost as if he were talking to himself. 'Once,' he said, 'I had the happiest home in the whole of Paris. I married the woman I loved, and after a year, we had a little boy. Three weeks later, my wife went mad and now she is in an asylum.'

He paused and wiped his face with his hand. Then he went on. 'He was beautiful. He was all the world to me. He was the first to greet me in the morning and the first to welcome me home in the evening. Until the sixth year . . .'

'When he died.'

'Yes.' It was as if he had forgotten Kate was there. 'Yes. He died.' He shifted and shook himself and ran his hand through his hair. 'Then I went to the devil. Before the open grave in the Père Lachaise cemetery with all my friends round me I held my hand up to heaven and shouted "If there is a God, then let him strike me dead!"'

'But He didn't.'

'No.'

'He is gentle.' It was midnight and very quiet in the deserted hall, tucked away from the main thoroughfare. 'And now we are here tonight. Doesn't it seem strange to you that out of all the millions in France and the millions in England, you and I should be here talking together at midnight? How do you account for it? Isn't it because God loves you?' There was a pause while he thought. 'Do you ever pray?' asked Kate.

'Pray? As a child, I suppose, but never now.'

'Well, I pray,' said Kate, and kneeling down she shut her eyes and prayed with all her might. When she had finished, the man was crying. 'I have hated God,' he said. 'I've hated religion. I've laughed at you and called you Jesuits.'

'But God loves you.'

'Then why did He let my wife go mad? If He loves me, why did He take away my son?'

Kate shook her head. 'I can't tell you that, but one day you will understand. One thing I do know, though. I know that God loves you.'

'Is it possible that He can forgive me?'

'It is certain.'

It was the first real victory. The dark-haired man was the first of the workers of Paris to be won to the Salvation Army, and from that night, he became Kate's bodyguard, clearing her way, quietening the crowds and fighting anyone who threatened her. Kate likened it to a flame which had at last been kindled, and would never die.

43

'Wherever we went in France, we brought the fire with us, we fanned it, we communicated it,' she said later. 'We could not help doing so, because it was in us, burning day and night. It was our symbol.

'I have not the insufferable conceit to suppose that it was anything in me that drew them. What was I? Dust and ashes. But if you have the fire, it draws, it melts, it consumes all selfishness, it makes you love as He loves. It gives you a heart of steel to yourself, and the tenderest of hearts to others. It gives you eyes to see what no one else sees, to hear what others have never given themselves the trouble to listen to. And men rush to you because of what you are. You are as He was in the world. You have His sympathy, His divine love, His divine patience. Therefore He gives you the victory over the world: and what is money, what are houses, lands, anything, compared with that?'

'Seigneur, ce que mon coeur réclame,' they sang in the dingy little hall.

> *'C'est le Feu.*
> *Le seul secret de la Victoire,*
> *C'est le feu.'*

Gradually, imperceptibly at first, the fire spread. New converts appeared, jeered at and ridiculed, wearing handkerchiefs round their necks and the letter 'S' for *Salut* sewn onto their collars. Kate endeared herself because she never pretended it would be easy.

'If you cannot get all you need from God, if you are not independent of human inspiration, then you are no use to us,' she told them. 'The discouragements and hardships are so great in the French war that nothing less than Jesus can satisfy here.'

With the first hint of success, opposition became more intense and vicious. It was, as Railton once said, a case of going 'where there may be little comfort, but where the most good may be done.' *'Elle est trop pure pour nous!'* shouted the notorious *'Femme du Diable'*, slapping a drunk across the mouth for swearing at Kate. 'I am your friend: I love you,' Kate told a man on the run for murder. 'The guillotine destroys the body. It cannot destroy the soul.'

After nearly eight months in Paris, Bramwell coined a new title for her – La Maréchale – uniquely French, untranslatable, and yet obvious in its connotations of admiration and respect. It

44

was to be the name she used for the rest of her life, and before long, she was signing it with a flourish at the end of her letters in preference to her Christian name.

She was called *'La cavalière'* and *'l'empaumeuse'* too – the bold Salvationist who manipulated the hearts of men and women – *'la prophétesse plus ravissante aux cheveux d'or'*. *'Sa verve,'* they exclaimed, *'sa diversité, sa liberté audacieuse, cette jeune Maréchale . . .'*

'Madame la Maréchale,' said a priest Kate met daily, walking to and from the Rue d'Angoulême. 'I want to tell you that since you began your work here, the moral atmosphere of the whole place has changed. I can tell better than you what you are doing. I meet the results of it everywhere.' Kate called his comment God's word of encouragement.

By the end of October, the hall at the Quai Valmy was finished, plain and white-washed with texts painted on the wall, tricolour flags, and the Salvation Army banner over the platform at one end, the initials of the French Republic with the letter 'S' on the blind concealing a large window over the entrance. The men who straggled in kept their caps on and looked, it was remarked, much like any other music hall audience.

'The second hall of the Salvation Army in Paris, at 187 Quai Valmy, was opened on 23 October 1881,' reported the *War Cry*. 'Somebody commented that people were saying "Is it wise to work without answering attacks?" Why do not people always do as the valiant little army in Paris? Nehemiah said "I am doing a great work and I cannot come down". To answer attacks is almost always to come down.'

The first meeting to be held at the new barracks – the *Caserne du Salut* – was 'owned by God, although the cold has been intense and our roof is yet out of repair.' The young editor of a French anarchist newspaper was routed by a deafening chorus of *'Come to Jesus'*, and Herbert took a bus to the hall in his uniform and received a lecture from the conductor on religion as a money-making machine. Later, he wrote home to describe the occasion when the white flag of holiness was hoisted.

'The call was well answered,' he said. 'Better than we expected, for the Christians have not, in time past, been altogether sure of us, and regard us as a very dangerous people.

45

Which we are.'

Kate's talk was described as a sharp and cutting appeal. 'Will you pay the price?' she kept asking those who listened. 'Will you be willing to leave all the dearest things of this earth to throw yourselves upon God?

'I do not promise you an easy life. You may have to sacrifice all that is dear to you. You are not to come to God merely to be happy or to gain peace, but in order to carry out His will.

'Will you do this? Will you pay the price?' And as she finished speaking, a forest of hands went up.

'The Army has commenced a work in Paris, and we are going on to conquer,' she said. 'The battle is the Lord's. It is all well, be it ever so dark. More courage, comrades. More boldness, more of the faith which laughs at impossibilities and rises triumphant over all. More of that love which suffereth long, beareth all things, endureth all things and never faileth but steadily and irresistibly seeks its object. The love that turns neither to the right nor to the left, but each day stronger and swifter than the day before, goes forward to seek the lost.

'Oh Lord, give us more of this love.'

Towards the end of October, as if in answer to her prayer, a Quaker from Ireland gave up a family fortune to sail from Dover to Calais and join the Army in France. He had brown hair and thoughtful eyes, and a voice which according to General Booth could penetrate the farthest corner of the biggest hall in England. Kate had met him once before when she was in England in the spring.

His name was Arthur Clibborn, and he was immediately nicknamed the Hallelujah Quaker.

CHAPTER 4

'Is there song in your soul, O my brother?
A melody born from above?
A hymn that will wake in another
A longing for Christ and His love?'

The gale which blew the boat carrying Sydney Arthur Clibborn into Calais was one of the worst for years. Before the ship was far out of Dover, the foresail was swept away. 'The force of the blast and the driving spray was so great that one could not stand upright on the fore part of the deck,' he said, 'but in spite of these adverse circumstances, we managed to snatch a few of the precious moments between the lurches of the ship to talk of the great salvation to a group of French sailors in the shelter of the bridge...'

Later, Arthur Clibborn was to be described not only as a poet and hymn writer – 'Is there song in your soul, O my brother?' – but as an apostle of abandonment, the perfect exponent of *'la mystère salutiste'; la foi pure, le coeur pur, l'amour parfait.'*

He had been educated in France and Switzerland, where he had gained an honours degree at Lausanne University. He could speak five languages. His father, James Clibborn, was co-founder of the linen mills at Bessbrook, the model temperance town in Armagh. His elder brother had emigrated to Canada, his young brother had gone prospecting for gold in America, and Arthur was the only son who had remained at home and trained to take over a directorship in what was by then an extremely successful and lucrative family industry.

He could weave and spin and control men and machinery. By the time he was twenty-six, he not only had eleven hundred workers under him, but had been appointed the youngest Quaker minister for over a hundred years. Under the persuasion of the General, who conferred on him the rank of Colonel, he was coming to France to assist Kate with the production of a French *War Cry*. Tall and good-looking, with a singing voice pitched between tenor and baritone, he came to France enamoured of the gentle revolution of Desmoulins who plucked a green leaf as a symbol of innocence. 'Guillotining humanity doesn't save it,' he said. 'Christ alone can do that.' Nonetheless, he deplored what he called the 'weep for me' Christ of the Pre-Raphaelites. His ancestry fitted him for something more resilient: for the blood and fire of Salvationism and the sword of the spirit, because like all Quakers – like his own forebears who had destroyed their guns during the Irish Rebellion – he was an ardent pacifist.

'Had you ever heard, as I have, an unearthly shriek ring up through five storeys of a huge factory an eighth of a mile in length, and then seen the countless revolving wheels slowing down while, as the hum of thirty thousand spindles and ten thousand rollers gradually ceased, the shrieks grew louder against the growing stillness,' he was to say later, 'and had you gone down, as the responsible manager, to find a poor boy lying in a huge heckling machine with his arm caught in up to the shoulder, the flesh torn off by the countless revolving needles, and had you seen the white, awestruck faces gathered round the rescuers, and had you joined in the quick and careful unbolting of the dread conscienceless machine while the blood dripped and the groans died ever fainter away, then – well, then you would like to do just a little to unbolt some of the machinery of war and set free, even maimed and crippled, some of the poor mothers' sons who have been caught in it.'

Clibborn claimed two illustrious Quakers among his ancestors: John Clibborn and David Barclay, who themselves were descended from Richard of Clibborn who came with the Conqueror, and the barons who compelled King John to fix his seal to the Magna Carta.

In what has been called the great revival of the latter half of the seventeenth century, a movement of men led by George Fox began teaching sinners to tremble at the thought of their sins; at the holiness of God, and at the doom of the impenitent. They were called Quakers because they quaked under the power of the Spirit: 'And who are we that we should not quake?' they asked. 'Does not grass bow down before the wind?'

It was at this time that 26-year-old John Clibborn, an officer in Cromwell's army, came with the parliamentary soldiers to settle in Ireland. When he heard that Quakers were holding meetings in a house on his land, he set out to burn the house down. Instead, he listened behind the door and became converted to Quakerism himself, remaining loyal to his Quaker pacifist principles during the Civil wars when James the Second tried to retain power, continuing to hold meetings on his land, caring for refugees, praying when he was about to be killed, and refusing to reveal the names of those who had ill-treated him.

Colonel David Barclay was descended from military men since the time of the Norman Conquest. Military governor of all Scotland North of the Tay, he was imprisoned in Edinburgh Castle for his political beliefs, and while he was there, he experienced what he would have called a new birth. From then on, he renounced war as anti-Christian.

Released from prison, he faced years of persecution and imprisonment for the stand he continued to take against war, his relations accusing him of having fallen into the 'scandalous errors of Quakerism'.

'None,' wrote the American poet Whittier, 'bore the indignities of the mob with greater patience and nobleness of soul than this once proud gentleman and soldier.'

'I find more satisfaction, as well as honour,' said Barclay, 'in being thus insulted for my religious principles, than when, a few years ago, it was usual for the magistrates as I passed the city of Aberdeen, to meet me on the road and conduct me to public entertainments in their hall, and then escort me out again to gain my favour.

> 'Happier, I, with loss of all,
> Hunted, outlawed, held in thrall,
>   With few friends to greet me,
> Then when reeve and squire were seen,
> Riding out from Aberdeen,
>   With bared heads to greet me.'

Years later, Arthur Clibborn was to tell his own story too, to readers of the *War Cry:*

'When I was only seven years old, my soul was stirred by thoughts of God and heaven and hell, and I often dreamed of Judgement Day,' he said.

'I was also harassed with violent temptations to childish infidelity. Often I would lie awake trying to get rid of the unbelieving reasonings which the devil suggested to me about the beginnings of the world, such as 'Who created God?' Finding no end to such thoughts, and filled with terror at their presence in my mind, I would find refuge in sleep.

'As a member of the Society of Friends, I was carefully and religiously brought up, but though I dimly recognised that, somehow, a great heart change must take place, yet eighteen years of my life passed without anyone ever definitely speaking to me about my soul.

'Having gone to serve my time in business in a place of much more spiritual life, I became, at almost seventeen, a teacher in a Sunday school. Prompted by a sort of vague desire to do good, I used to study the Bible and teach it to my scholars, but all the while, I had the inward conviction that really to do good, one must first *be* good. When, in the course of a lesson, I came to some burning passage about sin and Salvation, I would pass it over with as few remarks as possible, and those few, very indefinite and impersonal, and go on to discourse learnedly about Hebrew customs or the trees or flowers or birds of Palestine.

'I could tell the names of all the cities of refuge, and required that each scholar should know them, but I could not say 'I have run into the City of Refuge and live there. Flee from the avenger and come and live there with me.'

'Living in Bessbrook, a north of Ireland town of about 2000 inhabitants – called the model town from the fact that there was neither public-house nor police barracks nor pawn shop – I had many spiritual advantages. I often felt the call of God to my soul, but resisted the spirit again and again. A revival having commenced at Moyallon, about fourteen miles away, my closest friend there on a visit, was converted. I shall never forget the effect produced upon me when I saw the light of salvation shining in his face on his return. I was then under deep conviction, and evening after evening, we walked the country roads together while he sought to help my soul into light.

'The next Saturday I went down with him to visit my relatives, at whose place the meetings were being held.

'The pressure of the Holy Ghost upon my heart became tremendous, and as it increased, the powers of darkness sought to crush me with fears of what I should have to give up and suffer in the future, for I had always the conviction from childhood that if ever I gave my heart to God I should have to give up my life to Salvation work. Now, remembering my own case, when people ask me "Why do you press people so to surrender?" I reply, "Because the devil is on the other side pressing them to resist and put off. We should be at least as in earnest as the devil."

'After the Sunday morning meeting I was in agony, and went and knelt down in a field with my friend and spent several hours in fruitless attempts to believe. I did not then see that I could not believe because I had not really surrendered myself, and that true faith is the abandonment of the soul to God. In the night meeting the fight in my soul became awful. The devil made a last desperate effort, with the result that I seized my cane and rushed out of the hall rather than give in. But, thank God, kind friends pursued me, and when I felt my friend's arm gently thrust into mine, my throbbing soul broke through the hard crust of pride and I burst into tears, the first I had shed before others over my sins. After some more hours of agonising struggles to believe, I went to my room and lay down, feeling that as all my effort had failed, I could do nothing more than leave my soul to God, and thus, 'When I had ceased from my troubles, His peace Jesus gave unto me.'

'Never, throughout eternity, shall I forget the double dawn of the next morning, when the earthly and heavenly sunlight streamed into my eyes and soul. Never had the birds sung so sweetly or all Nature looked so lovely and radiant. The very fields and flowers seemed to be changed, or to have put on their Sunday clothes on Monday by mistake.

'A year later came the life call of God to my soul. I was to make a new business engagement with my relatives who owned the immense factory employing 3000 people, where I had for five years been learning the business. The engagement was to open to me an excellent prospect as far as this world was concerned, and though I had felt my heart drawn out more and more to Salvation work, I had had no direct impression that I was to 'leave all and follow Him.' But that evening, after I was alone in my room, the spirit of God came suddenly upon me in such a flood as to deprive me of bodily strength, and I sank into an armchair, while the waves of the divine glory rolled over and over my soul as billows from the great ocean of heavenly love.

'The glory of Christ's kingdom seemed to pass before me. No

words could possibly express what was then revealed to me of the loveableness of Christ, of the infinite tenderness of His compassionate love for the dying world. I seemed to see the Kingdom of God and to wake to the inexpressible joy of living and suffering and dying in the service of this sweet king of kings. The very music of heaven seemed wafted through my being like the soft murmur of a great ocean, vast as the universe. I felt that if I had a thousand tongues they could not tell out what I then felt and saw of the world of light.

'It seemed as if no one could possibly resist such a Saviour as I then saw. Could I but get others to see Him as then revealed!

'After a time I felt God tell me to go to the table and open the Bible. I did so, and it opened at these words, 'Lay not up for yourselves treasure upon earth', and as I read on to the end of the chapter it all seemed burned into my soul as the direct call of God.

'The next day I saw how God had prepared the way; had I been obedient? My friends, having recognised how I had 'been with Jesus', hesitated to press me to any formal engagement.

'That which I had refused to give up was taken away. All desire for a business career went.

'Four years of cloudy Christian experience followed. I worked very hard holding meetings on board foreign ships and in the country villages and teaching two Sunday school classes and visiting the sick, but I do not know of one soul being saved in all that time.

'I became an acknowledged minister in the Society of Friends.

'At length a testing time came when I felt obliged to take a stand for out and out work, and in doing so, go counter to the ideas of some older Christians.

'I went on to hold meetings every night, and on the Friday evening, fifteen or twenty people remained, nearly all in tears, to seek salvation. I felt carried along in the life and power of God, and went on for seven weeks holding meetings almost every night, doing all the praying work alone, and leading hymns, and speaking generally an hour. During that time about one hundred and thirty people professed to have found salvation.

'About that time I heard of the Salvation Army, and the rumours of its daring, desperate warfare and glorious results made me feel that the mighty power of the Holy Ghost was there.

I felt these people must be dead to self and filled with the holy boldness of the apostles.

'When I saw the first *War Cry*, the daring free-and-easiness of its language took my breath away and its direct, simple, definiteness seemed to open a new world. The methods of the Army were never a difficulty, as they seemed to me to be simply common sense applied to religion.

'I read Mrs Booth's books and longed for the full deliverance they spoke of. About that time, the Army invaded the North of Ireland, and when one day Captain Edmonds came and held a meeting at Bessbrook, I saw and felt that he had got that something after which I was pining, and in an All-Night of prayer, with three others, he showed us how the blessing was received, and I entered into faith.

'Next week I took about thirty of the young men converts to Army Holiness meetings at Moyallon, and I shall never forget the impression produced upon me as I entered the tent, and looked upon the rows of officers, all dressed so simply, with faces which spoke of the deep restfulness, the peace and power of 'the life hid with Christ in God'. My joy knew no bounds, and my heart cried out "Here is primitive Quakerism, primitive Methodism, primitive Christianity!"

'Having formerly learned French and German at school in Switzerland, I had often longed since my conversion, to go to work for souls upon the continent, and had a conviction God would send me there ultimately, but when Captain Edmonds mentioned to me one day how badly the Army, which had just invaded France, was in need of helpers, some time alone with God finally decided the matter, and I went and offered myself to the General for the war. I subsequently met Miss Booth, and as I heard of the desperate fight which she and her devoted little band had had to sustain, I had a still clearer view of all that Salvation War on the continent would mean. Alone on the seashore I made a fresh consecration of myself to God, and received from Him a promise of victory and soul-saving to which I have clung in many a fierce fight.

'One day, when under pressure from my friends, all the stronger through its kindness, I was alone in the study which I had fitted up several months before, and where souls had sought and found salvation, and all the realisation of my position came over me. Here I was, about to leave a comfortable position, friends, home and country, to join a despised and rejected people, and go out not knowing whither.

'Lost in thought, I opened quite mechanically a pamphlet lying among others on my table, and which I had never read before. My eye fell on words like these: 'He felt himself drawn to cast in his lot with this despised and persecuted people, though his friends were much opposed to it.' I turned to the cover and found that it was the story of one of my ancestors, Robert Barclay, author of *Barclay's Apology*, the standard theological work of the Society of Friends, who, two hundred years ago, was about to join the then poor and outcast Quakers, feeling that 'God was with them of a truth'. It seemed to come right from God to my soul as a word of encouragement.'

When Arthur told his father of his decision, James Clibborn bowed his head in silence. Then he said, 'Dost thee say, my son, that this is God's call to thee?'

'Yes, my father.'

'Then, my son, I have nothing to say.'

In return for Mrs Booth's tracts, Clibborn gave her a copy of *Barclay's Apology*, which set out the deepest held convictions of Quakerism: peace, prayer, the power of silence. 'Mrs Booth felt considerably drawn towards these views,' he wrote later. 'And she read *Barclay's Apology* with deep interest and fellowship of spirit.

'When called, in 1881,' he added, 'I stated that I could never forego any of the essential truths of Quakerism, and I entered the work on that understanding.'

The first meeting he attended at the Rue d'Angoulême factory hall, was typical. A group of roughs dominated the singing by howling in unison from the back of the hall. After leaving noisily, they attacked coachmen waiting outside by kicking them from behind and swinging iron bars at their heads until Army soldiers fought with them and they ran away.

Inside the hall was the cross-section of aristocracy and criminals which had become typical of an Army audience. They sat listening side by side with tears running down their cheeks as Kate sang the emotive words:

> 'Reviens, reviens, pauvre pécheur,
> Ton Père encore t'attend.'

Snuff boxes appeared in the collection as symbols of abandoned sin; rings and bracelets as gestures from those attempting to sell all and give to the poor.

'We all went home about as happy as we could,' reported Arthur Clibborn. Within a week, he was addressing audiences from the platform himself, standing side by side with the Maréchale.

CHAPTER 5

Kate was speaking to crowds of four hundred a night and telling stories which she said would draw tears from demons. Boys on bicycles were whistling her songs in the streets. She was just twenty-three. 'I am a different woman from the one who left England,' she told her friends. 'I did not know then what a wretch the devil is, nor what misery he brings his followers.'

Nursing drunken women in the gutter and putting her arms round street girls driven to attempt suicide, she suffered their sins and felt their shame and confusion to be her own. 'With them, I discovered what an awful thing it is to be stamped by sin,' she said. 'And with them I discovered the blessing of salvation.'

Teenage girls came in off the streets to mock, a shell of bravado cloaking deep inner misery. Kate praised God when they came, though their aim was to ridicule and disrupt, because usually they stayed until past one o'clock in the morning to listen. The rich and influential she called Pharisees, scorched by the fire and fleeing from it. Many turned to its warmth instead of running away, since her attacks were much as Christ launched on Simon: 'I have somewhat to say to thee . . .'

Summoned to the bedside of an old woman dying insignificantly among the dirty, cramped buildings above the canal, 'I knelt by her bed and said "Jesus came to save you", and she said, "*Moi? Ce n'est pas possible.*" And I said, "Yes. You are the very woman Christ came to save."

'I shall never forget the hope that lit up her woebegone face. "*Moi?*" she said. "*Moi!*"

'Jesus said God so loved the world,' she said later. 'He didn't say God so pitied it.'

They went visiting late at night when the factories closed; incongruous figures in navy bonnets and high-necked coats edged with braid, hurrying up the narrow hilly streets of Montmartre and into muddy ill-lit courtyards where police considered it unsafe to patrol at night. Oil lamps still flickered in the poorest neighbourhoods where there was no gas, and families lived together in one room with little furniture, seventy to a hundred families in one house with a drunken concierge asleep on the floor by the desk. Heads poked out of dark doorways as they climbed the shadowy staircases to smelly attic rooms, or peered into cold stone outhouses with crumbling plaster walls and leaking roofs.

The home of Madeleine, whose picture of the Virgin had so offended the Protestants, was typical of many, two dingy rooms with the children dressed in dirty clothes, a bottle of absinth on the table and pornographic pictures on the walls. Kate found it hard to hide dismay, and rarely tried. 'If ever I have a home of my own, I won't have anything in it that the Lord wouldn't like,' she said as she left.

On the next visit the children had clean frocks on, their hair had been cropped for cleanliness, the stove was bright and the room tidy.

'Where are the pictures?' Kate asked.

'I burnt them.'

'And the absinth?'

'I threw it away.'

'Who told you to?'

'You said if ever you had a home you wouldn't have anything in it that would displease Jesus . . .'

'I took her face in my hands and kissed her,' remembered Kate later. '"Follow the Lord," I said, "and I will help you with the children." Which I did.'

Back at the Rue Parmentier, moods changed swiftly and completely: Kate had always been contemptuous of compromise. Optimism petered out in despair; exhilaration bubbled up from nowhere – the retelling of a gift, a smile, a grunt of approval. Thinner and paler than when she left England eight months previously, Kate's spirit was as resilient and irrepressible as her humour and mealtimes were noisy, happy affairs, taken late at night with the nicety of a newspaper tablecloth.

Arthur Clibborn arrived in time to hear her preach on love, aggressive and reckless, invading enemy territory and staking its claim. Parents used the hall like a nursery, parking their children all day and picking them up in the evening when the factories closed, and the children played noisily among the long wooden benches, clattering up and down in clogs. Arthur picked them up and sat them on his lap, dangling his watch and chain in front of them to keep them amused 'until Miss Booth has finished speaking.'

'It would be too much for the decorum of a Friends' meeting,' he observed, as a man on his knees in prayer, apparently addressing no one, came under the puzzled scrutiny of a close-packed crowd of onlookers. 'I sometimes think I never understood what real, daring resolute faith was, until I came here,' he said.

He called Paris a city of gilded sin, commenting anxiously on the sensual aromas of the ballrooms and theatres. He saw shop names – Bob Diable and Le Petit Dieu – watched libre-penseurs parading the streets with placards advertising '*Jésus le déclassé*' – the socially unacceptable God – and described the scene melodramatically as the edge of a precipice: an awful river of human souls taking their final plunge into the lake which burns with fire and brimstone.

He and Railton were not dissimilar: innocent knights errant, charging, full-tilt and unabashed, at sin. Kate, on the other hand, was horrified less by the trappings of sin than by its potential for destruction set daily before her. As William Booth had proved on Mile End Waste, the wilderness as well as the mountain top was ground for holiness, requiring persistent invention and imagination. Arthur's letters home showed the ingenuous sincerity of a visitor from another world, looking on as 'these dear fellows' emerged blinking from moral darkness into light. Delightfully, in the face of blows and kicks and ultimate imprisonment, he was never to lose this first eager enthusiasm: the starry-eyed but justified hope that goodness might emanate from expected places, and that everyone retained a primeval resemblance to God; a purity not wholly forgotten. Finding his own niche in the corps, he began to work on the first issue of a French *War Cry*.

Kate wanted to call it *Amour* because love was the one word which summed up her presence in Paris. Admitting reluctantly that even she could not send her girls out onto the streets shouting '*Amour! Un sou!*' she settled instead for *En Avant* since the soldiers of Christ never stood still, but marched forward or went into retreat, and she was only interested in the forward march.

Arthur Cilbborn edited the paper from a little upstairs room on the Quai Valmy overlooking the Canal St Martin. 'Through the office window, at all hours of day and night, sounds come pouring in from far and near to remind one of the intense earnestness and energy with which men are rushing hither and thither on every business but that of salvation,' he said. 'Not a moment is silent. All is life, motion, and noise, the unceasing rattle of cabs and carts, the creaking of ships, the weird blare of the tram and bus horns on the distant boulevard, the ringing of factory bells, the dull thud of steam hammers, and now and then the quick splash of paddles on the wide canal below, and cutting clear through all these mingled sounds, the shriek of the trains on the Strasbourg line where, ten years ago, thousands of soldiers whirled off into the jaws of death amid the cheers of their friends.

'The more we travel,' he said, 'the more we see how well adapted are the measures and organisations of the Army to the glorious end in view. Every new discovery which facilitates travel and communication, every new railway, telegraph wire, or channel tunnel, is favourable to the Salvation Army. The Army fits this go-ahead age.'

'Forward is the title of our cry, and it is our word of order here,' wrote Kate in a call to arms contained in the first number of *En Avant*. 'The devil is doing all he possibly can to discourage and drive us back, yet forward we move in spite of everything. Faith looks beyond all difficulties and darkness, straight into the face of God.'

Patty and Little Johnny – Major Kate Patrick, a tanned, smiling girl from Ireland, and short, fair-haired Lucy Johns – were among the first to sell the paper. At the police station where Little Johnny presented herself to request a peddler's permit to sell in the streets, the policeman looked her up and down in astonishment.

'Vous voulez un permis de vende et de colportage pour les rues de Paris?' he said. *'C'est bien réallement ce que vous voulez?'*

On the coldest days, they wore mitts and heavy navy capes with hoods which drew up tightly round their faces, and men and women watching them exclaimed: *'Comme c'est shocking! Comme c'est invonvenant!'*

'Nous étions heureuses!' reminisced Little Johnny blissfully,

59

years later. 'From the beginning we had jettisoned our reputation and our respectability,' she said. 'We thought of nothing but souls. *Nous étions heureuses.*'

One girl sold 700 copies of *En Avant* in under a week. Soon sales averaged 15,000 a month. They stationed themselves at strategic points, with satchels slung across their backs: early in the morning outside railway stations; mid-afternoon outside the Bourse, the Paris Stock Exchange; by tram and bus stops in the evening, often standing for three or four hours until a sale was sparked off by a word of encouragement – 'I see you're taking the enemy by force!' – by someone kicking or swearing and rousing a wave of sympathetic buying in response, or by the sight of the Maréchale driving purposefully past in a carriage, stopping the carriage and sending the coachman hurrying across for half a dozen copies, so that others bought copies too out of curiosity.

At the end of a hard and cold day's selling, the girls met in the park, tired out, with aching feet, to sit on a bench and count their money to see who had sold the most. Little Johnny had a notebook where she jotted down each day's sales, and she still kept the book years later:

'Glorious victory after trial of faith: sold 351 *En Avant* at the Bourse . . .

'All Souls Day, alone at the entrance to the Père-Lachaise cemetery, 548 *En Avant* sold!'

'Vous vous perdez la réputation!' said French friends in horror. 'We can think of nothing but souls,' the girls replied obstinately, taking their cue from the Maréchale, who cheerfully proclaimed that she had lost her reputation a long time ago.

'Do you know *l'Armée du Salut?*' asked *Le Figaro*. 'We should probably never have thought it our duty to speak of it either good or evil, for everyone has a right to his opinions, if we had not witnessed on Saturday a strange scene in connection with the Society.

'At the crowded junction of streets at Drouot at six o'clock in the evening, just at the time when the circulation of cars and foot passengers was the most active, two young girls modestly but comfortably dressed, distributed profusely copies of a newspaper of which they had an ample provision in satchels.

'The crowd, whose mockery and curiosity were excited, pressed round these young girls who were easily recognisable as

English ladies of good family, and literally snatched at the little newspaper in question, which was none other than the organ of the Salvation Army.

'It is not our place to make reflections,' they concluded, making them nonetheless, 'but we think we may simply say that few young French ladies would be resolute enough to take a similar line in the streets of London. We will add, without the slightest hesitation, that we should be glad it is so.'

Bramwell paid a second visit to Paris, and so did Herbert: family affection and loyalty were of vital importance, and so was the erratic but generous correspondence which flowed between Kate and her father. Bramwell and Florence Soper met again – Florrie was due to go home to England after a year or two in France, and Bramwell was delighted with her courage and delicacy. Meetings were being held in both halls four nights a week as well as Sundays, and Bramwell commented on the rapidity with which 'they are becoming French', saying that he did not know how to praise the Lord enough. 'They sing, they pray, they respond, they work, like true Salvation soldiers,' he said. 'Fire is in their bones.'

There were French cadets, men and women, enlisting for training, and cadets from Germany, Holland and Switzerland as well, and he called it the beginning of an international work.

Kate was still forced to spend hours lying flat on her bed writing begging letters. In London, Army finances were low, and General Booth was sentencing new recruits to 'hard labour for life'. Cadets in England wore out a pair of boots in six months and ate meals of bloaters and mouldy bread, while parents dedicated their children to be 'despised, hated, cursed, beaten, kicked, imprisoned or killed for Christ's sake'. There was little time or money to spare for work abroad, and the General was convinced that successful Salvation work would pay for itself (though his own bank deficit did not always bear him out).

'The pressure is sometimes unbearable,' Kate said. 'France – the France we know – is poor. Our soldiers are poor. And the rich, with very few exceptions, do not in any way understand denying themselves for the kingdom's sake. And yet again and again, God comes to our relief and sends help from the most unexpected sources.'

Herbert saw a change in her, and called the whole venture

nothing short of self-sacrifice. 'Many thoughts entered my mind as I once more sat by the side of my sister upon whom months of severe fighting and unceasing prayer, months of tears and anxiety, made sadly too much mark,' he said. 'But I rejoice in the fact that He sees it, and I look to the time when they that turn many to righteousness shall shine like the stars . . .'

Then, in March 1882, as France was celebrating the festival of Mardi Gras, with carnivals and dancing beneath street lamps and music into the night, General Booth himself came from England to celebrate the first anniversary of the Army in Paris.

Seven nationalities were represented, and the General called them angels. 'I wish I could get our soldiers to wear uniform as yours do,' he said to Kate, who disliked rules, but relied on example, flying from exclusivism and egotism as she would from cholera, dreading what she called the lure of 'MY church, MY organisation, MY position, MY views, MY mission.' A *Daily Telegraph* correspondent, travelling to France to attend the meeting, said that 'no other form of religion could have boasted such an assembly of the lowest class of Parisians as that collected in the hall tonight.' There were, he estimated, 1200 'rough, brutal and unkempt men, more fitting to a socialist meeting or a wine shop.

'Though the proceedings were, to an unaccustomed eye and ear, decidedly eccentric,' he said, 'it must be acknowledged that they achieved success.'

The General returned to England declaring Kate to be his second self. British parents were already proclaiming her a heroine, and teaching their children French, with the careless prospect of growing up to become officers in *L'Armée du Salut*. Kate spoke of men and women 'bouleversés' or turned upside down by what they heard. 'They can scarcely believe that we simply wish to do them good,' she said.

WANTED, read a large notice on the back of the London *War Cry*, TO HELP IN ALARMING FRANCE! 30-KEY ANGLO GERMAN CONCERTINA; ALSO B-FLAT BARITONE, AND ANY OTHER KIND OF BRASS INSTRUMENTS. KINDLY FORWARD AT ONCE TO 187 QUAI VALMY, PARIS.

Within a month of her father's departure, Kate followed him to England, exhausted and unwell, visiting doctors and spending a good deal of time and energy talking to Dr Soper, Florence's father, a distinguished clergyman, eventually persuading him, against his better judgement, to allow Florrie and Bramwell to marry once Florrie was twenty-one. Never willing to rest for long, with the first sign of recovery, she was on the boat again for France. The sea was calm enough for her to stand on deck and watch the coastline coming into sight, misty at first, and then clear. Gulls flew overhead in upward spirals.

'I felt all as I stood there,' she said. 'And God promising "My presence shall go with thee". France shall hear of salvation. Every province and every town shall hear of it. Persecution, sorrow, difficulties, darkness, cannot hinder us. We hasten onward, faster than ever before, like the seagulls, upward and onward, with rapid flight to plant the colours of blood and fire.'

After a year's work in France, there were one hundred new soldiers and eighteen cadets on probation, all proudly wearing badges and armlets with the word *L'Armée du Salut* embroidered on them. The *Journal de Protestantism* invited its readers to join in condemning what it called the frivolity and folleries without number accompanying 'these attempts at evangelisation', but surprising support came from a correspondent of the *Feuille Populaire* in Marseilles.

'I do not approve of all the Salvation Army does,' he wrote, 'but I believe that those who direct it are sincere. I smile like other people in reading their songs, so incorrect that they are sometimes incomprehensible, but if the Lord choose by those hymns to save souls, I bless Him for it.

'Would they succeed better in other ways? Perhaps. But since it is true that they reach people who were not reached before, and since they have by the grace of God snatched souls from death, we ought to say thank you to them.'

Forty-kilo rocks were hurled against the great iron doors, as they probably were in the days of the Commune, but they did little more than break the lock, and Kate sang choruses like 'Fight on courageously, but fight on your knees, the world and Satan are in a rage,' with stones breaking the windows and glass falling into the hall.

'A visitor told us he was amazed at the perfect calm which reigned among us while the cannonade was going on at the door,' wrote one of Kate's soldiers. 'He forgot that Peter slept

63

soundly the night before he was to be killed, and Paul and Silas sang in the dungeon . . .'

'Pray for us,' the Maréchale asked the Army in England. 'We fight against fearful odds, but God is with me and holds me in His arms.'

Army tactics had always been offensive rather than defensive, and opposition inevitably provoked the pioneering spirit. *Cafés Joyeux* had already begun: the French equivalent of what English Salvationists called Glory Suppers, with white tablecloths covering long tables where a lavish if basic meal was laid out for those who rarely had enough to eat. Afterwards there were hymns and testimonies from soldiers in the two corps functioning in Paris – so far as Kate was concerned, the salvation of the soul had always taken precedence over the salvation of the body. 'Bring the prodigal back to his Father,' she remembered Railton saying optimistically, 'and all will be well with him.' In July she led her first all-night prayer meeting, and to coincide with the national independence festivities, she conducted the first open-air meeting and Salvation Army procession to take place in France. It was a calculated and impertinent risk. In England, corps were suffering near martyrdom from local 'skeleton' armies. Lassies in seaside towns had been thrown into the sea, landlords had been beaten and their houses burned down, and soldiers everywhere had been kicked and shot at and pelted with rotten eggs and paint.

Flags· and coloured lights decorated the Paris streets and thousands danced to the music of bands set up in the market squares. The Salvationists gathered in the park with a drummer, a violinist, a guitarist, and a girl banging a triangle. There they sang '*Jésus, marche avec moi*' to an enormous and surprised crowd which immediately gathered to watch and listen. Ballington, tall and handsome as a Greek god, nicknamed the Henry Irving of the Booth family, was in Paris for the occasion. 'The idea of having a Christ, a friend who would come and walk with men in Paris, caused the crowd to stand in wonder,' he said later. 'The soldiers mustered for the procession, and the verandahs of the lofty houses were filled with onlookers, and on every hand the people flocked to see this novel invasion!'

'Is it Catholic, this *Armée du Salut*?' asked people, as they marched past.

64

'Oh, no.'

'Is it Protestant?'

'No.'

'Well, what is it then?'

'It's a new religion,' they told each other, and the Salvationists called it the old religion come to life again. Pastor Theodore Monod, one of the Maréchale's staunchest French supporters from *L'Eǵlise Libre*, called it *'Methodisme porte à sa plus haute puissance';* Methodism at its most powerful, much like the primitive Methodism which had led William and Catherine to break with the New Connexion. 'The churches fail in France because France requires sacrifice,' Kate had told Pastor Monod months ago.

In England, those anxious for news of France read cameo descriptions of converts. A wizened woman selling pears from a basket in the doorway of a crowded street tormented by a passion for snuff: 'Suddenly her hand began to tremble about her pocket. "I *will* walk with my Lord!" she exclaimed, and the abandoned snuff box whizzed amidst the throng of passers-by and landed in the gutter.'

'My mother!' exclaimed a girl bitterly at a Midnight Glory Supper. 'She set me a good example. She showed me how to make an easy living – and she was good at it too.'

Turco-French soldiers from the Villette told tales of brutality, rape and murder, committed after systematically drinking brandy mixed with gunpowder, and a timid woman fingered the New Testament given to her by a girl in *L'Armée du Salut* and called it 'such a nice book.' 'I suppose that lady wrote it,' she added, pointing to Kate.

'I remember so well the moment and the place where the last spark of hope and faith died in me,' a highly educated man told Kate one night. 'I am now absolutely, eternally, unalterably in darkness.'

Inconspicuous girls enlisted and were to be seen out in all weather, kneeling beside drunks on the wet roads and in muddy alleyways, oblivious of passers-by; converts were taunted for being cowards when they refused to retaliate when workmates hit them. Young men, trying to stand by their new faith, were blacklisted and thrown out of their jobs; and quietly, day by day, a little misshapen woman took it upon herself to pioneer work which Kate was to take up later, touring the cafés in the back streets and inviting people to come to meetings, pleading with them for their souls, quite undeterred by the laughter and ribaldry that greeted her grotesque figure and the extraordinary mission she came upon.

'I can't find your God,' complained one old man. 'I'm going to buy a telescope and look for Him between the stars.'

'Go and do some cooking ... go home and sew ... go and get married,' they shouted at *L'Armée* girls in the streets.

A woman was turned out of hospital because she belonged to the Salvation Army. Another, turned out of her home with her children for rent arrears, found it impossible to claim from the authorities because she wore the Salvation Army 'S' and an Army brooch on her clothes. 'You're paid to go there every night,' said the state official. 'We're not going to help you. Stay at home and mend your stockings.'

A farmer in the South said peasants believed that an 'S' was branded on the foreheads of officers with a red-hot iron, and that they fasted for days on end, and a lady who visited England assured her pastor that all Salvationists wore swords.

'The papers and the people are writing against us,' Kate exclaimed rejoicingly, over in England to take part in the annual Salvation Army Congress at Clacton. 'Do you think they hurt us?' she went on like a second Saint Peter, giving a rousing sermon in praise of what she called the grand eminence of suffering persecution. 'I praise God morning, noon and night for it. I say hallelujah in my inmost soul because I am so glad. It is a great chance for our work in Paris.'

Arthur Clibborn was in England with her, and so were some of the most recent French officers. Colonel Clibborn shared the platform, translating their testimonies, and thousands gathered to listen and to catch a glimpse of the Maréchale, who had gained an almost legendary reputation. It was just before her twenty-fourth birthday.

'The papers blacken us,' she said. 'Why? Because, thank God, we have gone in for the losing. We have adopted the principles of John the Baptist: I decrease, but He must increase. We do not care for ourselves. We are content to lose. That is the secret of success and power.

'It is not an easy task. Twelve souls converted in France seem

66

like four thousand would seem in England. If anybody is afraid of dark days, let them get out of the Salvation Army.

'"You don't know the character of the people," a lady said to me. "I know that they have immortal souls," I replied. "And I know that Christ came down to the lowest."

'I could tell you so much more,' she said. 'We have bitter and painful work – work of which I knew nothing until I went to Paris.'

Before leaving England, she spoke at Florence and Bramwell's wedding, which she attended with Arthur Clibborn: six thousand people paid a shilling each to watch the ceremony which took place at the Congress Hall and helped to pay for the Eagle Tavern which Railton had persuaded William to lease in the City Road. Marriage was viewed as an efficient instrument for furthering the work rather than a romantic indulgence, with the junior officer, male or female, promising to obey the senior, and Catherine's blessing that Salvation might be propagated through all generations.

In November, Mrs Booth paid her first visit to Paris, and it coincided with the opening of a new hall in one of the most radical and revolutionary areas of the city, at the Rue Oberkampf, where four main roads intersected, marking the junction of the inner circle of the city with one of the most dangerous and thickly populated suburbs. Intellectuals condemned the move as simplistic and naïve and local police, wary of enflaming the intense anti-religious feeling which was at its height throughout Paris, refused protection. To the Salvationists it was an ill wind, since any personal risk was more than off-set by the chance of attracting those the police might have scared away.

Before the hall opened, a new entrance was built with double doors and iron shutters which slid down over them. Outside, a red gas lamp flared among the many others in a notorious red light district of the city.

At the first meeting Kate moved alone into the middle of a gang of two hundred or more who were shouting *'Vive la Commune! Vive la Commune!'* but she found it impossible to quieten them. The Editor of *Le Témoignage* called them a delirious mob and a pack of howling wolves eager for blood. 'I have been rejoiced and moved beyond all expression,' he said.

'I have never attended religious meetings before without

67

experiencing a piercing feeling of deception and regret. Always the same audience. But the public which it was the object to gain – the notoriously hostile public, the public of our atheist press, the public of the big political meetings in whose eyes Victor Hugo himself would pass for a cleric – where was that public?

'I have seen it at last with my own eyes at the meetings of the Salvation Army,' he said. 'In all my life I shall not forget the scenes at the opening of the new hall in Rue Oberkampf.'

Mrs Booth went first to the Quai Valmy, where she spoke from the platform, translated by Colonel Clibborn. 'It was glorious to see where we had so often imagined her,' said Kate. She spoke of the cost of sacrificing the Maréchale to Paris, and the reward, 'when I can look, as I can tonight,' she said charmingly, 'into the faces of my daughter's spiritual children: my grandchildren.'

Then she went on to a select drawing-room meeting where an audience of influential Christians were gathered, 'trying to scrape together all my patience to meet and answer all the old, time-worn objections to our work,' which she professed herself 'sick of hearing.'

'My mother defended the Army measures and explained our work in such a manner as to remove a great deal of prejudice and misunderstanding,' Kate said later.

In the evening, they went together to a meeting in the hall on the Rue Oberkampf, where they were met by a shrill and over-excited audience which Mrs Booth described afterwards as full of blood and hell. 'I would have liked those Christians to have been there,' she commented wryly. 'Especially one good pastor who talked to us about reading more Bible in our meetings. I should like to have seen him try. They would have torn his Bible to ribbons, and him too.'

Colonel Clibborn who organised the meeting, described the scene: 'The better-class workmen and shop-keepers held aloof on the outskirts of the crowd as if to say "We know what you're in for tonight . . ."' he said. 'And in they came, nudging each other with a cunning delight at finding themselves admitted. Once inside, they glided slyly to their seats, caps on, cigars alight, eyes bright with anticipation.

'There was a little fellow, all on springs, gliding restlessly from one knot of men to another. He could hardly have been more than fourteen years old, and yet his flushed cheeks, blood-shot eyes and blackened teeth told the story of a life far advanced in drunkenness and vice.

'And there was a blue-bloused workman in the centre of another fidgeting knot of men. They leaned over and kept whispering to him as he sat bolt upright in their midst with a half tipsy air of importance.

'As their numbers increased, they became more bold. They called to each other across the room and began singing snatches of songs and tumbling the chairs about as the moment of opening came. The first verse was hardly through before the whole band chimed in in a perfect babel of discordant voices. The prayer which followed was drowned in the general uproar, and from then on, we were on top of a volcano.'

At the height of the uproar, the Maréchale came down from the platform and walked through them into the middle of the hall where she stood on a bench and began 'pleading', said her mother, 'like an apostle.'

'We'll listen to you so long as you don't talk about Jesus!' shouted one man, shaking his fist in her face. 'We hate Jesus!'

'We hate Jesus!' came echoing shouts from all over the hall. 'Yes,' they shouted, 'Down with Jesus! À bas Jésus!'

'If Jesus was here,' the man went on shouting, 'I'd empty a slop pail on His head!'

'Vive la liberté!' came a shout from the back of the hall.

'Amen!' replied Kate.

'Liberty, but no amens,' they shouted back. 'No amens and no Jesus. We hate Jesus. Your Jesus brings us nothing but trouble and we've had enough of Him. À bas Jésus.'

'What makes you so patient with them?' asked a woman, pushing her way through the crowd and seizing Catherine Booth's hand. 'If it were us, we'd kill them!'

Led by the Colonel, the men linked arms and formed a line across the hall, gradually pushing the crowd towards the doors. Outside the doors, they joined those waiting, who had kept themselves amused during the meeting by banging on the doors and throwing stones at the Army sentinels.

'The mob swelled to enormous proportions,' said Clibborn. 'Crushing back on the entrance, they turned on us with savage fury. Fists, sticks, boots, anything that could hit or kick or wound was brought into play, and the little lad of fourteen or so seemed to lose all human semblance as he kicked and pinched and screwed his little body in behind us to force us out into the hands of the crowd.

'For a long time we could not work the handle to shut down the iron screen, and the missiles came flying in thickly from the crowd as they yelled "No religion! Away with religion! Down with Jesus Christ. *Frappé, frappé!* Strike, strike!"'

'Our comrades were kicked and beaten in the face, but never did I see one of them strike back. Flesh and blood could not possibly have stood its ground more coolly or resolutely or with such Christ-like forebearance.'

Eventually the iron plating was pulled down and secured, only to find that the back entrance was also surrounded. Resorting to an impromptu prayer meeting – 'such a blessed time,' said Clibborn placidly – a neighbour suggested they should slip away quietly by an exit which led through his house.

'How we got home, I can scarcely tell,' said Kate afterwards. 'They flourished their knives in our faces and followed us with cries of *"Voici Jésus! Voici le Christ! C'est Lui! C'est Lui!"*'

'My mother was deeply moved.'

Mrs Booth was so moved that she called it a sublime sight and worth coming from England to witness. For the first time, she referred to Kate as the Maréchale: 'I fear for the consequences on the Maréchale,' she said. 'It is such a strain on her.' Viewing Kate's performance, she seemed almost in awe of the person her daughter had become. At night, however, back in the flat, talking and praying together, sharing laughter and some tears, the passionate young Maréchale was Catherine's little Katie again, her own darling girl, and 'My soul shall not draw back, though He slay me and her too,' Mrs Booth vowed again. 'I will trust Him.

'Pray for us,' she cabled London spiritedly the next day. 'We go again tonight.'

Meetings continued at the Rue Oberkampf until the end of the month. 'We said "tonight we have been beaten, but a few more defeats and then victory will be ours,"' remembered Little Johnny. 'For the souls it was worth risking anything.' One soldier had his lip split open by a flying oyster shell. Another, Monsieur Moilliet, one of the first Frenchmen to write to

England requesting General Booth to send the Army to Paris, could be seen night after night, guarding the door with the rest, standing shoulder to shoulder with them, his feet firmly against the door posts, his jacket torn to shreds and his face bleeding.

Often the audience had to be barricaded inside the hall to safeguard them from the mob outside, while Colonel Clibborn went out to face the rioters alone and try to persuade them to go home peacefully. One night, a young man pulled a revolver on the waiting crowd. 'I shall never forget the scene that followed,' wrote Clibborn. 'Before he had time to fire, a dozen hands grabbed him and his upturned face disappeared, dragged down into the vortex of the crowd, while blows rained on him from all sides.'

A Salvationist, chased along the boulevard and badly beaten, had to hide in a friend's house until the early morning. 'I could have knocked half a dozen of them down with this,' he said grimly the next day, waving a large umbrella with a heavy handle. 'But I remembered how Jesus bore crucifixion without complaint and I couldn't strike back.'

'An Englishman may take to religion,' shouted one man at Kate. 'A German or a heathen even. A Frenchman never.' Kate turned and asked all her French soldiers to stand up, and when they did so, the audience was silent.

'The blacker it looks, the more determined we are to go forward,' she said. 'We have opposition on all sides. We stand almost alone. We are called extreme. How can we be extreme when on our faithfulness hang the mighty issues of life and death for thousands?'

On a cold Thursday in December, the hall was closed down by order of the Prefect. Police escorted the Salvationists out by the back door where a crowd threw mud and gravel at them. 'We got the Lassies into the middle and made a circle of the fellows around, and marched across the open streets to the tram stop,' described Clibborn. 'The conduct of our soldiers was apostolically cool, though one could not be surprised at the Lassies being a little white . . .'

As the trams pulled away, the crowd ran along the roads after them, pulling the Salvationists' coats, pelting them with mud, and shouting 'Jesus Christ!'

Back at the Quai Valmy, ladies were giving up the things they loved best – feathers, flowers, jewellery; gentlemen gave up beer, wine and tobacco. Kate talked of love, as she so often had done before, calm and trusting and brave as a lion. Shaken by the intensity of the hatred they had encountered, and by their comparative inability to make any inroad on it, her appeal was particularly personal. 'It requires a broken heart to love as Christ loved,' she said. 'It is only when we break, that sinners break.'

Nevertheless, the old year finished on a note of optimism, with glory's and hallelujah's, *'Faites feu!'* and fixed bayonets, hats in the air and rousing cheers for the Saviour. Volley after volley of shouts, amens, and raised hands greeted the Maréchale – 'our precious leader' – when she came onto the platform. As midnight struck, she asked her soldiers 'willingly to put all on the altar', and they stayed to spend Watch Night 'together with Jesus.'

'We have spent nights in that company before, holding mutual communion with the Master, as the French put it,' wrote one of her colleagues. 'But we felt that He came nearer that night, and blessed us more than ever before. Song after song we sang until the morning hours came up, one after another, and with them, a strong determination to fight, as the General has told us, hanging onto the omnipotent arm stretched out to every one of us.

'Then we left the hall and began the war of 1883.'

'My darling Blucher,' wrote the General, in a New Year note to Kate. 'I appreciate and admire and daily thank God for your courage and love and endurance. God will and must bless you. I feel I live over again in you,' he said. It was a theme constantly recurring, and especially dear to his heart.

CHAPTER 6

In November 1880, three months before his death and a year before the Maréchale entered Paris, Dostoevsky finished writing *The Brothers Karamazov*. In it, before telling of Christ and his terrible kiss, Ivan recounts the story of Richard, brought up like a chattel by shepherds, taught nothing and beaten for stealing food from the pigs, who robbed and murdered a man in Geneva. His story amounts to a cynical but shrewd indictment of the brand of Christianity predominant in Switzerland in the 1880s.

'He was caught, tried and condemned to death. They are not sentimentalists there,' Ivan said. 'And in prison he was immediately surrounded by pastors, members of Christian brotherhoods, philanthropic ladies and the like. They taught him to read and write in prison and expounded the Gospel to him. They exhorted him, worked upon him, drummed at him incessantly, till at last he solemnly confessed his crime. He was converted. He wrote to the court himself that he was a monster, but that in the end God had vouchsafed him light and shown grace. All Geneva was in excitement about him – all philanthropic and religious Geneva.

'All the aristocratic and well-bred society of the town rushed to the prison, kissed Richard and embraced him; "You are our brother, and you have found grace." And Richard does nothing but weep with emotion, "Yes, I've found grace! All my youth and childhood I was glad of pigs' food but now even I have found grace. I am dying in the Lord."

'Yes, Richard, die in the Lord; you have shed blood and must die. Though it's not your fault that you knew not the Lord when you coveted the pigs' food and were beaten for stealing it (which was very wrong of you, for stealing is forbidden); but you've shed blood and you must die.' And on the last day, Richard, perfectly limp, did nothing but cry and repeat every minute: "This is my happiest day. I am going to the Lord." "Yes," cry the pastors and the judges and philanthropic ladies. "This is the happiest day of your life, for you are going to the Lord!" They all walk or drive to the scaffold in procession behind the prison van. At the scaffold they call to Richard: "Die, brother, die in the Lord, for even thou hast found grace!"

'And so, covered with his brothers' kisses, Richard is dragged on to the scaffold, and led to the guillotine. And they chopped off his head in brotherly fashion, because he had found grace.'

It was to this philanthropic Geneva that Kate turned her attention at the start of 1883. If she had read her Dostoevsky, she might have been less startled at the events which were to take place.

*

Arthur Clibborn, kneeling in one of Geneva's halls on New Year's morning, 1883, saw the gas lamps turned down and darkness give way to dawn. He was the first *'avant-coureur'* taking the Anglican Plague – 'the malady come to us from England' – across the Jura mountains from France into Switzerland.

Kate had received letters as early as the previous October – 'God grant that we may ere long clasp hands. Our greatest wish is to see you soon cross our frontier' and Clibborn arrived at the lakeside capital in December, where he was met by wary pastors who advised him to postpone the attack since they were already doing all that could be done.

Two years after Dostoevsky's death, Geneva lay cold and calm as her lake, overshadowed by the slopes of the Jura and the snow-capped Alps, by Mont Blanc and the Dent du Midi, and by the lowering threats of successive reformers with their over-bearing certainty that light, as the city motto foretold, had exclusively – and conclusively – followed darkness.

Clibborn preached Joel on old men dreaming dreams, young men seeing visions, and handmaidens receiving a pouring out of the spirit, and said that with 40,000 people in the town who never went inside a church, the pastors needed all the help they could get. Brought up on Calvanism, on predestination and the salvation of the elect, they shuddered and begged him to go home.

On 10 December, the Swiss celebrated victory over the

Catholic Savoyards, with street carnivals and a meeting in the big Salle de la Reformation, with its impressive two-tiered galleries and a raised platform mounted like a massive organ loft at one end. Built with the help of money from England expressly for the purpose of holding evangelistic meetings, there was seating for 3000 people. For most of the year, it was used as a concert hall.

Taking, as always, the grand view, Clibborn booked the hall for the evening of the 10th, ignoring the danger of revellers breaking in. In the afternoon, a pastor retold the story of Protestant victory, as he did every year, to a packed audience who clapped and cheered when he described the Catholics running for their lives with pots of boiling soup poured down on their heads. As a band of young men wearing dark suits and white gloves grouped themselves on the platform to sing, Arthur handed a note to the pastor asking him to announce the evening meeting. The pastor glanced at the note and then tore it into little pieces which he threw on the floor in front of him.

Eight hundred people attended that night, with Arthur Clibborn thundering salvation from the rail, his officers ranged behind him, standards propped against the wall of the enormous building which was later to become famous as the meeting place for the League of Nations. Over the next few weeks, meetings were held in smaller halls as well – at the Rive Droite and the Casino, and at the Salles du Terraillet and des Grottes. By the time the Maréchale arrived, Clibborn had built up a strong congregation of cultured middle-class Swiss men and women, high-minded, well-meanning and pious, who viewed the Army with cautious approval.

'These are not the people we came to Geneva to seek,' Kate said as she left the first meeting she addressed. 'We must reach the others, by whatever means.' A very earthquake of sensation can alone suffice, Railton had once remarked.

Like so many countries with a tradition of religious and political tolerance – and in spite of her Calvinistic upbringing – Switzerland, and Geneva in particular, had become a clearing-house for the drop-outs, exiles, and hot-heads of Europe. Nihilists from Russia fled there, and so did anarchists from Paris. The gospel they preached varied, but certain points remained constant: negativism, destruction, and murder. They preached, however, on the corners of the back streets, in the cheap bars and the cellars, and in the dimly lit rooms of lodging-houses, which meant that respectable citizens either did not know of their existence, or did not care to acknowledge it.

Caught in the kind of society they had created for themselves, Genevans were forced to maintain double standards and a level of hypocrisy which Kate regarded with irritation and contempt. Since she was a small girl, she had found it hard to be patient with the Pharisees: 'to get a view of your own heart, will cure you forever of pride,' she said. While asserting that their city was free from prostitution and alcoholism, brothels and bars were licensed and received tacit support, and the men who ran them were among the most influential in the Canton. Prepared to indulge what they privately considered yet another in a long line of crack-pot evangelists, they were unwilling to assist in the salvation of those who entertained them and made them rich.

To comply with Swiss regulations, there had so far been no street processions, no cornets or drums, and placards advertising meetings had from the start been submitted for police approval. Just before Christmas, a new placard went on the streets advertising a meeting at the Casino Hall on 22 December. Lurid and provocative, the police passed it, as they had passed all the rest, presumably without paying too much attention.

'Blood and fire!' it said, with the picture of a sword. *L'Armée du Salut* would explain its strange and warlike device, and the Maréchale would open the attack.

Watching from a window before the meeting began, Kate said she had never seen such men in London or in Paris. Out of the cellars and the single rooms, from filthy drinking dens, brothels and sleazy dance halls, came a community that Dostoevsky's pastors and philanthropic ladies hardly knew existed, curious to hear what they thought to be a call to arms, an incitement to commit arson, and a declaration of war. Instead, they heard of the blood of Christ and the fire of the Spirit, from the impelling 24-year-old, fair-haired Maréchale and her handsome 27-year-old second in command, Colonel Clibborn.

Scandalised, the Christian community condemned the placard as crude sensationalism and an insult to the Gospel. In its élitest way, it considered itself betrayed. Influential citizens who had previously patronised the novelty of the Army turned against it, and those who had heralded Kate as a second Saint Joan, galvanised by her piercing eyes and striking manner, now viewed her with shocked dismay as a potent threat to dignity, law and order.

'*Quel audace!*' they exclaimed. 'What can a group of children teach the city of Calvin?' Kate spoke of the work of saving souls, which she called a supernatural science, a selflessness, a heart equipment, and Railton's words came back to her – dear Railton, so like Arthur Clibborn in his cavalier indifference to anything but the will of the Lord. 'The deadness of sin,' he used to say, 'when men are dead to sin none but fools should dream of awakening them without sensation . . . a very earthquake of sensation alone can suffice.'

With Railton's memory goading her, her father in her, Clibborn beside her, and the certainty of a fourth, like to the Son of God, she went, as always, straight to the point. 'Our mission is not directed at you, fellow Christians, but at a class of people whose tastes, views, ideas, and habits, are wholly different from yours,' she said.

'This announcement seemed to you startling and bordering on the profane, but it did for us exactly what we had hoped. It brought from the depths, from the cellars and slums and hells of your city, a vast crowd of beings whom no ordinary call would have reached. They were struck with the words; seized with wonder and curiosity; even amusement. And they came with a great rush to see this novelty and hear what the strange words meant.

'They came with every motive except the right one, but they came, thank God.'

From then on, meetings were riotous and disorganised, but effective. A Greek journalist who called Christ a fanatic and a layabout, under police surveillance as a political activist, wrote an article against his paper's policy, defending the Army, and received an angry letter from his Editor demanding a retraction. Persuaded that dynamite was not after all the universal remedy he had conceived it to be, he resigned his job and went to work as a labourer with the peasants in the fields. A newspaper correspondent, sent to report a meeting and confessing a lifelong desire to see burned every Christian church, priest and Bible, pronounced himself 'bouleversé'. 'I have been shot through,' he

77

said.

'*Tel que je suis, pécheur rebelle,*' they sang on their knees, '*Jésus, je viens à Toi*', while Kate came down the stairs from the platform and walked up and down the aisles among the people, going first among the rowdiest and singing to them, her eyes dwelling on them one by one, and then walking on a little, singing and speaking, standing still or climbing on a chair so that they could all see and hear her.

A pastor, disgusted by what seemed to him to be no more than showmanship and blatant emotive sensationalism, left a graphic description of the scene:

'The Maréchale,' he said, 'her body leaning forward, arms extended with ecstatic countenance, her look immersing anyone who saw it in a strange flame, with a supplicating manner, slowly called "Come, my friends, come my sister, come my brother, come, come!" and a man rose, his captive eyes attached to her, dragging himself forward on his knees, cast himself violently down, and in a series of inarticulate cries, threw his soul in a disorderly way at the Saviour's feet.

'A young girl rose, and as if struck with lightning, fell before her chair, which she then broke with her forehead by furious plunges, and then rising to her feet, with a bruised face, confessed her dreadful past to the public.

'Once more the Maréchale rose, once more she advanced. You could see her concentrate on one point the powerful fascination of her look, open her arms as if to enwrap and bring back to herself a friend whom the devil was trying to take from her. You might have heard her push her cry of "Come!" with such a vibration of anguish, terror, and compassion, that every eye sought to find out which way she was looking. The answer to this explosion of divine, irresistible and devouring love had not long to be waited for. Breaking away from her husband, who wished to hold her back, a woman rushed out, mounted the steps of the platform and fell at the Maréchale's side.'

Blanche Roussel, a clergyman's daughter, seeing the Maréchale in Geneva for the first time, called her '*une tragédienne instinctive, la belle salutiste*', remarking on '*le timbre ardent, le sourire plus tendre, l'emotion qui se peignait sur le délicat visage allongé*'. Even Kate's correct English accent − '*vous jetterez le mesque de votre faux bonheur*' was '*pas du tout désagréable*'. '*Qu'elle était jolie!*' said

Blanche years later.

On Christmas Day, the Reformation Hall was full, students shouting anarchist slogans from the boxes in the galleries and criminal and political refugees fighting in the pit. Among them, Genevan Christians said they were seeing the city as it really was for the first time in their lives. Prayers were laughed at and hymns shouted down, but Kate, hardly knowing whether it was excitement or fear that she felt, refused to be deflected. Taking turns, she and Clibborn interspersed the flurries of whistles with a brief phrase, shouted loud and clear into the hall, and gradually but steadily the whistling died down. Kate gripped the wooden balustrade in front of her to stop her hands shaking, and leaning towards the people, she spoke with all the volatile fire of her father and the gentle but dogged perseverance of her mother, challenging, whispering, calling out and bringing her hand down on the rail with force to emphasise her call, pleading for Christ with genuine tears in her eyes.

Josephine Butler, the social reformer from England, on the Continent to further her campaign against white slave trafficking, described it as a revelation. 'The uproar itself,' she said, 'seemed at times to render more pointed the words spoken in a clear, unfaltering voice which cut their way through it.' Afterwards, in a continuation meeting in the quietness of a smaller hall behind the platform, 'the roar of voices gradually died away, and a feeling of deep solemnity fell on those assembled,' she said. 'Some of the ringleaders of the disturbance had pushed their way into the smaller hall, but there they remained perfectly still, subdued and over-awed, with an expression on their faces of intense interest in the presence of a reality in religion which they had not encountered before. The officers did not fail to take advantage of the scene which had just been witnessed to urge their hearers to be as decided for Christ as the rioters were against Him, and there followed a scene such as, it was said, had never been witnessed in Geneva. More than forty people (careless or mocking a few minutes before), arose and one after another came forward and, kneeling down, surrendered themselves to God before the whole meeting.'

'Je rencontrai Dieu face à face,' wrote one young man, speaking later of *'ce mystérieux changement qui transforma ma vie entière'*. *'Je sentais mes pieds quitter le sol sous la pression de la foule, et cependant Dieu*

me sauva.' It was, he said, a question of being '*mis au pied du mur: il fallait être sauvé ou perdu'*.

Incensed and bewildered at the somersault threatening to take place in their midst, hard-core Genevans began striking back. A doctor swore that the emotional upheaval provoked by the Army was harmful to the mentally insecure. Men in charge of vice rings spread rumours that converts were paid to testify, while themselves paying four francs and a pint of beer to anyone willing to cause a disturbance. Soon feeling ran so high that those who joined the Army risked losing their jobs, and Colonel Clibborn found himself unable to hand out work or even the price of a meal for fear of being charged with bribery.

Having reviewed Kate's application to reside in Geneva, the Council of State for the Canton granted permission for a year. Four days later she was expelled. Monsieur Marc Heredier, President of the Department of Justice and Police which issued the expulsion, announced angrily that he was withdrawing police support from Army meetings, and shouted that if it had been up to him, he would never have signed a single English passport in the first place. Later, a Swiss lawyer called his words the most direct encouragement to mob disturbance ever heard from the lips of a magistrate.

La Scène, a theatrical newspaper with its own vested interests, called Salvationists cynical play actors parodying religion, and likened them to parasites feeding on public credulity. The *Theatrical Chronicle* accused them of living by speculation and promoting 'the cleverly designed plan of campaign of the bank of Booth and Co' in whose English coffers they said the Maréchale was amassing Swiss money.

'Why spare those who open a shop to sell righteousness just as formerly indulgences were sold?' they asked. 'It is high time for the Department of Justice and Police to appear on the scene, otherwise the people themselves would have scourged these sinners from the temple.'

As police began turning a blind eye to rioters, fifty Swiss gentlemen, many of them holding influential positions, formed themselves into a private police escort, manning the doors at each Army service, but Colonel Clibborn and a fellow officer, walking down the street in broad daylight, had stones thrown at them, and the Army offices in the Place Longemalle were attacked, the windows broken and the doors forced off their hinges, the inside ransacked and vandalised. Instead of arresting the law-breakers, the Geneva government issued a decree ordering the Army to cease holding meetings altogether.

The decree was posted on 2 February 1883. It read: 'In consequence of representations which have reached the Department of Justice and Police, whence it is understood that religious meetings held by a group of persons calling themselves the Salvation Army and acting under the direction of foreigners not established in the Canton, have been preceded by advertisements of a nature to agitate the population; and seeing that the exercise and operation of the above individuals give rise to energetic protests, and that the public peace is daily troubled in a grave and disquieting manner – Be it decreed: In virtue of Article 9 of the law of 11 March 1816, on the duties of the administrative police; and under the seal of the Department of Justice and Police, that the exercises of the Salvation Army be temporarily suspended.'

Within twenty-four hours, 900 people had signed a petition calling the decree an incitement to public disorder, and the leading Geneva newspaper, *Journal de Génève*, had condemned the measure as illegal and accused the police of complicity with the rioters. Article 9, cited by the Department, charged police to inspect shows, dancing saloons, cafés, billiard rooms, cabarets, wine cellars, public houses, inns, and all public gatherings, and it gave the Council of State the right to close any such places. Unable to discover precisely what was meant by the word 'Exercises', it soon became apparent that all Salvation work and all meetings, even those held in private houses, were at an end in Geneva. To support such action legally, it was said that the Council would have had to delve back to the days of the Inquisition.

'If from the first the police had seriously wished to hinder the disturbances, they had abundant power to do so,' said the *Journal de Génève*. 'They might then have brought into play Article 9. But instead of this, they tolerated and encouraged the rioters with the motive of reaching the end which Monsieur Heredier confessed in the Grand Council, namely of driving out of our midst people whose religion does not please him.

'Doubtless their religion does not please. But what merit

81

would there be in tolerating it if it entirely pleased us? And what motive would there have been for inscribing this guarantee in our Constitution if it were only meant to be applied to cases in which it would be manifestly useless?

'Now we must see that we do not any longer deceive foreigners who, in the faith of our Constitution may imagine that Geneva is a country of religious liberty.

'It will be necessary to change the text of the articles of the Constitution in which this mention of our rights is found. It must in future run thus: "Freedom of meeting is guaranteed. Nevertheless, persons who know how to persevere in making sufficient noise, coupled with abuse and personal assaults, shall always be able to obtain from the Government the closing by the police of any meeting whatsoever, even in a private house, which happens to displease them.'

Sensing he would do well to entrench his position, Monsieur Heredier judicially swapped one charge for another, which was equally inappropriate. Fifteen or twenty years earlier, Jesuit nuns had made a nuisance of themselves begging, and a new law had been introduced forbidding house to house collections. The Salvation Army had never taken house to house collections, but making much of money handed in at meetings and of literature containing subscription forms, Monsieur Heredier summoned Kate to his office and demanded to see her account books, which she was unable to produce since her treasurer was away.

On 12 February at six o'clock in the evening, she was expelled from the Canton of Geveva: on the printed form of her expulsion, the word 'days' in which she must leave was crossed out and replaced by the word 'hours'. On the road that led out of the town to the railway station, Swiss Salvationists, hearing what had happened, surrounded her and walked with her as she talked to them of the purifying fire and of the work they had to do until she returned. Then they recited the 46th Psalm together like the knights of old at Agincourt, punctuating every verse, the shaking of the mountains and the heathens' rage, with amens and hallelujahs:

> 'God is our refuge and strength,
> A very present help in trouble.
> Therefore will we not fear . . .'

Arriving exhausted the other side of the lake at Lausanne in the Canton of Vaud, Kate climbed four flights of stairs to a hotel bedroom which had been booked for her. Hurried feet clattered up the stairs and there were whispers exchanged with the porter: '*Salutistes* . . . we cannot have them here!' and she was forced to find another hotel prepared to let rooms to the tired young English evangelist and her colleagues who knocked on the door late at night.

Kate was twenty-four, with her father's passionate intensity and her mother's terrier-like determination: an inherited committal to the cause of Christ. Many of those who worked with her were young, or younger than she was. Almost all were in their twenties.

Adelaide Cox and Elizabeth Clarke were with her from the first days in France, Liz Clarke with her capacity for praying far into the night and showing no apparent sign of exhaustion – 'and who can tell what her prayers accomplished,' Kate was to say years later – and Adelaide with her unfailing optimism and faith. Patty – Kate Patrick – was still there, her dark hair drawn back from full cheeks, her face deceptively untried: sometimes the stones thrown at her in Paris had torn her bonnet and cut her head.

There were French and German Swiss, Emile, Bouillat, Zitzer, and 'Tall Jacques' who never tired of testifying to his previous 'life of sin'. Captain Richard Thonger, fair and hefty with a fresh complexion had come to Switzerland from the north of England, and Sylvester Rabey, small, dark and lively, had come to the Continent from the Channel Islands with Captain Becquet whose catch-phrase – 'Amen, my friends!' – was always on his lips. Athletic and humorous and indomitably cheerful, Edward Becquet's carefree good humour annoyed his enemies as much as it impressed and encouraged his friends.

Maud Charlesworth, the youngest of them all, was only seventeen years old, a clergyman's daughter, from an eminently respectable home in England. Adventurous and self-composed, she was legally in Kate's care while away from home. Respecting her father's wishes by not joining the Army as an officer, she nevertheless accompanied Kate wherever she went, wearing the Salvation Army 'S' pinned on her dress like a brooch. Only five foot tall and able to speak fluent French, she and Kate had survived for several days when they first came to Switzerland, on chocolates provided by a sympathetic chocolate factory owner.

Maud leaves behind her, in an account printed in *The Times*, an endearing picture of the guileless devastation Kate's colleagues wrought on the bewildered Genevan authorities who were now committed to harassing Salvationists wherever they could be found to be operating. Ordered with Captain Zitzer to attend police headquarters, Maud was shown into 'a small and very hot office' to be questioned by a 'savage-looking' magistrate, and officers with 'cross and unsaved-looking faces,' who were evidently no match at all for the forthright young lady before them.

'The last thing Katie said to me was "Do not sign anything,"' she said. 'So when I got into that little room, I made up my mind that when they came to the end and asked me to sign, I would refuse.

'My questioners, of whom most of the time there were five, all possessed very quick tempers. Their object was to frighten me so as to make me answer unwisely, but they were disappointed, for they had never had to do with a Salvationist before, and could not make out why I was so calm and answered so clearly. They were also disappointed to find that I understood their language, and no matter how fast they read, I was always prepared with an answer.

'They began by asking me about the private meeting at which I had been present. They said it was a public meeting, because three detectives had got in without being asked at the door for their cards of invitation. I denied the false statement, and made them write down my answer plainly. Then they asked me how we dared wear uniforms at the meeting when we had been told of the law forbidding the wearing of religious dress.

'Now I knew this law by heart. It says that no one is to wear a religious dress on the public highway. My answer was that I did not think the words "Public highway" could apply to the kitchen of a cottage in which a private meeting was held.

'"Have you a passport or leave to stay in Geneva?" asked one of the crossest of the examiners (with whom I was now quite alone), and I could see by his manner that he thought I had not got my papers. I answered that I had my leave to stay, and that my passport was in the hands of the police. You should have seen the rage he got into. He rose, threw down his chair, stamped out of the room, shouted for some under-officer, and asked the man what he meant by having said that I was not provided with a passport. This man also lost his temper, went off to look for the passport, and in a few minutes returned and saw I was quite right and that they had my passport and I my "leave to stay".

'The inspector then flew into a greater rage than before and scolded the man who had misled him. When he was more composed, he continued. He asked me if I had my father's leave to remain in Geneva, and when I said yes, he wanted letters to prove it. I asked him how he dared to doubt my word, and told him to write down that Miss Booth had letters from my father authorising me to stay.

'A little later, he said that I had prayed in a private meeting according to the form of the Salvation Army. I insisted that the Salvation Army had no form of prayer, and asked him in what way their prayers differed from other prayers. He said they differed very much, but he could not tell me how. He repeated that we had a form of prayer and began to storm so loudly that an inspector ran in from the next room saying "Gently, gently, there is somebody outside..."

'At last, after a great deal more questioning, my paper was finished. I knew all my answers were true, and that there was no harm in putting my name to it, but I said I would not sign until Captain Bouillat had read it through. They were angry, and tried to frighten me, all talking as fast as they could at the same time. Then they said they would read the paper all through again, which they did, three times, but nothing could move me.

'I said I would go with Zitzer and fetch Bouillat. They answered that I might go, but not with Zitzer, and I said I could not think of such a thing – that it would be very improper for a young lady to walk through the streets after dark, especially as I knew there was a plot on foot to do us harm. In the end, two gendarmes were sent for Bouillat, I and Zitzer waiting meanwhile in the hot little office.

'All at once it struck me that we would have a prayer meeting. "Zitzer," I said, "we will pray. Let us go down on our knees and pray for these people, for if ever we wanted the Lord with us, it is now." So down we went, and prayed out loud for about ten minutes, and it did us good. The inspector was much surprised. He cleared his throat, grunted, and finally got up and went to the door of the outer office. At length Bouillat came, and on his recommendation, I signed the deposition.

'The great fun was that all these cross magistrates and inspectors were kept from their dinners. So were we, but as I told them that was a very secondary consideration to us. We left that office at half past seven, singing "Glory to His Name". I had been there four hours, and the whole town knew it.'

Told to report back to the police the following day, Maud and three other Salvationists sent a letter explaining that since it was Sunday, they could not 'conscientiously go on that day'. At 12.30 Sunday lunchtime she received a warrant instructing her to leave the canton of Geneva by six o'clock in the evening. It was alleged that she had spoken at a public meeting; she had failed to present herself at the police station as requested on Sunday morning; and she had nothing to prove her parents' consent to her being on the continent with the Maréchale in the first place.

The *Journal de Génève* called it the case of 'two young foreign girls of honourable character whose only crime is that they have held religious services of a rather eccentric nature.' They criticised Monsieur Heredier for being secretly present, like a grand inquisitor, hiding behind a curtain during each interrogation, and pointed out that he had chosen Sunday, a holiday when the majority of the members of the government were away in the country, to enforce a law which was illegal in the first place.

'Never have foreigners – young girls, almost children – been treated in such a manner among us,' it said. 'By whom are we governed? Into whose hands have we fallen?'

'A woman', writing anonymously to another newspaper, attacked the Maréchale and called her officers saltimbanques or charlatans, a word promptly taken up and used by strip cartoonists and satirists, and a religious paper suggested that the Army's success was due to its powers of mesmerism. 'If mesmerism can work such a change as has been worked in my house,' said a mother, 'then I wish all Geneva were mesmerised!'

'It is no delusion,' wrote another. 'It is not imagination. Still less is it by mesmerism that my five children and I have been converted. Consecrated lives and hearts filled with the love of souls have spoken more clearly than ten thousand discourses.'

A Swiss evangelist running mission halls in Geneva said that since the arrival of the Army, blessings had increased at his meetings proportionately with the increase of violence, and a pastor wrote to tell of relationships healed and enemies reunited. 'The spirit of God has been working in a marvellous way all round my parish, inspired by the fire lit in my heart by the Army,' he said. 'On all sides I am now called to minister to broken hearts.'

'As mothers and as women who love their families and their fatherland,' proclaimed a letter signed by nearly a hundred women, 'we can only bless the Lord for the good which He has brought us and our children, by means of the Salvation Army.'

'Is it really possible that they have driven from among us the friends who have done us so much good?' wrote one of them to the Maréchale.

As if to put the matter beyond all doubt, it was at this time that Comtesse Agenor de Gasparin, an apparently devout Christian woman of great influence, distributed a venomous letter attacking the *l'Armée du Salut* for degrading the Gospel. Never having attended a meeting, she based her knowledge on gossip, and painted a picture of mass hysteria, rowdyism and abandon.

Madame de Gasparin called her brochure *'Lisez et Jugez'* – read and judge. In it, she purported to set out extracts from the *Rules and Regulations* of the Army, and Kate had to listen to the words which her beloved Railton had laboured over, his black eyes blazing with excitement, being twisted, ridiculed, and turned into blasphemy. Salvationists themselves were condemned as a regiment of Amazons talking religious claptrap: *'le boniment religieux'*. Accusing Kate of Machiavellian methods and Jesuitical tendencies, the Comtesse denounced Army procedure as hypocritical and scheming, and prophesied that if Jesus were in Geneva, He would be the Army's bitterest judge, tearing their banners to shreds and overturning their platforms.

Strengthened, as always, by persecution, Swiss officers of the Salvation Army increased. Denied permission to meet even in private, they began holding clandestine rendezvous in Hallelujah kitchens, Hallelujah parlours, Hallelujah shops, defying local thugs who had been given carte blanche by the police to disturb and inform on meetings. Sometimes they met early, at four or five o'clock in the morning, out on the slopes of the mountains or by the lakeside or in the gardens of big houses.

Arthur Clibborn went to Berne to see the President of the Republic and the British Ambassador, and when he returned, with the help of Swiss lawyers, he prepared a long and detailed appeal for Kate to send to the Federal Council in Berne, who sent an equally wordy refusal, reiterating the erroneous charge of house to house collecting and accusing Kate, 'styled Maréchale', of exploiting the credulous. Attending a succession of overcrowded meetings in stuffy Geneva back rooms, Clibborn, with several other Swiss Salvationists at that time, contracted a mild form of TB and had to leave for the fresh air of the North.

'For the first time in my life I feel ashamed of being a Swiss,' said a gentleman living in London, writing to the citizens of Geneva. 'If my people are autonomous, if every man can make his opinion felt, how can such an infamy be perpetrated? Is it possible that two ladies have been banished from your midst? And why? Have they broken any law? I will speak boldly. It is not for this that you have driven them out. You have driven them out because you felt that they have more real power and virility than all of you put together and because you could not drive them away by mockery, that weapon which you have hitherto considered all-powerful.

'You have driven them out, or permitted them to be driven out, because you felt impelled to get rid of them, and because you dared not burn them as would have been done in the old times.'

'Precious Maréchale,' said one of the many letters sent by the Swiss to Kate after her expulsion, 'we all pray for you and believe hard for your return. Your crown will be very bright when you go home to the Lord, for you have gone through so much fire. I pray that I may have a place at your feet there, as near the dear Lord as I can get.'

On the day of her expulsion, the Maréchale had addressed an appeal to the Grand Council of Geneva. On 26 February, under a safe-conduct, she was allowed back from Vaud to appear in Geneva before the Counsellor of State delegated to hear the appeal. Insisting that she had never incited violence, she pointed out that permission to reside in Geneva for a year had been granted just at the time when meetings had been at their most rowdy, and when permission could have been withheld.

The Counsellor shrugged his shoulders and said that this was nothing more than a pretext for expulsion. 'It is not the real reason why you were expelled,' he said. It was the *'bruit'* he explained, the noise caused by such meetings, the palaver and the embarrassment.

'It is not in accordance with our ideas and customs that young women should appear in public,' he went on, quoting at length from Madame de Gasparin's circular, which he had on the table in front of him. *'Nous sommes froissés,'* he said. 'We are offended.'

Kate was angry, as she always had been since childhood when faced with ignorance and injustice: once upon a time, it would have seemed impossible that men could be so blind. 'It is contrary, you tell me, to your sense of what is right and becoming, sir,' she repeated, watching him steadily, 'that young women should preach the Gospel.

'If Miss Charlesworth and I had come to Geneva to act in one of your theatres, we should have met with sympathy and approval. We could have sung and danced on your stage. We could have dressed in a manner very different from, and much less modest than, you see us dressed. We could have appeared before a miscellaneous audience, men and women, young and old, of every class. Members of the Grand Council, Monsieur Heredier himself, would have come to see us act. Geneva would have paid money ungrudgingly and you would all have sat and approved and clapped your hands and applauded us. You would have brought your wives and daughters to see us, and they also would have applauded. There would have been nothing to "offend" you. No immorality at all, according to your ideas and customs. The "noise" we would have thus made would not have been a cause for our expulsion.

'But when women come to try and save some of the forty or fifty thousand of your miserable, scoffing, irreligious population, who never enter any place of worship, when they come with hearts full of pity and love for the ignorant and sinful, and stand up to tell the glad tidings of salvation to these rebels, many of whom accept the tidings with eager joy, then you cry out that this is unseemly and immodest.

'You would not bring your wives and daughters to hear us speak of Jesus, though you would bring them to hear us if we danced and sang upon the stage of your theatres. Now you have expelled us. But still there are these multitudes in Geneva who are dark, lost, unsaved, and you know it. There they are. They exist. What will you do with them?

89

'Say – what will you do?' she repeated urgently. 'Are they not a danger? Does not their lost condition cry out against you?'

The Counsellor was silent, sunk down in his chair, listening and thinking. Discomforted, he recognised the truth of what Kate said, and he found it unaccountably moving.

Several weeks later, the Council of State turned down the Appeal. This time they found a third pretext for refusing the Maréchale permission to stay in Geneva, in consideration, they said, of Article 28 of the Law of February, 1844:

'The Council of State, in virtue of its supreme administrative power, always possesses the right of sending out of the Canton foreigners whose presence may be a danger to the interests of the country or to the safety of the State.'

It was a law at once so vague and yet so immense that its effect was equivalent to a temporary suspension of the write of Habeas Corpus, and left the Salvationists with no room for manoeuvre at all.

'Since the departure of the Salvation Army, our theatre has lost a formidable rival,' reported the *Theatrical Chronicle*. 'The crowds are beginning to find their way back to us . . .'

CHAPTER 7

'You will never know what a moving of the Spirit it was among *la jeunesse* of Switzerland,' said an old aristocrat in his late eighties who travelled across Switzerland to meet two of the Maréchale's children because he could not forget what had happened seventy years earlier.

'I was an officer then in the Swiss Military Army,' he said. 'I came with other young men, and we came not to worship but to ridicule. The hall was packed and instead of being amused, God met me. I can't remember a word that was said, but my life rose up before me, all the uselessness and the selfishness, and I cried to God for mercy as I knelt there among the benches.

'When the Maréchale was forbidden to speak in the casinos and the theatres and in the Reformation Hall, we would flock out in hundreds after work, along the lake below the Dent du Midi to God's natural amphitheatre where the trees seem to grow right up the hillside, and there in the wide valley below, we worshipped together.

'It wasn't a passing whim. I wasn't mentally disturbed as many people would have said. I didn't join the Salvation Army on a wave of emotion, but I offered myself instead to *l'Église Nationale*, and I have been a pastor ever since.

'I can never forget it. It was a moving of the Spirit. It was God bringing conviction to the youth of Switzerland.'

*

'We would walk eight leagues to see her,' they said, slipping and slithering across the border into the French mountains to hear her speak. 'God gives us strength and takes away our hunger.'

The first meeting the Maréchale held after her expulsion was in a quarry hidden in the Savoy mountainside high above Geneva, sheltered by an overhanging rock. Appropriately, the nearest village was Ferney, with its history of passion and cynicism, where Voltaire had lived his last bitter years writing *Candide*, sniping at what he saw as religious fanaticism in the French and Swiss authorities, throwing open his home to victims of oppression.

Ferney was four miles from Geneva, and the Maréchale arrived by train the night before the meeting which began at first light, five in the morning with mist still hanging on the mountains and clinging wetly to the grass.

Salvation Army soldiers stood in the roads below to direct troops as they arrived from Switzerland with their cheeks red in the frosty air and their hair damp in the mist. Each troop marched in unbroken ranks, as if endeavouring to prove that their spirit, too, remained unbroken. Beside them, mothers wheeled prams and carried children in their arms. 'S's gleamed on their jerseys and high-collared coats, and many of the women already wore dark blue bonnets with dull red ribbons.

As they began to pray together, 300 of them standing on the cliffside gathered round the Maréchale, Geneva suddenly became visible through the mist in the valley below, roofs glinting in the early morning sun as it rose above the mountains, making the hollow of the quarry where they stood seem darker and more chill. Then, as one of the soldiers voiced the certainty of them all that the Salvation Army would soon re-enter Geneva, the first rays of sunshine broke above the precipice and flooded the meeting, and loath, as always, to let the parable pass, they spoke delightedly of the light of liberty which would seem all the more bright for the temporary shadow.

Later in the day, more people arrived, some loyal, some merely curious, drawn by the sound of singing and by the sight of smoke from a bonfire lit in the brushwood by local Roman Catholic boys signalling that the Salvationists were at prayer, and police pushed and grunted their cumbersome way up the slippery paths and through the undergrowth, prowling round the gathering and making notes in their notebooks as the Maréchale spoke of shooting to kill as Napoleon did, and of all that God gave to those who dared to follow at all costs. In the evening, there were more police waiting for Colonel Clibborn at Geneva railway station and calling at his lodgings in the town, searching for him in cupboards and under the bed, but he had returned with the Maréchale to Lausanne.

In England, General Booth went a second time to see Lord Granville, the Liberal Foreign Secretary, to ask the British Government to intervene with the Swiss authorities to restore his daughter's freedom of movement, and in the Canton of Neuchâtel, *'Neuchâtel, cette ville froide et intellectuelle'* with its old twelfth-century buildings and modern watch-making factories, set between the Terrible and the Tender Mountains of the Jura on the banks of Lake Neuchâtel to the north of Geneva, Major Kate Patrick and Captain Edward Becquet were being chased down the streets by crowds wanting to throw them into the water, and accompanied home by police with drawn swords. 'Are you persecuted enough?' asked Railton in a *War Cry* Editorial.

The first meeting held in Neuchâtel in January had been calm. Because of rioting mobs at the doors on following evenings, Captain Becquet decided to close the hall for a few days, re-opening with admission by ticket only, which caused worse riots outside, with windows broken and stones thrown at the door of the Hôtel Mont Blanc where the meetings were held.

The Grand Council of Neuchâtel, hearing of the scenes already taking place in Geneva, issued a commendably liberal proclamation calling on the people of the Canton not to let it be said that 'the glorious rights of our Constitution are a dead letter.'

'Dear Citizens,' it read. 'The Council of State is determined to enforce respect for public order, liberty of meeting, and liberty of worship. Its duty is to protect the liberties and security of all. It will not fail in this duty.

'One of the most glorious conquests of our Revolution of 1848 was the securing of liberty of public meeting, and absolute liberty of worship. These liberties are enshrined in our Cantonal Constitution. We appeal, dear Citizens, to your feelings of justice and tolerance. Let us give full liberty to the manifestation of all opinion, of all creeds. Let us discuss them, if we will, and even judge them severely; but let us beware of seeking to suppress them. Let us avoid even the appearance of persecution.

'Citizens of Neuchâtel, we boast of being a free and civilised people. Let us show that we know how to respect the public manifestation of convictions, religious or otherwise, however absurd they may appear to us. Let us carefully guard all our liberties, and let us not destroy them for ourselves by ceasing to respect them in others. Let us know how to be tolerant, if we desire that others shall be tolerant to us.'

It was a clear enough call, greeted by the majority with as much enthusiasm as Voltaire's Candide, who said that it was all true enough, and then got on with his gardening.

From Geneva, Monsieur Heredier contacted his friend, Monsieur Cornaz, his opposite number at the head of the Department of Justice and Police at Neuchâtel. Judging that Colonel Clibborn and the Maréchale would move into Neuchâtel from Geneva, Monsieur Heredier sent duplicated copies of Madame de Gasparin's letter and had them circulated to everyone of influence in Neuchâtel by the time the two notorious Salvationists arrived. 'Suddenly little children began to shrink from us as if we would do them harm,' said Kate Patrick. 'Doors were shut in our faces. Former friends crossed the street to avoid us.' The Grand Council began speaking of 'this sect', with its 'renown for eccentricity and peculiarity', and, distastefully, of 'the erection of platforms, the monotonous repetition of hymns sung to vulgar airs', and worst of all, 'appeals to public confession'.

Evening meetings were closed, and another Cantonal decree issued, the nub of it hingeing on a nicety of the law:

'Considering the establishment at Neuchâtel of a sect known as the Salvation Army,' it read.

'Considering the extracts from the Orders and Regulations of the Sect as published in Geneva by Madame de Gasparin;

'Considering Article 72 of the Cantonal Constitution, which prescribes that no religious corporation shall establish itself in the Canton without an express and always revocable authorisation by the Grand Council;

'Considering that it is necessary to decide by a formal inquiry whether the Salvation Army does possess the character of a religious corporation before calling upon it to claim the authorisation of the Grand Council;

'The Council decrees: that it charges the Department of Public Worship to proceed to the above mentioned inquiry.'

For the moment, the buck had been neatly and hastily passed on. While investigations were begun to prove whether or not the

Salvation Army could legally be considered a corporation, Salvationists continued to hold demonstrative meetings in the face of accusations of profanation and blasphemy. 'When I left Neuchâtel, there were only a few soldiers and a very small platform,' wrote a soldier returning from France. 'Now the platform is three times as large as any in Paris.'

A twenty-year-old German, unable to speak French, throwing mud and shouting insults, became calm when Captain Becquet stopped the meeting and began praying for him. Pleading in German with Becquet afterwards, he was taken to a German-Swiss pastor who explained that he wanted to be forgiven. From then on, he followed Becquet everywhere, shouting the only two words he could master from his new universal language, 'Hallelujah!' and 'Amen!'

As Monsieur Heredier had guessed, the Maréchale entered Neuchâtel from the French mountains in February and preached to over a thousand people squashed into the Mont Blanc Hotel hall which was meant to seat five hundred. She spoke of the righteous who dwell in the holy hill and speaketh the truth in his heart. Addressing crowds on Sunday morning, she likened herself to Miriam who took a tambourine and sang unto the Lord when the Red Sea parted and the Israelites went across.

Crowds collected outside the door, fighting and shouting, and Kate came down from the platform and walked through the hall to confront them in the open air. 'There were no police to enforce order,' she said later. 'I was powerless. I threw myself on God and asked Him to silence the people and He heard my cry.'

'Go away!' they chorused. 'We have our pastors.'

'You don't do them much credit,' she retorted grimly.

'This is my God,' said one man, waving a pipe in her face.

'You will need another when you come to die.'

'Money is your God!' said another, provoking an uproar of jeering approval.

'Do you really believe we would have left our homes, our friends, our country and everything we love, to come to Switzerland and be treated as you treat us, hooting at us, pelting us with mud and stones, swearing at us and spreading lies about us, just to get money?' she asked. 'You know that all we want is to see you delivered from the slavery of sin. You know that all we want is to bring you into the glorious liberty of the children of God.

'Follow me,' she commanded the man with the pipe, who stared at her with his mouth open and then followed without a word. 'Follow me and listen to me.'

Nonetheless, the reputation of being 'purse-cutters and comedians who drive people mad' clung to the Army. A group of soldiers were caned and padlocked inside the hall where they were holding their meeting, and then had mud and stones thrown at them as they escaped through a back door and went home. 'Few of our friends come now to the afternoon meetings,' they said, 'as they don't like stones and mud thrown at them and they are afraid of being blown up by dynamite . . .'

In the streets, boys sang raucous choruses and hooted with laughter: 'I do believe, I will believe, that Jesus died for me . . .'

'The great news of the day is the presence of the Salvation Army,' commented the Neuchâtel special correspondent in *L'Aurore* in March. 'They have hired an immense hall in the Hôtel Mont Blanc. Their meetings have been disturbed from the outside by a noisy and evil-disposed crowd. There has been an outburst of hatred and exasperation such as one would not have thought possible in our little town – windows broken, blows, ribald songs and savage cries. Everything has been done to upset the meetings which have, however, continued with calmness and courage, God evidently being with these people.

'Immense crowds rush to their meetings – men in rags, poor women, porters, workmen, together with altogether different classes. These evangelists present an immediate, present salvation, with much power and with so much simplicity that every child can understand it.

'I was, for my part, much prejudiced against the Army and their manner of working. But since I have seen them at their work, and witnessed their ardent love for souls, and the strength and power which this consecration of body and soul to the Saviour gives them (the sacrifice even of their lives), I am fully persuaded.'

While meetings continued under duress in Geneva, with shouts of 'Hallelujah for Geneva!' and 'Geneva for Jesus!', the second Swiss corps was formed from soldiers in Neuchâtel, and 'Decree followed Decree,' said Kate Patrick. Without warning, the Prefect informed the Army that Sunday afternoon meetings were also to be forbidden by the Council of State. 'Why didn't they send two or three policemen to keep order?' asked Maud Charlesworth indignantly, discovering that the meetings had been stopped because trouble had been anticipated. 'Why didn't they wait and see? How can they justify breaking their own laws and sacrificing the religious liberty of which the people of Neuchâtel are so proud? It's the same old story: we are the cause, and so we must be stopped.' Even a little boy, asking why there was no afternoon meeting and being told that the government had forbidden it, demanded to know why it was put in the catechism he had to learn by heart that religious liberty was guaranteed by the State.

Making last minute arrangements to hold the meeting instead in the 'Lord's great cathedral' of the forests, six or seven hundred people trekked through the trees although they had been given less than a couple of hours' notice, shouts of '*Toujours en avant!*' resounding to the sky.

'*De l'audace, de l'audace,*' Kate urged. '*Vous n'êtes pas belles roses de printemps à metter sous globe, vous savez.* You aren't lovely little primroses to be kept under glass. *Vous êtes soldats de Jésus-Christ. La guerre veut des âmes guerrières,*' she said. 'A war requires warrior souls.'

Kate Patrick, Edward Becquet and a young Swiss Salvationist from Lausanne, called Anna Furrer, wrote boldly and lucidly to the Grand Council of Neuchâtel: Salvationists, when put to it, could be as cunning as children of the world.

'The Salvation Army is not a religious corporation, nor does it seek to be recognised as such,' ran part of their long letter. 'Hence we do not understand in what manner the Council of State is able to attribute to it that character.

'The Salvation Army is simply an association of persons who enter it and leave it freely at will, and who never take any vows of obligation. As such, it has a right to the protection of the Cantonal Constitution...

'In the letter addressed to the Prefect of Neuchâtel, the Council of State alleges absolutely nothing which could justify the exceptional measures adopted against us. Our meetings take place in private houses and they have not in any way troubled public order or tranquillity. Consequently, basing our appeal upon Articles, 49, 50, and 56 of the Federal Constitution,

97

we respectfully beg you, gentlemen, to be so good as to annul the decree which you published on the 14th of this month, and to give us freedom of meeting.'

The Grand Council, in reply, contented itself with admitting little surprise 'at the sight of two foreigners and a young lady of Lausanne taking upon themselves to give us a lesson in Constitutional Law,' since 'the same persons take upon themselves to preach lessons of Christianity to our pastors.'

In the neighbouring canton of Vaud where Anna Furrer came from, a country said, with its forests and vineyards, to be widowed by drink, Salvationists were hounded out of private houses with fire hoses and buckets of water poured down on their heads. Instead, they went out to worship at three in the morning, meeting in the mountains among the pine trees in snow or pouring rain, or hiring a boat on the lake where they could sing and pray on neutral ground. The Maréchale's reaction was one of encouragement rather than comfort. 'I have told you before,' she said without surprise. 'We have all said goodbye to comfort; goodbye to every selfish impulse, *pour aller après les perdus*.'

In Neuchâtel, over two thousand people from the surrounding country villages, most of whom had never heard of the Army, signed a petition complaining of 'perturbation, speculation, profanation and demoralisation.' Salvationists, harried wherever they went by cries of *'Au lac!'* and *'À l'eau!'* met furtively like the disciples in the upper room. Kate was preaching several times a day, taking as her Ascension-tide text the upper room story of the men who continued together with one accord in prayer and supplication, waiting for the coming of the Holy Ghost.

'I feel impressed that God is about to undertake for us in a wonderful way,' she wrote to England. 'The spirit of prayer has especially come upon me lately. If only we had a barn to meet in: any place to pray.'

When she did pray, however, in a church lent by *L'Église Libre*, following a Sunday evening service – 'though I had not intended, the Holy Spirit led me,' she said, 'and I dared not disobey' – the church was promptly closed down. Kate was struck in the street, sticks and stones and blocks of wood were hurled at her as she walked along, and ink and water tipped out of the windows of the houses as Salvationists walked in the streets beneath. Strangers spat and swore at them and anonymous letters began to arrive.

'*God* was not angry,' commented Kate Patrick. 'We stood and wondered. What had we done? A *woman* had prayed in chapel!'

While a local and eminently respectable army instructor called the Salvationists 'Christians such as I've never known' practising a gospel 'as in the times of the primitive Church' – ('This,' he said, 'is the reason why I love them') – indignant publicans likened them to vine pest, preaching a gospel 'not at all to our taste'. The Grand Council, augmenting its already thick dossier of information on the Army's eccentric behaviour, recorded tales of family secrets being openly confessed in public, women and girls leaving 'the domestic hearth' to go to Salvationist meetings, and citizens being treated 'like pagans' by 'these modern apostles.'

'We are accustomed to dignified religious ceremonies, not to consciences paraded outwardly,' said informants. 'A certain instinctive modesty tells us that the religious man must always remain modest and reserved.' Religious fanaticism could not become the ideal of modern society: after all they asked, 'what will become of the housekeeping. . . ?'

Le Réveil, the official organ of the police force, of which Monsieur Cornaz was the head, referred to Salvationists scathingly as British importations, wretched mountebanks and Salvationist acrobats. 'Our people, who toil from morning till evening,' it said emotively, 'do not quite understand that there is any obligation to show particular respect to people without education and without talent, who pay themselves out of our pockets for gesticulating for two or three hours a day and shouting "Hallelujahs" and "Amens".

'They think that the Maréchale and her female companions would be better employed – and more usefully – knitting stockings or studying a cookery book.' The police, commented the paper inaccurately, had no more right to preserve the peace of a private meeting than of a tea party. 'The public force,' it said, 'has no business to be accompanying the Maréchale wherever she pleases to walk, following her at a distance as though she were a Princess of royal blood.'

Those who were brave enough to continue opening their homes to private prayer meetings, risked having them wrecked.

Several did so purposely, in open defiance. Monsieur Convert, a well-known and respected Neuchâtelois, was one; magistrate Monsieur Aimé Humbert, a progressive educationalist and promoter of religious freedom, one of the founders of the Canton of Neuchâtel when the struggle against the Prussians culminated in the founding of the Swiss Republic, was another.

Monsieur Convert openly flouted the decree forbidding weekday meetings, because he believed it to be unconstitutional. Returning from the police station after lodging an appeal with the Prefect, he found his windows smashed, his door broken down, and his house surrounded by 300 angry rioters who plastered him with mud and threatened to throw the police in the lake.

'Sir, I invite you to abstain henceforward from calling together at your house any members of the Salvation Army, either Swiss or foreign, or to take part in any meeting of this kind, whether in a private house or in public,' Monsieur Cornaz, the Prefect, wrote in a letter to Monsieur Convert.

Not easily quelled, Monsieur Convert wrote back citing three Federal Articles and two Cantonal Articles which he felt the Prefect's letter contradicted. 'According to the terms of your letter, Sir,' he said, 'every meeting whatsoever which may have a religious, moral, or philanthropic character is rendered impossible.'

Monsieur Cornaz was patient and thorough. 'This protest leads me to think I have not clearly explained myself, or else that you wilfully fail to understand me,' he said. 'That being so, I will be more clear.

'The decree of the Council of State to which I called your attention does not, as you appear to think, contemplate interference with all meetings whatsoever which have a religious, moral, or philanthropic character, but the meetings of the Salvation Army, or (in order to be still more explicit), such meetings as those which have taken place at the houses of Monsieur Aimé Humbert and your own house, Sir, and which have been occasions of tumult and disorder.

'There are circumstances, and this is one, in which men should know how to give way, and to wait patiently rather than to run counter to public opinion.'

Monsieur Humbert had already 'run counter to public

opinion' by putting his name to Mrs Josephine Butler's British and Continental Federation for the Abolition of the State Regulation of Vice. When the Army arrived in Switzerland he wrote to friends in England to confirm that it was genuine. Attending one of the first meetings at the Hôtel Mont Blanc in order to judge for himself, he came away calling it 'the strangest phenomena of our great social, political, and religious crisis ... one of those enterprises which neither ridicule nor violence will succeed in annihilating.'

Like Monsieur Convert before him, he risked opening his home to the homeless Salvationists, and with much the same consequences. Paving stones were ripped up from the street outside and thrown through his windows, and his daughter, answering a knock at the door, found herself assailed by insults aimed at her father and his social work.

'Public opinion has been grieved to see a man whose name is connected in the most honourable manner possible with the establishment of our Republic, entering into the debates relative to the Salvation Army,' commented *Le Réveil*. 'The lunatic asylums will have a large number of additional inmates presently.'

By now there were over eighty soldiers in Neuchâtel, braving rotten eggs and buckets of water to hear the Maréchale talk of Calvary and demand a show of hands from all those prepared to walk the road there with her. 'Pray for Switzerland' ordered the *War Cry* in a front page banner headline. On 15 June, the Grand Council of Neuchâtel, having considered all the information put before them, issued a decree:

'The Council forbids, provisionally for as long time as the officers in the Salvation Army shall not have received the authorisation prescribed by Article 72 of the Constitution,' required of all religious corporations, 'all meetings whatsoever and wheresoever of the Army.'

Kate Patrick, who, with the Maréchale, attended the sitting of the Grand Council, likened it to the appearance of the apostles before the Sanhedrin. 'There was the same hatred, the same false accusations, the same evident purpose to stamp out "these who exceedingly trouble our city",' she said, quoting the Bible. 'It pained us to see how little they understand the Gospel, and how little they know Him who is the friend of publicans and sinners. They show this in accusing us of trailing religion in the mud by exhibiting on our platforms jailbirds and drunkards who say they are saved.'

'If they knew what we are, and what we mean,' asked Adelaide Cox, 'how could they try so completely to shut the door against us?'

The Christian called the debate interesting, but very, very sad. 'This precedent will serve as a justification for the tyrannical suppression of any movement in future which may not happen to please the dominant party of the day in Switzerland,' it said, calling that party 'hostile to religion and leaning towards a strongly despotic form of government.' But on the whole, those who supported liberty were dismissed as war-mongers. 'It is finished!' said *Le Réveil*, unconsciously echoing the words of Christ when His work was done.

'57 to 14 against Christ!' exclaimed the *War Cry*, reporting the Council votes. 'They might as well try to stop the growth of the corn as the growth of the Army in Neuchâtel now.'

Colonel Clibborn, on his way down from the mountains in the north where he had been recovering, called the furnace one degree hotter, and the ruling as arbitrary as that of Nebuchadnezzar. 'Our comrades have paid as much attention to it as did the three Hebrews,' he said – a comment borne out by Kate Patrick, staying behind in Neuchâtel 'to encourage the Swiss soldiers,' who called the fire fiercer than ever before. Police trailed her movements, she was jostled off the pavement into the road, and a man chased her down the street with a hatchet shouting 'If you're saved, then you're ready to die!' Captain Becquet, marooned in a house surrounded by police waiting to arrest him, escaped across the rooftops to his home.

Leaving appeals in the hands of Swiss lawyers sympathetic to the cause, Kate and Clibborn went to Paris in July. News of La Maréchale and her skirmishes with Swiss bureaucracy had preceded them, and when Kate spoke in a crowded Paris hall, men like Henri Rochefort, the notorious journalist and Communard, were prominent in the front rows of the gallery to hear her. Tricolours hung from the windows of the houses and in the street there were horses with flags tucked into their harnesses and donkeys with *'Vive la République'* on their headpieces. French Salvationists caught a steamer to St Cloud 'to spend a day with

Jesus in the woods with our beloved Maréchale', polishing up their 'S's and wearing little pieces of tricolour ribbon in honour of the Independence celebrations, carrying a tricolour banner with the words *L'ARMÉE DU SALUT* embroidered across it. At St Cloud, they marched through the park holding the banner above their heads and singing, until they reached the top of the hill, where they were to meet with the Maréchale. Below them lay the busy panorama of Paris, the river glinting in the sun, and the metal glinting on the building site on Montmartre, the hill of martyrs where Joan of Arc once worshipped, and where foundation piles were now being driven thirty metres down to support the great new church of the Sacré Coeur, planned by rich and poor as a peace offering and as a plea for better things to come.

The sunshine soon gave way to rain, but crowding together under a chestnut tree, there were delighted cheers as the Maréchale came in sight, 'weak and very worn' reported a French soldier, 'but with the bright smile we love so much.' Another called it the meeting of a mother and her eldest children, for the soldiers who gathered on the hill in St Cloud were the first French corps, singing their welcome in the familiar salute to the glory and the crown.

'The crown,' said Kate soberly. 'Ah, the crown. I hope we'll be worthy of the crown. It's only for those who fight, you know,' she said, looking round at them. 'For those who stand against the storm and come through victorious.' Then she began to preach.

'It's not enough to pray and plead for blessing,' she said. 'You must receive it. I see more and more that it is God alone who can satisfy.

'Everyone in this world seeks something, but we miss the object of existence unless we find for whom our hearts were created. We must get to know God. How do we get to know God? By seeking Him. And what does this mean? Does it mean knowledge? Does it mean understanding all about the Bible, having theories, being wise and learned? No. It means knowing Him as a friend: experiencing His love and holding communion with Him.

'How can we attain this?' she asked. 'We must be ready to die to self; to crucify ourselves so dead that we don't care what people say or think about us; so dead that we are ready to be spoken evil of, written against, despised, rejected – crucified. We must be living sacrifices.

'Give your all to Him,' she said, her eyes boring holes in the faces before her. 'He is looking down. He sees you. He has chosen the weak things of the world to confound the mighty, and we can do all things through Christ who strengthens us.

'There are two things I wish you to be – two things God wishes you to be – saints and soldiers. It is good to pray, good to read your Bibles and sing hymns, but you must be soldiers too, and fight. Let all who are ready to fight say Amen!' she finished, and they jumped to their feet, carried away less by her words than by the way that she said them, shouting 'Amen! Amen!' over and over again.

From Paris, Kate went to stay with a Swiss friend in a château built on terraced gardens in open parkland at the foot of the slopes of the Jura mountains in Vaud. Influential Swiss came to her from Neuchâtel as soon as she was rested enough to talk with them, and they discussed tactics: a field-marshal surrounded by her generals. As British subjects provided with passports and permits of residence in the Cantons of Geneva and Neuchâtel, the members of the Army were entitled to all the benefits guaranteed in the *Treaty of Friendship, Commerce and Establishment* of 1855, made between Switzerland and England.

'The subjects of her Britannic Majesty shall be admitted to reside in each of the Swiss Cantons on the same conditions and on the same footing as citizens of the other Swiss cantons,' runs an extract. 'They may hire and occupy houses and warehouses for the purpose of residence and commerce and may exercise, conformably to the laws of the country, any profession, business, or occupation.' In conformity with the provisions of this Treaty, full liberty had always been accorded to British subjects to hold evangelistic meetings in all parts of Switzerland. Nevertheless, there was still no news from England; no support from a Foreign Office unwilling to make a fool of itself, and Kate felt lonely in spite of her friends, bewildered and betrayed.

'Your government could, with such good grace and with so much dignity, address a grave remonstrance to ours,' they told her. Meetings had now been forbidden in the Canton of Vaud as well, and police from the local station came up on the railway, creeping across the lawns and looking in at them through the deep drawing-room windows. 'England is so great and powerful, and Switzerland so small . . .'

Taking a boat across the lake to Tougues in the French Savoy, where the Mayor of Tougues met them on horseback and welcomed them, the first French-Swiss corps, three boatloads of them, met with the Maréchale, welcoming her with fixed bayonets and rousing cheers: 'There is a better world, they say . . .' There, she presented them with the first Swiss colours, and orders not to rest until all Switzerland rang from end to end with salvation.

'*De l'audace, de l'audace* . . .' On 9 September 1883, purposely flouting the Neuchâtel decree and putting the Anglo-Swiss Treaty to the test, the Maréchale met her soldiers in a wood five miles outside the town of Neuchâtel, at Prise-Imer in the Jura forest. The clearing where they met was near the home of Monsieur Convert, who announced that he would attend, and that he was happy to answer to God for his actions, which he knew to be illegal, rather than to the Prefect of Neuchâtel. Before the meeting took place, one of the invitations had been intercepted in the post and taken to the President of the Council of State.

'The decree was illegal,' Kate was to say later. 'We considered the matter with Swiss friends and Swiss lawyers, all of whom were united in believing that it was unconstitutional and that meetings ought to continue.

'Besides,' she added, as if the rest were irrelevant, 'I judged it right and better to obey God rather than man, and I considered it my duty – to my Swiss comrades, to Switzerland, and to my opponents.'

Three hundred gathered in a clearing shadowed by tall fir trees, sitting down on the grass and pine needles before the Maréchale. As they sang the first hymn, the Prefect of the local police and his chief inspector appeared, accompanied by fifteen policemen: an inordinately large posse for one girl, considering there were apparently no police available at all to keep order at the Hôtel Mont Blanc. Kate shut her eyes and went on singing, while the police stood on the edge of the crowd, their hats in their hands, waiting awkwardly for nearly four hours until the meeting ended.

Kate spoke of the aims of the Salvation Army: to save the lost and the outcast and to lead the nations to God. She prayed for Switzerland, for the government, for the Prefect. 'We are one great family,' she said. 'We fight under the same colours. We love our General; we love one another. All the persecution, the lies and the cruel things said against us can only bind us more closely together and make us love more.' When she had finished, as always in a Salvation Army meeting, converts stood up and gave their testimonies.

'That policeman knows me well, he can vouch for my story,' said one, pointing to a gendarme leaning against a tree and listening. 'I was in gaol for three years, and he put me there!'

'I will fight for Jesus,
I will, I will, I will!'

they sang triumphantly.

It was six o'clock in the evening when the meeting ended, and the Prefect came forward, holding a piece of paper in his hands. 'Miss Booth,' he said, embarrassed and apologetic, 'I am afraid you have violated the Decree of the Council of State.'

'I know that,' said Kate.

'I'm sorry – I really am sorry to have to perform this duty,' he said reluctantly, calling it 'an extremely awkward one.' 'I quite agreed with him that it was, the Lord bless him,' said Kate afterwards. 'Why didn't you come forward earlier?' she asked.

'I couldn't. I had judged you without seeing you, just like everyone else has done,' he said. 'Now I've seen you, and I know you're doing good. Please don't blame me for doing my job.'

The sun was sinking behind the mountains, the pine trees towering above them, tall and black and commanding against the sky. Everybody seemed very small. 'The trees are standing idle now,' said Kate as they left the forest. 'Such beautiful trees, silent and unused. How strange that we can't even worship God in the woods.'

With Captain Becquet, the Prefect escorted her in a carriage which he had waiting, to the house of the President of the Council of State, where they were put under arrest.

Kate was tired out, as she always was after a meeting. Begging to be allowed to attend the funeral of a young Swiss soldier in Geneva, she gave her word of honour to return the next evening. 'Words of honour have no value in Neuchâtel,' said the President, and Monsieur Convert put up 6000 francs bail.

106

Arrested a second time in Geneva at the private funeral – 'I cannot, with the best will in the world, go to two prisons in two cantons at the same time' – she returned to Neuchâtel. Ignorant, until then, of the system of granting bail, and discovering that her freedom rested with Monsieur Convert and not with the Neuchâtel constabulary, she promptly presented herself at the police headquarters and confounded the already baffled authorities by announcing that she and Captain Becquet no longer wished the responsibility of their actions to rest on their friends. Neither did they wish to ease the passage of the Neuchâtel authorities, who had no alternative but to put them in gaol.

Perplexed, much like Pilate, at an intransigent and apparently innocent prisoner, the magistrate sent the Maréchale to the Public Prosecutor, who, unwilling in his turn, to assume responsibility, sent her to the President of the Council of State, who signed her committal to gaol.

CHAPTER 8

Neuchâtel prison was at the end of the Rue du Château, built around an ancient castle on a hill. The Maréchale's cell was on the third floor at the top of the castle tower, number 24, seven feet by fourteen, with thick stone block walls, a stone floor, and two tiny high windows with double bars.

The gaoler's wife unlocked the door with a large key which she took from a table in the passage outside. Friends had accompanied the Maréchale, and Kate Patrick, who had persuaded the authorities to allow her to share the imprisonment.

Two iron bedsteads were made up with straw mattresses and straw pillows covered by coarse brown blankets, and there were two wooden chairs pulled up to a deal table. By taking one of the chairs to the window and standing on it, it was possible to see the tops of the mountains; otherwise, there was only a meagre glimpse of sky.

Kate, for all her determination, was momentarily at a loss, and reacted spontaneously, as anyone else, at such a moment, might have relieved the tension by making a joke. 'Let's say a prayer,' she said, getting down on her knees. When they had finished praying, her friends were ordered to leave. It was nearly six o'clock in the evening, and dismal in the fading light. 'It was the first prison I had ever seen,' Kate said later, the baldness of her words conveying her sudden and unaccustomed sense of desolation.

At dawn the next morning, cow bells clanked as herdsmen brought the cattle down to graze, and the sound had a clear sweetness before the coarser noises of the day. The cell smelled of garlic and dirt, and the smell made Kate retch, until she found that by climbing on a chair and forcing her face between the bars, she could catch a whiff of fresh mountain air. Friends brought in some carpet and a cushion for her back, and the wife of the Public Prosecutor, unexpectedly gracious, sent flowers and some grapes. Monsieur Humbert, allowed a visit a day, brought in the mail.

'We were awakened by telegraph messenger with a wire from Geneva to say "Blucher detained till trial,"' wrote General Booth, enclosing a copy of *The Times* for Kate to see. 'It is flying all over the world. If you do not suffer in your health, I don't care. It will all work for good.'

'I feel it a great thing to have a child in prison for Jesus' sake,' wrote Mrs Booth. 'There could be only one greater, namely to be there myself. God wants the attention of the people, and this is the best way to secure it. Nevertheless', she added, 'words cannot convey what I have suffered about you during the last twenty-four hours. This is a test of one's consecration certainly, both for you in the prison, and for me lying awake in the night, imagining what you are passing through.'

'*Oh, là, là!*

'*Oh, là, là!*' chanted errand boys in Paris.

'*La pauvre Maréchale,*
Qu'a t'elle donc fait là?'

La Suisse Libérale pointed out that imprisonment prior to trial could only be inflicted in cases of extreme gravity, or when the defendants were of no fixed abode, in which case Miss Booth was being treated as a vagabond. 'That which troubles us,' they said, 'and that which ought to trouble every citizen, whatever his religious or political opinions, is the fact that at this hour in our country there are persons in prison for conscience sake.'

In England, newspapers like *The Times* and the *Daily News*, apparently ignorant of the questionable legality of the arrest, condemned the Maréchale for deliberately breaking a decree issued against her, and *Punch* printed doggerel:

Hey for our Catherine, blushing so feminine,
Rousing the Swiss to conviction of sin;
Out on their 'beak' who, the tide of grace stemmin', in-
Sisted on brutally running her in!

List to dear Catherine's fervent beseeching,
Even for prefects, policemen and all;
Poor old St Paul rated women for preaching,
Catherine knows rather more than St Paul.

Lord Granville, out of patience with the whole affair, wrote to say that he had instructed someone to 'look into the case', which was much what he had said several months previously, and Catherine Booth wrote irately to Mr Gladstone, who was Prime Minister at the time.

'Sir, allow me to intrude on your valuable time for a moment in order to call your attention to the perils of my daughter, Miss Booth, and her companions in Switzerland,' she said. 'Six months ago, after this illegal and groundless persecution commenced, Earl Granville promised my husband that he would interfere, but although we have made two or three applications to his Lordship through parliamentary friends since then, so far as we can see, *nothing has been done*,' she said, underlining the words heavily and putting an exclamation mark. 'I beg with a mother's importunity, your timely interference . . .'

September 18 was Kate's twenty-fifth birthday. 'The devil takes great advantage of us at times of solitude,' she said. In the long hours of quietness, her mind dwelt on the accusations levelled against her: vanity, immodesty, unwomanliness, and worse than these, blasphemy, degradation of the gospel, insulting the very person of Christ. To her dismay, each indictment still had power to wound, and to wound deeply, and she was shocked at her vulnerability.

'Ready to die,' she had said, 'ready to crucify ourselves . . .' The words spoken so confidently in Paris such a short time ago came back to her, empty and arrogant. 'To crucify ourselves so dead that we don't care what people say or think about us – so dead that we are ready to be spoken evil of, written against, despised, rejected . . .' By her own strict reckoning, she now found herself guilty of a far greater sin than any of those for which she was in prison: the sin, she told herself sadly, of being hollow as a sounding gong or a tinkling cymbal, and utterly lacking in humility.

Early that morning, she had discovered a slate hanging on the cell wall. Taking it down, she began purposefully making a list of each accusation, as if trying to rivet it all in her mind by spelling it out, letter by letter. When the list was finished, she read it through, and then went on to add further trials, anything she could think of, loss of health, loss of reputation and the misunderstanding of family and friends, extending her imagination to its limits in order to leave out nothing.

110

'Can I write my name underneath and say I accept it all?' she asked herself when the task was done, and she knew that the honest answer was no, and she hung the slate back on the wall, determined to leave it there as a reproach, until she was able to sign it.

That afternoon, she began writing an article for the *War Cry*. 'They all joined in the cry "Crucify Him!" What evil had He done? No reply. The devil never can answer straightforward questions, and they only cried louder, "Crucify Him!"

'But I turned in the tumult to look at that face. The crowd, the great public demonstration, had not in the least made Him shrink. There was no sign of shrinking. No shadow of turning. No word of complaint as they led Him away. And He was alone, for they all forsook Him and fled.

'I gazed on that countenance as they led Him to Calvary, and my soul will ever gaze there. What patience! What strength! What love! What victory! A world against Him, and yet His next step is forward to die for it.'

Outside, a group of Salvationists had made their way along by the lake from a friend's house where they had been holding a meeting. As they reached the terrace below the prison, they could see a light burning in the tower. It was a quarter to ten at night, and they began to sing:

'Soldats du Christ, Le Maitre nous appelle!
Serrons nos rangs, que chacun soit fidèle!
Si de Satan la force est redoutable,
Le Dieu des Cieux est puissant, secourable.'

'God is strong and He will save.' Putting down her pen, Kate took her chair to the window and stood on it on tip-toe, waving her handkerchief through the bars, and a chorus of 'Amens' came from the darkness below.

'I was in great sadness,' she wrote to Josephine Butler later. 'Many things pressed on my heart. My body was tired out and my spirit overwhelmed. But I cried out of the depths, and He answered me – all at once I heard singing. It was our people! The singing seemed glorious in the silent night, and the burden fell from my heart as I listened. I slept, and am so thankful.'

Monsieur Cornaz, who lived near, sent police to take down the names of all those who had been singing, and in the morning, there were police stationed round the gaol to prevent Salvation-

ists from coming near. The gaoler threatened to move the Maréchale to a cell without windows, and nailed a list of prison rules
on the wall. When he had gone, Kate fastened another piece of
paper beneath it: 'My peace I give unto you,' she had written on
it. 'Not as the world giveth, give I unto you. Let not your heart be
troubled, neither let it be afraid.'

Instead of continuing with the article for the *War Cry*, she
turned back again and again to the slate on the wall, with its
daunting list of hardships drawn up on it. Before she could begin
to write, she took it down and read it through again, word by
word from start to finish. 'All right, Lord, I accept it,' she said at
last. 'However much they misunderstand, I accept it. It's
nothing to what they did to you. I accept it for your sake.' Then
she signed her name at the bottom.

'A man of sorrows cheered me,' she said later, writing to Josephine Butler. 'I have been led by a way I knew not, nor even
dreamed. My prison is all brilliant with the presence of Jesus.'

The song which she sat down and wrote that day, sublime and
certain in the face of insurmountable odds, became known
throughout the world as her prison song: later she was to look
back and covet such clarity of faith.

> Best beloved of my soul,
> I am here alone with Thee,
> And my prison is a heaven,
> Since Thou sharest it with me.
>
> All my life is at Thy service,
> All my choice to share Thy cross;
> I am Thine to do or suffer,
> All things else I count but dross.
>
> Wicked men may persecute me,
> Banishing to solitude;
> They should know my joy is Jesus,
> Whom they never understood.
>
> At His voice my gloom disperses,
> Heavenly sunshine takes its place,
> Bars and bolts cannot withold Him,
> Hide from me His lovely face.

Calm amid the raging tempest,
We can well afford to wait;
Truth and justice soon shall triumph,
Christ our cause will vindicate.

That night, the lamp flickered again in the window, as she sat up late, writing. Undeterred by the police, a gang of local youths gathered on the terrace where the Salvationists had sung the night before, and they jeered and shouted obscenities, whistling and making cat-calls. At one point, the noise was so fierce that the thick prison walls seemed like paper, and Kate Patrick, watching the Maréchale, saw her begin to tremble. Later Kate likened their howls and curses to cries for mercy and pardon: 'their anguish shook my heart,' she said. Those who lived in the neighbourhood of the Castle prison said the noise was like a pack of wolves. Nevertheless, by morning, the *War Cry* piece was written.

'Jesus was crucified:' she picked up where she had left off. 'Ever since that day, men have tried to find an easier way, but the easier ways fail. If you would win thousands who are without God, you must be ready to be crucified: your plans, your ideas, your likes and your inclinations.

'Things have changed, you say, there is liberty now. Is there? Go and live Christ's life, speak as He spoke, teach what He taught, denounce sin wherever you find it, and see if the enemy will not turn on you with all the fury of hell.

'Make no mistake, in spite of all the science and enlightenment of the nineteenth century, Calvary is Calvary today. Christ wasn't crucified in the drawing-room. His was no easy-chair business. The world needs an army of men and women who can face Calvary, and that means coming down low.

'Do you shrink from being bated, misrepresented and spoken evil of? It is time you were crucified. Come down, my brother. Come down, my sister. There is such wonderful blessing and peace down here. Make haste and come down. Lose your life. You will never be happy, never be free, never be more than conquerors, until you do.'

The next day, Captain Edward Becquet arrived. Arrested at the same time as the Maréchale, he turned up cheerfully a couple of days late, since he had been away in Berne when the summons was served. Apologising, he was given a tiny cell in the basement, and soon after he settled in, and every day afterwards, he heard the voice of his German convert shouting 'Hallelujah! Amen!' outside.

Warders said they had never dealt with such prisoners before. Some were astonished at their light-hearted manner and their courtesy. Others called them a scandal. Kate, hearing a warder shouting at a prostitute in the next cell, speaking to her as if she were an animal, dressed him down like a school child. 'How dare you talk to a fellow prisoner of mine like that?' she said. In the cell the other side of her she heard a baby crying, and she persuaded one of the warders to let her look inside.

'I saw a young woman with an infant in her arms,' she said. 'The child was crying, for it was cold and its feet were bare.

'I asked her how old the baby was, and she replied – eight weeks. I tried to cover it up and we made it as comfortable as we could. We got some milk and tried to feed it.

'The woman seemed unwilling to speak. I knelt down in the prison, bare and uncomfortable, and thought "What can I say?" She said nothing – just rocked to and fro. I said, "I think I know Someone who will help you. Let's speak to Him," and I prayed, and she burst out sobbing.

'I thought as I left her that I might have been that baby.'

Letters of encouragement arrived every day, some from single people, some from whole communities:

'Dear Maréchale, not a day passes but I do not think of you and go before the prison to see you at the window . . .'

'If there had been found ten just men in Sodom, it would have been saved. We are more than ten in Geneva to pray for Switzerland. We are more than ten who pray for you . . .'

'They have expelled you from our Canton, but from our hearts, never, no more than they can expel our Saviour or shut our mouths from praising Him; no more than they will have enough chains to tie us down with, nor enough prisons to shut us up in.'

'I feel as if you had mounted away to a land where I can call you Katie no more,' said Bramwell's wife, Florence. 'If only I could beseech you to remember that your health is everything. Just let me know – your Flo – if it is as bad as a prison cell, and

114

whether it is doing your body the least bit of harm.

'I wish you could know in your solitude how we all love you – I wish the breezes over the lake could bring you some whispers of what we have said of you.'

'What *can* be said at such times compared with what is felt?' wrote Emma. 'I will not attempt to write. I am praying. It would have been easier to be with you, but I'll fight harder than ever in my corner here.

'It is your poor back I must tremble for,' she added in a post-script. 'I wonder if you have pillows', while Mrs Booth, persis-tent as ever, wrote as she had written to Kate when she was a child at school, about health and food and bedding. 'Give those officials to understand that although we do submit to suffer for the sake of Christ, nevertheless, we have influence in this country which will make itself felt if they treat you unreason-ably,' she said. 'Even if your imprisonment were legal, you have a right to be treated as a State prisoner before trial. The Lord wants you to fight another day and perhaps for other nations besides Switzerland.'

In London, the Exeter Hall was packed for an emergency meeting called at short notice by the General. Kate had sent a telegram, which was read out – 'No need for anxiety: Jesus is here' – and her prison song was distributed and sung. 'What are we doing in Switzerland?' demanded the General, echoing a question asked by many leading British newspapers. 'A bishop was once accused of overstepping his brief, and the Duke of Wel-lington asked him what his marching orders were. He said his marching orders were to go into all the world and preach the Gospel to every creature. Those are the marching orders of the Salvation Army.'

'Dear Maréchale Prisoner,' wrote Railton when he arrived home that evening, 'I have just come from that tremendous prayer meeting, one of the biggest and best this world has ever seen ... the way the volleys burst out at the right time and went ringing all round the hall sounded splendid.

'My impression is that as the Swiss have outraged law all along, they may very likely do it when it comes to the sentence. God only knows what is coming next, but anyhow, we shall win.'

Kate spent twelve days in Neuchâtel gaol. 'I was blessed there,' she said later. 'I think that there, I accepted the cross more really than I had ever done in my life before.' During that time, she decided to conduct her own individual defence, backed by the two Swiss lawyers engaged to defend all six Salvationists who were to stand trial. 'Pray for me during the trial,' she asked Josephine Butler, whom she called her second mother. 'God will teach me what to speak. Surely he has a great work in these times for women to do. We need an army of holy, consecrated, brave women who will dare to obey God. What a shaking the world would have!'

On the final day in gaol, dawn broke with the sound of the cow bells again, jangling through the clear air as they had done every day: a friend brought her one to take away as a souvenir. It was made of rough beaten brass, and she kept it with her all her life as a memory of 'the time I looked at Jesus again, and was bowed in the dust by the sight.'

'I could kiss these walls, they have been such friends to me, because Jesus has been here,' she said, touching them with her hand as she left, and hesitating at the door, almost as if reluctant to go. 'Nobody will ever know the glory and the wonder of the presence of Christ I knew in that prison cell,' she told her children, years later. 'As I left, I said, "Lord, will you stay with me so that I may always know Thee as deeply and as closely as I have done here".'

*

Salvationists from all over the three cantons of Geneva, Neuchâtel and Vaud, met at Neuchâtel railway station at seven in the morning on the day of the trial, Saturday, 29 September 1883. From there they caught the train to Boudry, five miles outside Neuchâtel near the forest of Prise-Imer, where the trial was to be held. When they arrived, a dense crowd was already waiting for the doors of the court room to be opened. As well as a curious public, equally vociferous in demonstrations of friendship and hostility, there was the British Ambassador from Berne, Mr Adams, an independent observer sent by the British government, and journalists, lawyers and eminent literary personalities from all over the Continent, drawn by a trial which Swiss papers were calling an event of immense political significance. 'This decision,' they said, 'will take its place in the history of the

116

Republic.' That it did, is proved by the fact that in Switzerland today, it is still the subject of animated debate among students in schools and universities.

Monsieur Cornaz had already been accused of jury rigging, since an article in his police organ *Le Réveil*, ordered jurors to 'take care that they act in harmony with public opinion and do not attempt to brave that opinion.' To do so, said the article, would be more than impolitic, it would be immoral.

'Is it possible,' asked the *Suisse Libérale*, 'that a jury can thus, in our day, be so intimidated? If so, it ought to be thoroughly understood that the tribunals, according to M. Cornaz, exist not to perform public services, but to pronounce decrees at his dictation.'

Before the trial began, friends met in an upper room in a house opposite, saying prayers and singing hymns together, ending with a chorus of Luther's defiant *'C'est un rempart que notre Dieu...'* – 'A safe stronghold our God is still.' At 9.30 the jury assembled and the defendants were brought in with Kate at their head, looking pale but composed. Edward Becquet sat beside her, and beside them the four Swiss who had also been accused, though not imprisoned: Monsieur Convert, middle-aged and eminently respectable, 25-year-old Madame Boillot – 'Pardon me, sir,' she interrupted the Prosecutor, 'but I am a Sergeant' – Monsieur Cost, a Salvationist gardener, and Monsieur Hess, a good-looking young carpenter who had frequently been brought before the police courts for drinking and now professed himself a Salvationist and total abstainer. Two lawyers, hired to defend them, spent the majority of the morning objecting to over half of the jurors, since their names had appeared on the petition against the Salvation Army, and they could not therefore be considered impartial. Just before the morning adjournment, when the crowded little court was becoming unbearably hot and airless, the door opened, and Herbert Booth edged his way to a seat near the front, raising his hand to his sister and smiling.

In the afternoon, the prosecution began, presented by the Public Prosecutor, Le Procureur-Général, a liberal free-thinker, manoeuvred against his will into performing a distasteful task to the best of his ability. In contrast to his evident discomfort, the Salvationists looked calm and relaxed. Captain

117

Becquet, jovial as ever, afforded a laugh or two. The Prosecutor rose to begin his speech, aware of his colleague, Monsieur Cornaz whom he disliked, sitting near to him, vindictively complacent.

'Fanaticism,' he said, calling Calvin a fanatic of the worst kind, 'contributes one-third of the patients to the lunatic asylums.' Voltaire, Rousseau, 'the entire enlightened nineteenth century', had put all that right, but 'if the Salvation Army is not suppressed, we shall have to enlarge our asylums.'

Basing the nub of his prosecution on the law involving corporations, by which the Army could be said to have met without the specific permission of the authorities, he drew heavily on Madame de Gasparin – 'an eminently Christian woman,' he said, 'a Christian if ever there was one' – quoting for a full twenty minutes from her circular, calling Salvationists intolerant fanatics beating drums and the Maréchale a young woman flinging insults in the face of the Grand Council.

Christ, who was, he said, perhaps the most religious man who had ever lived – which made Christ sound like Madame de Gasparin and caused Captain Becquet to burst out laughing – 'Christ,' he continued, 'advised men to retire to their closets in order to pray to God. He who lifts up his soul in this manner is more religious than he who thumps on the pulpit or shrieks "I'm saved!"'

'What do we find before us?' he asked, warming with professional skill to his job. 'People who show the slightest sign of repentance? No! A handful of people who come here with a coolness and aplomb simply superb, to tell us that they have done nothing wrong! A handful of people who presume to talk to us about law and to declare they are in their rights and mean to stick to them.

'Miss Booth thinks she has more science than our Constitutional authorities, and places herself above the law,' he said, glancing across to where Kate sat opposite him, her face white against the stiff navy serge of her uniform. 'No, no one is above the law. The President of the Council of State is as much bound to obey the law as the lowest of the people. The Queen of England herself – who is not, however, a Marshal of the Salvation Army,' he added, with a touch of sarcasm, 'is obliged to submit to Acts of Parliament.

118

1. William Booth, founder of the Salvation Army

2. The portrait of Catherine Booth which hung in Kate's bedroom

3. Kate Booth, later to become La Maréchale, on her departure for France in 1881

4. The Maréchale with her first group of officers

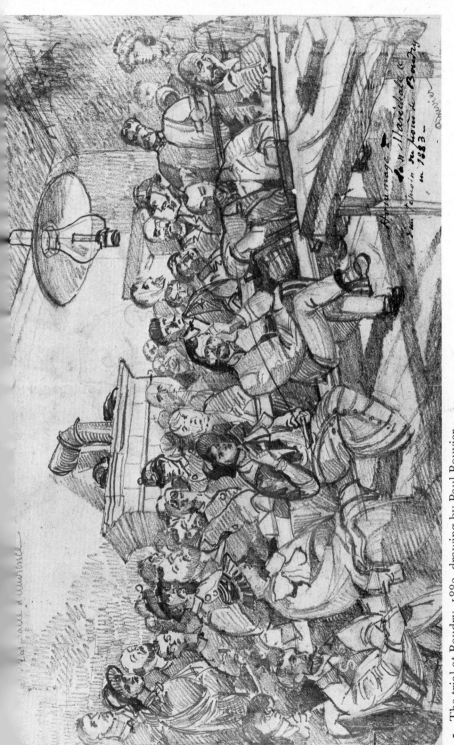

5. The trial at Boudry, 1883, drawing by Paul Bouvier

6. La Maréchale in 1890

7. La Maréchale with two of
her children in Amsterdam

8. Arthur and Catherine Booth-Clibborn
1887

'The law may be bad,' he conceded, 'but no human being can rise above it.'

As he finished speaking, a telegram arrived from England. It came from Lord Granville, and was addressed to Mr Adams, who opened it, read it and presented it to the court. It said: 'The Salvation Army is not a corporation', and the Prosecutor had no alternative but to withdraw his major accusation.

It was six o'clock in the evening, very stuffy and smelly in the closely packed court house. Kate was feeling faint, and as she left with Herbert and the other Salvationists, glad to be outside in the cold mountain air, women waved pitchforks in her face, and men who thought she should have been taken back to gaol shouted, *'Au clou!* Back to the cell!' and spat at her. Inside the empty building, officials stacked away benches which had been broken by the excited crowds, and noted down how many new ones would be needed before Monday. When Monday came, the crowds were bigger and more uncontrolled than ever.

Monsieur Monnier of the Neuchâtel bar gave the speech for the defence, referring wryly to 'our beautiful inalienable rights, framed and glazed at the Zurich Exhibition'. 'The decree and warrant of arrest are based upon Article 72 of the Constitution which refers to corporations,' he said. 'Now this Article was absolutely abandoned on Saturday by the Public Prosecutor. From that moment, the whole groundwork of the decree was overthrown.

'What is a corporation anyway?' he asked, in a momentary aside. 'The Council of State adopted the meaning which it looked up in Littré's Dictionary, which was an unlucky choice. According to Littré, a corporation is defined as a body having "particular and special rights and privileges". Splendid things they are,' he said, 'these rights and privileges of the Salvation Army! The privilege of having been interrupted in their worship and of having had to submit to imprisonment before trial!'

Next, he dealt with the charge against the Federal Constitution, which, he said, guaranteed the right of 'association, liberty of conscience, and of creed'. 'This latter,' he said, 'the Public Prosecutor carefully distinguishes from liberty of public worship, but does he not see that liberty of conscience and belief only come into effect when men unite in order to exercise the same form of its outward expression.

119

'In England,' he said, smiling, 'they understand perfectly the liberty of meeting and worship. There was formed there, in opposition to the Salvation Army, a "Skeleton Army",' he looked towards Kate for affirmation. 'I see Miss Booth smile. A Skeleton Army has collisions with the processions of its rival in the streets. A magistrate in England had put down the processions of the Salvation Army on one occasion, but the Judge of Assize, on the contrary, condemned the Skeletons as the aggressive party, and gave a verdict for the Salvationists, who had been disturbed in the exercise of their right.

'We come now,' he said finally, 'to the Cantonal Constitution. Our Neuchâtel Constitution tends to prevent all interference of the State in the exterior exercise of forms of worship. If this were not so, the principle of equality as well as liberty, would suffer. Why did you treat the Salvation Army differently from other sects? Why did you prosecute only six of the accused? There were three hundred people in the forest of Prise-Imer. If you are convinced of your ground and wish to be logical, you should prosecute them all. I know your prisons would not be large enough. Well then, knock them down and build new ones. When you have entered on the path of religious persecution, you will want many more prisons than those you now have. You will require immense barracks for your prisoners.'

Captain Becquet, called on to make his defence, provided, predictably, something of a side-show. 'I prayed to God after my fashion, the police forbade me, and I continued to do so notwithstanding,' he said, commenting that although they had used neither drums nor cornets, he considered that they had the right to use as many instruments as King David. As an example, he gave an energetic rendering of what he called a specimen of old-time religion from the psalms:

'Praise the Lord!' he thundered.

'Praise Him with the sound of the trumpet; praise Him with the psaltery and harp.

'Praise Him with the timbrel and dance: praise Him with stringed instruments and organs.

'Praise Him upon the loud cymbals: praise Him upon the high sounding cymbals!'

Monsieur Convert, rather more soberly, called it a post of honour to stand with the accused. 'Why was I chosen among

120

three hundred?' he asked, but as Kate stood up to make her defence, a woman at the back of the court shouted, 'Give me a chance and I'll kill her with a pitchfork!' Youth and fatigue masking for a moment the spirited fervour which had already been denounced as fanaticism, those who saw her inevitably likened her to Saint Joan in petticoats; Portia pleading at the bar, her fair hair taken back, emotions expressed in every movement: eyes, face, hands.

'I am aware that we are not here to enter on a disquisition about Christianity,' she began, speaking in the broken colloquial French which by now came naturally to her. 'However, as Monsieur Le Procureur-Général himself went off the ground of law to discuss at great length the doctrines and methods of the Army, I feel I cannot for truth's sake be silent.

'If the Conseil D'État had any doubts concerning the methods and aims of the Salvation Army, they should have sought information from competent judges, from those who know us and have seen and heard us, before accepting the opinions of persons who have done neither.

'Our only message has been "Repent, and turn ye to the Lord that your sins be blotted out". We want to see drunkards, thieves and outcasts, changed into peaceful, loyal citizens. This being our end, it is to the interest of all governments to protect us, and in protecting us, they protect themselves.

'The great accusation against us is that we disturbed the public peace. In a word, we were the cause of scandal. If to preach the Gospel, to denounce sin, and to pray over the masses is a scandal, then we are guilty of a scandal, even as Christ and Paul were.

'The Procureur-Général has attempted to describe in detail our proceedings, yet he has said that he has never attended a single meeting. He cannot therefore be considered capable of judging. He has said that we attacked the town with drums and trumpets and other extravagant things. I ask Monsieur le Procureur-Général how many drums he has seen in Neuchâtel, or how many trumpets? Not one. No musical instrument, with the exception of a piano, has been employed. There have been no flags and no processions. The only bill that has been issued, I have in my hand,' she said, holding it up for everyone to see. 'It simply announces that the Salvation Army will have meetings

121

at seven, three, and seven.

'Monsieur le Procureur-Général has referred to the language of the Salvationists. He says we teach that all that is necessary for Salvation is for one to jump on the platform and say *"Je suis sauvé!* I am saved!"* No one in Switzerland has ever heard us make such an outrageous statement. It is not true. Nevertheless,' she added, glancing up, her eyes resting for a moment on Monsieur Cornaz, who had climbed the stairs of the dais to sit watching her from a seat beside the Public Prosecutor, 'there may come a day when Monsieur le Procureur-Général – and others – would give all the world to be able to say *"Je suis sauvé!"*...'

'Stop her!' muttered Monsieur Cornaz angrily, turning to the Prosecutor. *'Faites la taire* – why don't you silence her?'

'But what were our proceedings?' asked Kate, returning to her notes. 'First, we have sung hymns in a hall that we had hired. Second, we read the Bible. Switzerland has not waited till the Salvation Army came to read the Bible: you know it already. Third, we pray, and fourth, we persuade men to leave the road to sin and death.

'Is that a scandal? It is not we that throw stones or break windows or howl and hoot after respectable people in the streets. It is not we who violate private houses. It is against all logic to say that we are the scandal of your country. Allow me to read an extract from one of your own journals: "Cantonal governments, the Federation, neighbourhoods and families," it says, "see with alarm the flood of demoralisation rising menacingly higher and higher, and instead of seeking to destroy the causes of this deluge, they only take away the remaining dams."

'You ask what is the need for the Salvation Army? The question which every intelligent man ought to ask is, "what are we to do with the masses?" If they are not won from sin, a day will come when they will turn round against you, with awful consequences. Then, Messieurs, you may have reason to regret your actions. If these disturbers are capable of manifesting such hatred and rage against citizens who pray for them, they will also be capable of manifesting the same hatred against any other opinion or any other law which may not please them.

'We have not made your people like this. We have broken no law since we entered your country. We have submitted and sub-

122

mitted again and again until you have taken away from us the right to meet and pray. We have now no more choice. We must obey God. We are not here to plead "Not guilty". Like the early Christians, we weighed this matter. I weighed it in my room on my knees. We have all told you that we did violate the decree. We have no wish to hide it. I note, however, that the devil has full liberty. I was struck the other night when I was in my prison, by the howling and singing of bands of roughs, which continued till past midnight without any interruption that I am aware of from the police, while our people were followed home because they had sung a hymn, and a strict watch was kept that they should not do it again.

'All we demand is that which is guaranteed by your Contitution – religious liberty. But there are people in Switzerland who are interested in, and gain by, sin, and they fight against us ...'

'That's enough!' Monsieur Cornaz leaped to his feet, forgetting himself. 'She has spoken long enough – tell her to be quiet,' he shouted angrily, conscious that those who knew him well were nodding knowingly at each other. The Prosecutor put out a restraining hand, and motioned to Kate to continue.

'Monsieur le Procureur-Général referred to our Queen,' she went on, glancing again at the notes she had made during the Prosecutor's speech. 'He said that even she was subject to the decrees of Parliament, but that I placed myself above her in refusing to become subject to the decrees of the Grand Counseil. There is no parallel. No Act has been passed to forbid her praying in a wood, or I think her Majesty would have something to say on the subject!' Several of those listening, laughed loudly, and there was a sprinkle of clapping from former enemies as well as from friends. 'Monsieur le Procureur-Général has spoken in a way that has astounded me on public opinion, which, he says, he cannot afford to take lightly,' she continued. 'Let me remind Monsieur le Procureur-Général and all here that it was public opinion that crucified Christ. Do you justify that?

'One word in conclusion,' she said, folding the notes which she had hardly used during her speech. 'You can punish us. You can imprison us. You can persecute us. But what you cannot do is to stop this work or suppress it. Beware what you do, for your country's sake. Take care that in banishing us, you don't banish the light.

123

'You can laugh at me, you can mock me, but you cannot deny what I have said.' Loathe, as always, to end, when a captive audience was showing signs, however faint, of conversion, she hazarded one last observation.

'We have suffered terribly from all the misrepresentations wilfully circulated about us,' she said, 'but we aren't discouraged because we know that truth and justice will triumph. I love Switzerland all the more for what we have endured,' she said earnestly and emphatically, still under the spell of the glorious closeness to Christ she had experienced during captivity. 'A little while, and Switzerland will love us,' she added, and a spontaneous burst of cheers and 'Amens' broke from the Salvationists who listened to her.

While the jury retired, soldiers in the court house passed the word round to begin praying, silently, intensely, and to the discomfort of everyone else. Outside, men broke into a nearby Temperance Hall, emptying chocolate onto the floor and filling the cups with brandy. It was eight o'clock in the evening when the door at the back of the court opened and the foreman of the jury came in followed by his colleagues.

'Did the accused take part in a meeting?' asked the Prosecutor.

'Yes.'

'Was the meeting in violation of the decree?'

'Yes.'

'Did they act with culpable intention?'

'No.'

'In consequence of this verdict, the accused are acquitted.'

The Prosecutor, to his surprise, found his hand grasped and firmly shaken by a beaming Captain Becquet, while Monsieur Cornaz, intractible to the end, dismissed his police on the spot, leaving the Salvationists to the mercy of the drunk and indignantly hostile crowd at the door.

124

CHAPTER 9

'Oh là, là! Oh là, là!
La pauvre Maréchale!
Qu'a t'elle donc fait là?'

Paris was agog when the Maréchale returned, acquitted though still exiled from Switzerland. Harnessing the movement of the Spirit with the mood of the moment, she began – presumptuously for anyone of her age and experience – a series of lectures which she called Conferences, some, at which Parisians blanched, advertised for men only (since religion, she contended unfashionably, was not a woman's prerogative), held in a hall on the elegant Boulevard des Capucines beyond the Place de l'Opéra, with its flower market and expensive dress shops.

'We believe,' said Clibborn, to the dismay of Railton in London, 'in saving the rich as well as the poor.'

The owner of the hall suggested that Kate should give an intellectual talk on ethics and moral theology, but *Le Figaro* had run an article on *'L'Abolition de Dieu'*, and she called her first talk, given in retaliation, 'Without God and Without Hope in the World'.

'The enlightened spirit of the nineteenth century was a very grand thing in its way,' she said, 'but it was a light that went out just when it was most needed.' Then she went on, characteristically, with a slap in the face for the wise.

'I will destroy wisdom,' she said, quoting Saint Paul. 'Hath not God made foolish the wisdom of this world? Not many wise, not many mighty, not many noble, are called, but God hath chosen the foolish of the world to confound the mighty.'

Colonel Clibborn, impressive and emotional, with his great beard and sonorous voice, called for revolution: the revolution against sin of God's enslaved (which was what he called the wise); a revolution daring, desperate and energetic as that of Marat and Robespierre.

Politicians with spats on their feet and top hats in their hands

125

sat next to respected journalists like the Editor of *Le Temps*, revolutionaries like Rochefort and modernist theologians like the Roman Catholic, Henri Lasserre. Free-thinkers and philosophers jostled for entry with anarchists and state military leaders. Working men and women and Salvation Army cadets in red jerseys – 'God's liveried servants,' said Clibborn; 'God's red shirts,' said Garibaldi's son, who was among the audience – sat on velvet seats beside aristocratic ladies with opera glasses in their hands, flipping the pages of *En Avant* as they might toy with a programme at the theatre, all of them prepared to be verbally thrashed into submission by a 25-year-old girl with fair hair whirled neatly into a bun beneath her bonnet, a long thin face, and burning eyes, who talked of a purity greater than the purity of a child, which she called the purity of experience: 'the purity of gold that has gone through the fire.'

'She has profoundly astonished the citizen sceptic,' reported a leading French newspaper. 'And the citizen sceptic has been out of the habit of being astonished.'

'God has given you the ear of the nation as it is given only once in a hundred years,' said Lasserre.

'Miss Booth is young,' wrote the radical Quaker politician, John Bright in his diary. 'She has a sweet countenance. Her conversation is interesting and impressive and her faith great. There is a goodness about her which is charming and attractive. What would not anyone part with to be like her?'

For once it seemed no coincidence that in the French language *'spirituel'* meant witty. Kate's wit could be disconcerting, bursting on the head of a terror-struck woman who confided in her: 'but you see, I am a fallen woman.' 'You are a fallen woman?' exclaimed Kate. 'So am I a fallen woman. So is everyone in this elegant hall, in all Paris, all France, all the world. We are all fallen.'

She talked, impertinently, of a new politique for France: the politique of love; the politique of the heart. 'Politics dictated by the heart rather than by cold intellect,' she said, 'can alone attain the improvement of the moral and material state of the people.

'There is an innate desire to know where we are going; an infinite need of pardon, purity and peace. Do you think that by laughing at these needs or by ignoring them, we stifle them? Do you think that you can abolish from the human heart these long-ings after holiness, these longings after God?

'Is it thus,' she asked incredulously, 'that you have studied human nature?

'A nation which is neglectful of these great subjects will perish in one sense even while it exists in another. It will perish in its highest domain: in its influence over that part of man which is most noble and most capable of self-sacrifice. It will lose the life without which everything becomes mechanical and animal.

'You say you see nothing of all this, but the truth is that you will not take the trouble to look. There is a light which lightens every man who lives in the world, but you have put it out. You possessed it once. You have seen, but you have voluntarily and persistently closed your eyes to this inner light until you have lost the power of seeing. Then you say that religion is a delusion.

'Wake up!' she challenged them, as they were so used to chal-lenging others. 'Rouse yourselves! Be among the first to show France the path which assures the truest interest of her children. Do not remain in ignorance on a subject about which you ought to know.

'If you had followed that light, who can say what you could have been today? Instead of wandering about in a labyrinth of doubt and materialism, you might have been above the clouds on the mountain tops of assurance, under the rays of the smile of God, and helping poor suffering humanity to climb up there too.

'Wake up! Wake up!' she pleaded, having brought the packed auditorium to total silence, intensity and weight in every word, her eyes resting on one and then on another of the people before her, entreating them, as she ended, almost whispering with a final intimate plea: *'Si dans la nuit,'* she said, *'si vous sentez dans la silence le besoin d'une amie . . .'*

It was not often now that her French let her down. When it did, the denouement was complete. Laughter broke out, and a round of good-natured applause. 'If, during the silence of the night, you feel the need of a lady friend . . .'

It was part of her charm that she laughed with them. As the laughter died away she endeavoured to pick up the thread: *'Si vous sentez,'* she began again, *'le plus petit besoin . . .'* An immacu-lately dressed young man with spats, top hat, gloves and a silver cane, stood up and hurried to the exit, apologising to right and

127

left as he went, demonstating only too clearly the colloquial meaning of the phrase *'un petit besoin'*, and order was only restored when he had returned a few minutes later, smiling and relieved, to his seat.

Clibborn sent exuberant and lengthy reports to London for inclusion in the *War Cry*, and Railton, who was Acting Editor, systematically cut them or omitted them altogether. 'How can I convince you once and for all that your reports are never delayed unavoidably,' he wrote crossly. 'I thought spiritual work was to be your speciality.' Every time the Maréchale visited England, the Colonel was with her, her Chief of Staff and right-hand man, 'a mighty man for God,' she said proudly, as handsome and besotted by salvation as Railton, and as magnetic too, eccentric, strong-willed, urbane and obstinate, influencing Kate with his overwhelming enthusiasms, stimulating her with his sacrificial zeal. Railton instinctively resented what he saw, despised his own resentment, and married a woman who loved him to distraction, – 'I almost worshipped him,' admitted Marianne Railton, – teaching her Spanish, French and German, since 'I marry with a view to more than redoubled fighting.'

'I hope you will now be content on finding that you have a column of *War Cry* space next Wednesday, all the long speeches omitted,' he wrote to Clibborn. 'Do make a salvation report in a salvation way about a warlike Sunday, and hang these wretched newspapers and the local bigwigs.'

'What we want to do,' said Kate, leaving Paris for the south, for Provence and the Mediterranean, 'is to move all the nations under the sun. I never wished so much that I was rich.'

She had already visited Nîmes the previous summer during her expulsion from Neuchâtel, *En Avant* sold at bullfights in the local Roman amphitheatre, silk and cotton workers taking time off to sit in the cool on the banks of the Gard, away from the shimmering heat haze of the plains. Kate spoke at the Casino, the open windows letting in more heat than air.

She spoke as she had done long ago when she was fourteen: 'Beware *le dernier jour*, the day of judgement, when the despised and the rejected will come in glory.' Men clambered out of the windows, clinging to the sills and dropping down onto the earth outside. 'Many will want to run away and hide,' she said. 'But they won't be able to. There will be no windows to climb through; no way of escape.'

Roman Catholics knelt to pray, and Protestants – for Nîmes was a largely Protestant town – stood. Sceptics laughed and stared. Rich ladies in colourful raw silk gowns and gentlemen in silk shirts and cravats sat beside workers wearing the cottons they had woven in the mills. The Protestants, pastors and laity, influential and conservative, organised a secondary meeting, and Kate preached on holiness: that God keeps His children from sin.

Grace was an illusion and an arrogance, original sin a valid excuse: 'Let him that is without sin get up and testify!' they challenged, and when a girl, beckoned by the Maréchale, stood up to talk of the saving grace they shouted that women were meant for the home: 'In church, women should be silent!'

'The soul has no sex,' argued Kate. 'Salvation, pardon, purity, peace, all the gifts of the Spirit, are for men and women alike.' Both Protestants and Roman Catholics claimed conversion, and a local citizen, Judge Albin Peyron, congratulated the Maréchale on being the first to bridge the gulf. Before she left, she held an all-night meeting of prayer, which she called spending a night with Jesus and Albin Peyron junior, who was just fourteen years old, stayed until morning came and everyone went home. Salvationists were leaving Nîmes for the surrounding countryside, Provence, Ardèche, and the Haute-Loire, the barren mountains and sudden harsh valleys of Languedoc and the Cevennes, and Albin, on holiday from school, joined them on his big-wheeled bicycle, his Hallelujah bike, through Hérault with its olive trees, the wine-making country of the Rhône, and the wheat fields of the Tarn with its rows of solid little stone bridges reflected in the water, to the borders of the Basses-Alpes. Salvationists called him one of the Lord's grass-hoppers: *les cigalles du Seigneur*. *'Nous allons, nous poussons, nous avançons!'* he sang out wherever he went. 'All the world for God!' Back at school, they threw bricks at him and mud in his eyes: *'Pauvre benêt, pauvre fol, il a perdu la carte . . .'*

Now, a year later, they travelled to Valence – 'We were so quiet before you came,' said the Commissaire, 'why didn't you go to St Étienne instead?' and then on up into the mountains by horse-drawn buses through wild and beautiful countryside with olive and almond trees, figs and vines, and old castles in ruins

129

with streams cascading through them into the rocky ravines below.

A small corps sprang up spontaneously at Les Ollières where there was a busy silk factory, young girls coming in from the surrounding villages, to live in crowded conditions in the silk mills, working from four in the morning until seven at night, their fingers thin and shrivelled from spinning and plunging their hands into boiling water. Kate held a meeting in an old barn and it was so hot and crowded that there was condensation running down the walls and sweat running off the people's faces. Hens squatted on the wooden beams above their heads: 'I asked the Lord to keep them quiet while I preached,' said Kate, 'and for more than an hour, they never moved.'

Much of the summer of 1884 was spent working at Les Ollières, sitting on the wooden benches with the women, sharing their chestnuts and talking to them, listening to the sound of their heavy wooden clogs on the cobbles. Kate and her officers lived in a ramshackle cowshed, which was the only accommodation they could afford, and when the intense heat of the summer gave way to the ice and snow of the winter, the mountain streams freezing as they trickled across the rocks, deep snow blanketing the figs and vines, they stuffed straw in the cracks round the doors and windows and lit fires of damp logs that spluttered and fizzled on the cold stone floor.

The only meeting place large enough to hold everyone who wanted to come, was an old flour mill with no seats and sacks of flour for a penitent bench. Many walked miles, their food tied in coloured handkerchiefs, to hear Kate talk of Jesus, 'the greatest fact of all.' The inside of the mill was long and dark and narrow, lit by flaring paraffin lamps, with a makeshift platform erected above the flour pit, and old women who came with boxes of hot cinders to keep their feet warm insisted on offering them to the Maréchale. One man brought six francs every week, which was the money he used to spend on drink. Another brought a barrel of nut oil. An illiterate sent a letter written for him by a friend enclosing enough money to train a Hallelujah lass like the one who had converted him, and an old woman, a very poor Catholic, brought a loaf of bread: often there was nothing to eat but chestnuts, roasted over the fire. When the weather was good enough, Kate travelled from post to post, meeting her little groups of soldiers who turned out in the cold to welcome her off the bus.

At St Jean du Gard in the Cevennes, where 'it is natural for men to drink and for the tongues of women to wag as it is for the wind to blow', a soldier was hit hard on the head with a clog. At Lamastre in the Ardèche, inn-keepers made an effigy of an Army captain and carried it shoulder-high to the market-place to burn. In Calvisson, men complained that the dance halls were empty of girls, and in Privas, in the Rhône valley, soldiers were stabbed by publicans who could no longer sell their stocks of drink and tobacco.

Professor Henry Drummond, the scientist theologian who called love the greatest thing in the world, likening it, as Browning did, to energy of life, landed in Marseilles on his way home from Africa, and said that after visiting cathedrals and listening to famous orators, he felt more of the presence and power of Christ in the Salvation Army hall listening to the officer, a young French peasant girl, than he had experienced in all his wanderings.

By the end of 1884, there were nineteen corps on the Continent, eight of them self-sufficient. There were Salvation Army stations in six of the departments of France, and in Switzerland there were two corps in Neuchâtel alone, each with over a hundred soldiers. There were two *Écoles Militaires* or training schools for cadets in Paris, *En Avant* was selling at the rate of 11,000 a fortnight, and the report of the year so impressed the notorious missionary, Hudson Taylor, that he sent a copy to every missionary in China.

'Can you imagine the bewilderment that comes over me when I sit down to convey some idea of the wonderful way God has led and helped us during the year?' wrote Kate. 'It is not too much to say that during the past twelve months, we have passed from the position of a small and almost unknown mission to that of a great spiritual power, recognised and felt throughout France and Switzerland.

In Switzerland itself, soldiers were still encountering what they called 'that heavenly manna, persecution'. So many had been pinned to the ground while the brass 'S' was cut off their uniform that they were now embroidering the letter onto their collars, and meetings had to be held with the shutters barred and

131

bolted, doors taken off their hinges and nailed to the windows, the tallest and broadest soldiers testifying with their backs against the shuddering wooden barricades as stones were hurled against them from the outside. Open air meetings were disrupted by youths who threw gunpowder crackers which exploded in smoke.

At the start of 1885, the majority of Swiss authorities changed their tactics and began imposing fines without the option of imprisonment, and poor Salvationist peasants were forced to sell their meagre possessions, their tables and chairs and the beds they slept on, with little chance of ever earning enough money to replace them. One of them, Louis Jeanmonod, converted at the last Swiss meeting to be held by the Maréchale in the forest at Prise-Imer, was systematically terrorised. His tools were stolen, a reward of sixty francs was offered to anyone who could throw him in the lake or duck him in the fountain, and one night as he lay in bed the skylight above him was broken and he was showered with splinters of glass and buckets of ice-cold water.

'We have a real devil and not a paper one,' said an officer in Lausanne. 'Thank God we have a real Saviour, and not just a paper Saviour.'

The first German-Swiss corps sang rousing German hymns: *'Wenn auch starken Stürme'* – 'When heavy storms are blowing' – and Arthur Clibborn, speaking in a hay barn on the hillside, lowered the lantern he held on a long stick, hiding the light for a moment to illustrate the responsibility to those who walked in darkness. Jeanmonod had arranged to emigrate to America to evade further persecution, but as he looked round at the faces, shadowed and dark in the half light, he decided to stay.

Captain Becquet was in charge of one of the Neuchâtel corps, with 103 soldiers under him. 'You have the state against you, the police against you, and the entire power of public opinion against you,' a man said to him. 'In the Bible, it says "and whosoever shall not receive you when ye depart out of that city, shake off the dust of your feet."'

'I'll do that,' said Becquet, 'if you will take care of the soldiers I leave behind. Where Christ has a hundred and three sheep, that text doesn't apply.'

'A soldier goes on, whatever the results,' said the Maréchale.

'A soldier goes on whether it's hard or whether it's good, whether there is a response or not. You go on. You're under orders.'

Typhoid crept across the borders from Switzerland into France, and cholera came from London with the merchant ships docking at Marseilles. 'Are you ready to die?' asked the *War Cry*. 'Are you ready for cholera? Is there anybody you haven't warned? Is there any of your work still neglected?'

Travelling uncomfortably by train between Paris and the south, Kate read of Napoleon who scorned *'ce bête de mot, impossible,'* and said that what she had read initiated her into the secret of true faith. One incident stuck in her mind. When cholera broke out among Napoleon's troops, he visited them where they lay in the field hospitals, talking to them and touching them to show he had no fear, until gradually his courage transmitted itself to them and they got up and rode into battle. Kate called it faith in action. 'Napoleon consecrated his gifts and genius to wordly ambition,' she said. 'If that could be done through faith in man, Oh Christ, what we could do through faith in Thee!'

In Paris, there were posters on the walls – *BOUILLEZ L'EAU* – ships were quarantined, government carts patrolled the streets with disinfectant, and officials inspected backyards. 'Cholera brings disease and death,' she said. 'All this energy and expense won't stop it spreading. Christianity brings healing and life, and it also spreads in the most unfavourable conditions.'

Arthur Clibborn was reading the newly published revised Bible, intrigued by the theological implications hidden in a nuance or a juxtaposition of words, comparing it with the modern French translation by Dr Segond of Geneva. He was becoming convinced that a belief in pacificism presupposed the belief that faith and prayer had power to heal what he called the sins of the body, and when Kate told him the story of Napoleon, he saw it not so much as a feat of personality or persuasion, as of the power of faith to heal. Quoting, in support of his theories, Isaiah's picture of the man who 'himself took our infirmities and bore our sicknesses', he spoke of divine healing within the terms of the atonement, praying over cadets and soldiers who were sick, laying his hands on them, and sending them to homes of healing outside the Army (since there were none in it), for 'God values human life,' he said, 'more than an ecclesiastical barrier.'

133

Kate declared she had two aims, to conquer the conventions of the world, and to awaken faith. Often she travelled miles across France to spend time with someone who needed her. 'If I am a minister today,' said a man at a meeting of French pastors and evangelists years later, 'it is because someone fought hell's legions for me. Someone deprived themselves of supper and sleep for me. Someone watched far into the night for my soul.'

'I believe in nothing,' said a man one day, thrusting a handful of banknotes into her hand.

'You believe in nothing, and yet you give me this?'

'I believe in you. I wish you had a hall in every town and village and hamlet in France.'

Kate looked at him, astonished at such illogicality. 'Take out your watch,' she said. 'It tells the right time. I believe in it. Why shouldn't I believe in the maker? *La force motrice* – the mainspring of my life – is Christ and the love of Christ. You believe in me: believe in Christ who makes me what I am.'

At the Boulevard des Capucines, intellectuals reacted spontaneously and unpredictably. 'I need more and more the spiritual atmosphere of the meetings: this opens the heart and at the same time deadens the opposition of the mind,' wrote one man, in what was more an indictment than a compliment. Others were less willing to be ridden rough-shod: 'You would like me to say I am converted. I cannot say that I am. But you have made me love the Christ I never loved.'

At the isolated Quai Valmy, thugs with crowbars and gunpowder attacked the hall between nine and ten o'clock every night, when police on duty changed patrols. Young girl cadets returned to their quarters, their faces covered with blood, and Kate was hit so hard that she was ill in bed for several days. Sometimes, on her way to the evening meeting, she walked along the Seine, watching the water and the reflections in it, and the faces of the people who went by, lovers, beggars, the drunk, the lonely and the sad. One night there was a girl leaning with her elbows on the wall, gazing into the water, and Kate sensed that she was contemplating suicide. 'The water's cruel,' she said. 'Don't keep looking at it. Come with me and have a hot cup of coffee.'

The girl shrugged away, sullen and suspicious. 'Please come with me,' insisted Kate. 'It's warm and comfortable, and there's singing too.'

Her name was Eugenie. In the end she agreed to come, and she listened to the singing and the prayers and drank her coffee without saying a word, her face bitter and closed. When the service ended, Kate sat down beside her. 'I'm glad you came,' she said. 'God is very good . . .'

The girl let flow a torrent of words, harsh, vehement and full of contempt. 'What has God done for me?' she spat. 'Don't talk to me about God – I hate God. What have I done to deserve a life like this? It's not my fault, but God doesn't care. He took my mother. He wouldn't have done that if He was good. I wouldn't have been born in prison if He cared for me. He cares for you all right though, doesn't He – you weren't born in a gaol.'

Kate kept on and on. She talked and prayed and persuaded, and in the end, Eugenie softened. She came to the meetings at the Quai Valmy, and a little of the bitterness left her face. Whenever Kate saw her, she thought of the baby in the prison cell next to hers in Neuchâtel, crying, with its hands and feet blue with the cold: 'I thought as I left her, that I might have been that baby . . .'

Travelling in a train across France, two gentlemen in a railway carriage recognised Kate as the Maréchale. One of them had seen her at work at Valence in Drôme, and he had read *En Avant* with interest and genuine enthusiasm.

'I go to church every week,' he said, as if trying to persuade her that he, too, did his share.

'Is that all you do?' she asked, amazed. 'For a dying world? You go to church.'

'That is all I have time for,' he said sharply, taken aback. 'Everyone has different gifts, Madame,' he added respectfully. 'I am a businessman. That is my talent. Yours is to do what you do. Your courage is marvellous. I don't always approve of your methods, but the work that you do is creditable. *Oh, que je vous admire!* How much I admire you.'

When he left the compartment, the Maréchale was alone. The words had been said so often, '*Je vous admire,*' more often than she could count or remember, until she was tired of hearing them and they no longer had any effect. It was always the same story: 'Your methods we do not agree with. The means you employ are suspect, and we take exception to them. But your courage, your consecration, your devotion – oh, *comme c'est admirable!*'

It was, she was to say later, an admiration which made the loneliness and isolation all the more intense. 'What are these means and measures they disapprove of?' she asked in a Christmas message sent to London. 'Only doing all we possibly can to snatch souls from hell and turn men from darkness to light. This is why we sell our *En Avant* and form night brigades to tour Paris in the dark, and challenge people in the open streets to ask about their soul.

'Hell is real. The devil is in earnest. Surely if we who hold the same beliefs as our blessed Master are not doing all in our power to save souls, we are monstrous impostors.

'They take exception to the means, and yet at the same time, they admire the courage and consecration needed to carry them out. How many victories does admiration gain? How many souls does it save? How much does it help those who are fighting? Admirers who come so far and no further awaken in us the hope of help and then draw back, only disappointing us and making the fight harder. If Jesus did more than admire, if He did not walk beside us when we got out in the night seeking the lost, if He did not appear to us face to face with the mocking crowds, our hearts would fail us.

'Jesus did not say "Admire me". He said "Take up thy cross and follow me". He made no exception for the nervous and timid,' she ended harshly. 'Though it does appear that the timid shall not inherit heaven.'

1886, they said, had everything: blood and death. In Switzerland a soldier was drenched in black train oil, travelling to a mountain rally. A man threatened to throw a woman officer out of the train, holding the door open and pushing her towards it as they hurtled fast across a ravine. 'You can throw me out,' she said to him, 'but if you do, you'll always be responsible for what you've done.' Captain Thonger was in gaol for a fellow officer – 'He is a married man, and as I am not yet in possession of a wife, it is better so' – and Colonel Clibborn had been expelled from Neuchâtel after being forcibly carried away from an open-air meeting.

In Ardèche, police stood guard during meetings with revolvers and drawn swords, and at Nîmes, the first rescue home was opened, the start of a chain of rescue homes, each one called *Le*

Phare because to the girls who came to them, they were beacons of light.

In Paris, Louis Jeanmonod, training to be an officer, was on duty one evening at the hall of the Quai Valmy when there was a knock on the door. Opening it, he was punched hard in the stomach. Four days later, he died. When the police came to his bedside for a statement, he refused to describe his assailant, but he described him to the Maréchale so that she could pray for him and speak to him if she saw him.

Mourning cards were sent out with borders of brilliant red for the blood of martyrs. At the funeral, officers wore a white sash of rejoicing across their scarlet jerseys and cadets wore white armbands. A white cloth covered the coffin with a branch of palm as a symbol of martyrdom. Grave-diggers waited, leaning on their spades to shovel earth into the insignificant pauper's grave, while Salvationists sang hymns and took the opportunity to preach conversion to those who gathered round to watch.

Jeanmonod was big and strong, twenty-two years old and six feet tall, and his death was heralded as the first Army martyrdom on the Continent. By the fifth anniversary of the Army in France, 200 had been injured, 142 had been up before the police, and 33 imprisoned.

In June, the General held what he called an International Congress, all the Salvation Army leaders from abroad brought home for the event. There were Buddhists from Ceylon, Hindus from India and Chinamen with baggy trousers and pigtails, black Americans from the southern states and white Americans in army blue, Scandinavian girls in national costume and Red Indians with beads and moccasins, all playing instruments, beating drums, blowing trumpets, waving flags, and singing hymns in a cacophony of languages to the tune of 'Marching Through Georgia'.

Thirty brass bands led a procession through the East End, with carriages for all the members of the Booth family. It was a direct contrast to the cold, ugly nights on the Quai Valmy, and while the Booth in Kate felt a sense of pride, there was an underlying distaste and an unaccountable sense of apprehension. Disharmony, especially with those she loved, was a sacrifice she dreaded.

'What is our life but a mystery and a misery, unless faith be

137

our guiding star and hope our stay?' Bramwell wrote to her in an impetuous note scribbled on a train to York before the year ended. 'Do not think you will ever be less dear to me than you have been. You cannot be.

'I am old and worn – often stupid, sometimes mistaken, with the work and cares of three men and a body that is like a broken-winded horse, and a nature that makes its burdens heavier, but I love you and admire you, and if you were my General tomorrow, I should follow you to the last gasp and stick while there was one limb of me left.

The warmth, the love, and the humility, and the phrase that had come to mean so little when it fell lightly from the lips of others, 'Oh, *que je vous admire*: how much I admire you!' It was one of the last exchanges of spontaneous affection between them.

CHAPTER 10

'Are you really decided to live the life of Christ, to seek and to save the lost? Are you ready to renounce yourself and a life of ease for His sake, and to live and die fighting? Are you willing to learn the best way to succeed?

'In your letter, you say you are ready for all this. If so, then *come*. My girls are being wonderfully used, and although there is plenty of difficulty and persecution, yet there is not a happier people under the sun.

'Can you pay your own voyage to Paris?

'When can you come?

'Yours, praying that He may make you a soldier who will never look back, but follow Him all the way.

'*Coûte que coûte* – whatever the cost.

'Catherine Booth.'

Thus new recruits were received at the two *Écoles Militaires* in Paris. The Maréchale called her cadets missionaries, spiritual Samsons, not made of tissue paper. 'No words can express the importance of training missionaries,' she said. 'We had no scholastic degrees, no profession, no money. The only justification for our existence was the need all round us.'

Male cadets occupied dormitories converted from the galleries above the hall on the Quai Valmy. Girls lived in apartments in the Villette, guitars, tambourines and concertinas cluttering the hall, chintz tablecloths and curtains, and chintz coverlets on the beds. They embroidered slogans on their jerseys: '*De progrès en progrès*' and '*Que ton règne vienne*' – 'From strength to strength' and 'Thy kingdom come'. There were no servants, in accordance with '*l'ésprit republicain véritable*' of liberty, equality and fraternity: 'Good stuff does not go under because it's put to wash dishes,' commented the Maréchale. Usually they ate cabbage soup, potatoes and beans – '*C'est la vie apostolique!*' – but occasionally there was horsemeat: '*C'est délicieux, ce bifteck, n'est ce pas!*'

'We are sometimes told,' said Kate, 'that our uniforms, our young women speaking in public, our tambourines and our processions, bring contempt on religion.

'It is a mistake. That which is the laughing-stock of the world and of hell is a religion without sacrifice. People will never believe in Christians who, while professing to be disciples of Him who had not where to lay His head, live in luxury, seeking first the comfort of their family and the health and position of their children, and letting their souls perish for lack of that Gospel which they profess to believe.

'That is the secret of the unbelief of France. That is what makes the young, who are in search of the truth, cry "Comedy!"'

They held *Sémaines de Renoncement*, and Clibborn taught abandonment which he called 'la mystère salutiste', the self-sacrifice 'which is the secret of apostolic strength', encouraging tongue-tied cadets with a display of personal inadequacy: 'When I don't know what to say, I throw myself on God'. The Maréchale led intensive all-night meetings, searching the hearts of new recruits: 'Why do you want to become an officer?' Escapism, wanderlust or a thirst for adventure were no good, she said, quoting Saint Paul who called himself an apostle by the will of God and Saint Peter the servant of Christ. It had to be *'Dieu le premier':* nothing short of vocation would do.

'There is a power emanating from those who have renounced all and are reckless of their own destiny,' she said, shamelessly sending the sweetest and the purest to the ugliest places, often with the result that both they and their hearers were reduced to tears. 'The people are not looking at your Bibles, they are looking at you. They want to see whether they can detect Jesus in you.'

'Throw your gold in the dust,' read Lucy Johns, preaching from Job before returning reluctantly to work with the Army in England. 'Throw the gold of Ophir among the stones on the bed of the fast-flowing river and the Almighty will be your gold and your silver and all your wordly wealth.'

'Do you remember the last time I saw you?' she wrote to Kate from England. 'You said "I trust you". You do not know how much those words have spurred me on.'

Kate was reading Catherine of Siena, and what she read

influenced her words in *En Avant*, candid and bracing one moment, feminine and winsome the next, like the saint who sometimes stamped her foot and shouted at the Pope himself, as well as at her 'bella brigata' of Caterinati.

'*Debout, ne dormons plus! Au combat!*

'*Camarades, ce n'est pas avec les autres que nous devons nous mesurer, c'est avec nous-mêmes. Il faut monter, monter . . .*

'*Rappelez-vous que vous êtes salutistes, ce qui veut dire: toujours plus haut. Prenez garde que le froid ne vous saisisse; l'eau stagnante est plus vite gelle que l'eau courante.*'

And underneath it all lay the same refrain: '*Pour l'amour de la France, je ne me tirai point. Pour l'amour de Paris . . .*'

Frederick Tucker, who had given up a career in the Indian Civil Service to take the Salvation Army to India, living in caves like the fakir and preaching to princes and untouchables, told her that he would rather have the task of evangelising the whole of Buddhist Ceylon twice over than the city of Paris.

'That's fine,' Kate told him. 'Leave Paris to me. That is all I want: just to keep Paris.'

'Order is the first rule in my house,' said a friend. 'Not so in mine,' replied Kate firmly, listing her three fundamentals as principle, example and love, and citing Garibaldi, whose followers understood his motives: the *Écoles Militaires* were founded on this law of the spirit of life rather than on rules.

'Garibaldi gathered a magnificent army although he promised no rations, no arms, no comfort,' she told her cadets. 'They flocked to his banner because they recognised his disinterested love for his country and his willingness to share their hardships and dangers.

'Organisation and order are essential, but order can supplant mercy and kindness, and you can organise a beautiful thing to death. The spontaneity, the individuality, the fresh breeze from another world, the song that bursts from the soul, all these can be ruled out, and the Holy Spirit grieved away.

'Who can estimate the force of example,' she said. 'Be what you want your followers to be.'

Determined not to allow her cadets inside the cafés, open all night on the French streets, until she had been inside them herself, she set off one night in 1884 with Kate Patrick and Blanche Young who played the guitar, wearing patched skirts and shawls thrown round their heads like itinerant Italians or French factory girls. They went to the Rue Lafayette which led to the centre of the city, starting in the noisy, hot little dives full of labourers from the slums by the canal. As they reached the door of the first, Kate hesitated, walking uneasily backwards and forwards along the pavement outside: 'You have never known your Maréchale until now. See what a coward she is!' Later she admitted that it had taken all her courage to push open the door and go inside.

Men sat at tables drinking and playing cards in the warm smoky atmosphere. A big fat man in a white apron was serving drinks from a long bar. 'May we sing something, monsieur?' He stared, open-mouthed, for a moment, and then shrugged his shoulders. 'Very well.'

The Maréchale began singing while Blanche accompanied her quietly on the guitar: *'Le ciel est ma belle patrie . . .'* A man got up angrily from his chair, but his companions pulled him down impatiently: *'Tais-toi! Écoute.'* Kate Patrick went from table to table with an armful of *En Avant*, and someone offered money: 'We haven't come here for money. We want to show you the way to God.' The card-playing ceased, eyes following them registering amazement and disbelief as they moved from table to table: *'En marche, en marche, soldats, vers cette belle patrie'*. When they had finished singing they turned to go, leaving an atmosphere of stunned incredulity.

'May we come and sing again?' The man in the white apron bowed. *'Certainement, mademoiselle.'*

They visited sixteen cafés that night, ending up in a smart café next door to the Opéra, where men stood by the bar while groups of people sat at tables eating sandwiches and drinking chocolate. The Maréchale noticed men whispering in a corner while she sang, and as soon as she finished, one of them got up and made his way towards her, his hand held out and a mocking expression on his face.

'Don't you dare touch me,' she snapped out intuitively. 'We are not on our own here. God is with us and He knows about all the women you have wronged. One day you will have to meet Him.'

The man backed away, overawed by her forthright manner, and his friends laughed at him because he had been made to look foolish. Walking back along the Rue Lafayette, the Maréchale felt ashamed. 'I must go back and find that man,' she said, sending the others on without her. 'I condemned him, but I didn't preach the Gospel to him.'

Turning round, she saw that he had followed them, standing under the light of a street lamp, watching. 'Come back into the café again,' she begged. 'I want to speak to you.'

They sat down at one of the dimly lit tables and began to talk quietly. 'What you said was true. If someone had spoken to me like that long ago, things might have been different.' Before she left, the Maréchale gave him a New Testament with his name written in the front of it, and when she reached home at last, she felt she had obeyed Christ: 'Let your light so shine before men and then they will see what you do, and glorify your Father.'

From then onwards they made what they called regular café bombardments, starting between nine and ten o'clock at night and visiting as many as thirty cafés in an evening. Sometimes they were greeted with pleasure, sometimes with ridicule and ribaldry.

'Wait until I've finished drinking.'

'No, I won't wait. I've come to speak about God.'

'God! Your infamous God?'

'Call me infamous if you like, but don't call God infamous.'

'Mademoiselle, religion has destroyed France. Religion has made Paris what she is today. I vowed never to set foot inside a church again, and I never will.'

Kate studied him for a moment. 'I don't want you to do anything your heart doesn't urge you to do,' she said quietly. 'But you have been deceived. You have been sold shoddy goods. If you came in here and the landlord gave you coloured water instead of wine, would you go away swearing never to go inside a café again because they all sold bad wine?'

'Bravo!' applauded the others who were listening. 'Bravo!' echoed the man thoughtfully. '*Mon Dieu*, what you say is true too. I'll go and find my Bible and read a bit of it tonight.'

Kate was unpredictable. 'You don't have to do that,' she said. 'Just kneel down and pray to God to give you light, because if you don't, you'll be in the dark for ever.'

Pattie pleaded quietly at a corner table at the far end of the smoke-filled room. '*Venez, venez à Jésus. Venez . . .*'

'*Venez à Jésus,*' the repetition annoyed them, but sometimes it penetrated. 'Come to Jesus. He will make you happy.'

'It is strange,' said the Maréchale later, 'but it is in the lowest cafés, among the most degraded men and women, where we are given the most attention. They sit and listen as if spellbound. At times, we are treated with profound respect, and I think of Jesus "walking through the midst of them", because crowds of rough men gather at the doorway listening, and when we finish singing, they fall back to let us pass without laying a finger on us or saying a word against us.'

'You will read it, won't you?' she said, selling a copy of *En Avant* at the door.

'Oh yes, mademoiselle.'

'Because the Lord sent me to this café to speak to you.'

'The Lord?'

'Yes.'

'Sent you to speak to me?'

'Yes.'

'He sent you here?'

'He sent me here.'

Baffled, he clutched at straws. 'But have you a certificate to sell?'

'Yes. I have my certificate. My name is written in the Book of Life.'

In the cafés near the centre of Paris were the cheap, chattering girls who haunted the world of Toulouse-Lautrec, with their red hair and chalk-white faces, sardonic, sophisticated and sad. At the café called L'Enfer, there were pictures of hell painted on the walls and waiters dressed as devils served the drinks. Men crowding round an open coffin with a skeleton inside it, vied with each other to win a prize for the wittiest joke about death.

'My soul?' echoed a man incredulously. 'This is how it will be with my poor soul, mademoiselle. I shall die. I shall be put into the earth. My soul will fly out of the coffin, and the first bird of prey that sees it soaring to heaven will snap it up and swallow it, and that'll be the end of my soul.'

When the Maréchale and her girls began singing, the band struck up softly, accompanying them as if it had been paid to do so. '*Pécheur,*' they sang, '*pense à l'éternité.*'

On the way out, they passed a girl who was younger than the

144

rest. 'You should be at home in bed,' Kate whispered in her ear. 'You shouldn't be in a place like this.'

'This is the only way I can afford supper and a bed,' replied the girl.

'Come with me, and I will give you both,' promised Kate, taking her back to the villette and giving her a home there before helping her to emigrate to America where she trained to be a teacher, sending 500 francs from her first wages, 'To save another as you saved me.'

The café called Hell was macabre: a joke which Kate, in her naïve way, found it impossible to share. At Les Singes, the waiters were dressed to look like monkeys, running up and down the winding staircase.

'I have more hope for an avowed infidel,' she said, 'than I have of the man who holds the Bible up in his hand and professes to believe some of the most extraordinary beliefs in the universe, while living a life in total disharmony with those beliefs.

'Remember, they are looking at you and not at your Bibles,' she told her girls again and again as they set off from the *École Militaire* for each nightly café bombardment. 'They want to see Jesus in you.'

At Christmas time there were special shows at the theatres and the Opera House, and eight of them hurried off with satchels of *En Avant* on Christmas Eve and Christmas night after evening prayers were over. Newsboys ran up and down outside the brightly lit foyers calling out the programmes and selling pictures of the actors and actresses, and the girls joined them shouting, *'En Avant! Un sou!'*

'Think of Heaven and Hell,' cried one eighteen-year-old. 'Nothing is more important than Heaven and Hell.'

'Your soul is immortal!' cried another.

Not surprisingly, the Maréchale, who had stationed herself at the foot of the theatre steps, talked later of 'the effect of such words uttered on a Paris boulevard . . .'

Horse-drawn carriages pulled up where she was standing while the ladies were helped down in their beautiful evening dresses. As they waited for the gentlemen to pay the cab, Kate suggested they 'take a paper to read during the interval.' Embarrassed, they turned away and pretended to fiddle with their gloves, as if they had heard nothing, looking anxiously to see

145

how much longer the men would be. Kate could challenge as well as plead: 'It is time you thought about your soul,' she said, presumptuous as a beggar on horseback. The men came across with sheafs of newspapers and magazines in their hands, and the party hurried inside, whispering to each other, glancing back and glaring at her.

'*En Avant!*' she called again. '*En Avant! Un sou!* Buy one – it will do your soul good.'

'My soul! Where do I keep that?'

'You'll discover when you die.'

When the last stragglers had gone inside, they moved on to other theatres, waiting in the crisp night air and talking with the shop-keepers until the interval, when the doors opened and people strolled outside to stretch their legs, and selling began again in earnest. One young man who refused to buy, rushed back impulsively after his friends had gone inside.

Moving on, to wait outside two last theatres as people left, they pushed their way through the Christmas crowds milling round on the pavement.

'Prepare to meet thy God!' called the eighteen-year-old, her voice clear and piercing, causing people to stop and stare, and sometimes to laugh.

'You won't always laugh.' Kate's quiet comment came at their elbow. 'Think of your soul.'

'Prepare to meet thy God!' rang out through the people crowded together, straining to see the reflection of a play in a window above them, as it was being acted on stage in the theatre inside, and they turned, confused, to see where the cry came from.

'Prepare to meet thy God!' she shouted again, high and clear, as the crowds came out of the Opera House, aristocratic Parisian society in festive spirits. 'Mademoiselle,' remarked a gentleman who had been standing watching them. 'I am shocked to see young ladies here at this time of night selling outside a theatre.'

'I am shocked that you are shocked,' said Kate.

'But your ways are so eccentric.'

'So is hell,' she retorted, busily selling papers. 'These people are on the road to hell. What are you doing about it?'

Silently he gave her two francs and went away with a copy of *En Avant* under his arm.

146

Kate called it the happiest Christmas she had ever spent, impossible to describe, with thoughts which made her heart cry. 'We went home feeling we had done something to celebrate Christ's birthday,' she said.

By the end of 1886, there were 32 girls and 24 men at the two *Écoles Militaires* in Paris: an explosive mixture, so soon after the war-torn 1870s, of English, French, German and Swiss. The Maréchale was receiving requests for French-speaking Salvationists from Canada, Brussels, and South America, where there was a colony of Vaudois, as well as from Seine, Haute-Saône, Doubs, Drôme, Ardèche, Gard, Hérault and Tarn, the regions of France where the Army was already established.

Ill-matched and differing in class and temperament, they arrived eager for battle, *prophetesses en herbes*: greenhorn evangelists full of unrealistic dreams and fervent enthusiasm. Often the first day was spent mending curtains, cleaning someone else's shoes or sweeping the floor. Sacrifices were trivial but unpleasant – drinking cocoa without sugar – and at the same time, immense in their implications: a French boy refused to clean the boots of *'un sal Bosch'* until the Maréchale told him to go back to his trade unless he could win this victory which she called greater than Bismarck's victory, 'the victory of Christ over Pilate and the Pharisees.'

Nourished on overturned values, unlikely friendships sprang up. Nadine Schindler, an ebullient, loud-mouthed, tawny-haired factory girl from the Swiss mountains where she used to run around barefoot climbing trees, flicking cigarette ash onto Salvationists or creeping up behind them and pinning their skirts together, went everywhere with Blanche Roussel, the shy, ladylike daughter of a Swiss pastor. Wearing patched clothes and secondhand shoes – 'only the poor can understand the poor' – they took *En Avant* out on the streets, several hundred copies in satchels slung across their shoulders, slopping along in the black mud, the snow and the rain, taking the horse-drawn double-decker or the funicular to the top of Montmartre, singing and talking to people in the overcrowded, smelly courtyards of the dilapidated slum tenements:

'Do you know Jesus Christ?'

'I don't know the name. But then, we're new around here . . .'

Nadine had overcome alcoholism by drinking vinegar from

the bottle, but she still only controlled her temper with difficulty. She punched publicans and boxed the ears of urchins who interrupted open-air meetings. When a butcher swore at Blanche, Nadine flew at him. 'You swine!' she shouted. 'No wonder you work in a slaughter-house where they stick pigs. You're nothing but a pig yourself.'

They visited the communal wash-houses wearing peasant bodices and handkerchiefs over their heads, talking to the workers in the vast steamy hangar-like buildings until the women in charge chased them out, throwing bars of soap at them as they went. Then they sang quietly in the backyard and the women came to the windows to listen, throwing down money in return for copies of *En Avant*.

Often on their way back, they stopped to sit on benches in the Buttes-Chaumont Park, the lungs of Paris, made out of the mountainous quarry which had once been little more than a rubbish dump, with its rocks and lake, and the sad little brick Bridge of Suicides. During the day, urchins ran after them throwing mud which stuck to their clothes. Returning home after midnight from a meeting on the Quai Valmy, Blanche found a girl – 'une de nos soeurs de la rue' as she called them, without condescension – sitting on a seat sobbing, her face thin and pale and her clothes in rags. Blanche put her arm round the girl and prayed with her before taking her back to the Villette for a cup of hot coffee: *'Seigneur, nous voici,'* she said, *'nous deux, Tes filles . . .'*

A century later, such gestures of tenderness and comradeship appear false and sentimental, and yet they came from the heart and drew a response from the heart: the majority of street girls in Paris had come naturally to use the intimate *'tu'* when talking with Salvationists.

They sold *En Avant* at the fairs around the Clignancourt Gate on the outskirts of the city, knocking on the doors of the caravans and going into the circuses with their fairground booths and painted wooden horses.

They sold in the *'assommoirs'*, the stale-smelling pot-houses where men drank themselves to oblivion. Then they caught the bus back to the main street in the early evening as people hurried from work for buses and trains or ambled up and down the street in search of excitement.

148

They went into the roadside cafés, refusing drunken offers of cherries soaked in liqueur – 'Thank you, but we only drink water' – and braved fashionable meeting-places like the Café de la Paix, consmopolitan and international, more frightening to many of the girls than the sleaziest backstreet clip-joints, where they sang hymns to the catchy tunes of modern French songs, or the Maréchale's 'Marseillaise': *'Allons, enfants de la lumière!'*

On Saturday nights, they went to Montmartre, jangling, colourful and noisy, stopping outside the dance halls in the doorways decorated with strings of lights inside coloured glass balls, and in front of the Moulin Rouge, the brightly lit sails turning silently and slowly above them. Men sidled past, lingering, touching them, whispering in their ears. There was grit and mud churned up with the snow at the crossroads and the girls were hunched up in their cloaks, huddling into themselves trying to keep warm, blown in the wind like the flames in the street lamps, and Blanche called Paris unbearable, a wilderness of disbelief and indifference; kindness, an impossible sacrifice to give in return for all the filth and bitterness thrown at them.

The Maréchale was in the south, desolate before the primitive paintings on the walls of the crumbling stone churches, which to her seemed remote and insensitive. In Paris that spring, the General had called her girls angels. 'To be cool under fire is the quality of the very best soldiers,' he said as they battled nightly with toughs on the Quai Valmy, adding, with unaccustomed honesty, 'I fear I have not excelled in this direction. It is a difficult property in our family, seeing how full of sympathy our hearts are.'

Resigned nuns with sad eyes wearing little rings engraved with the motto 'service is worship' preached a sterile religion, and Kate longed for the joy emanating from the 'free faces of free creatures', which was how a leading woman socialist and feminist had described her girl cadets.

Back in Paris again among them, a French baron suggested she should buy some holy pictures to adorn the bleak walls of the Salvation Army hall. Accepting her invitation to attend a Sunday meeting, he left saying there was no need of paintings on the wall: 'Your faces are your pictures.'

CHAPTER 11

When they became engaged, Arthur Clibborn was thirty-two and the Maréchale, twenty-eight. Many years later, after Arthur's death, Kate was to call it the entrance to a Garden of Eden. 'It brings a wealth of fresh hope, strength and courage,' she said. 'When a great human love is ours, all nature assumes a new aspect. The birds sing a new song, the flowers give sweeter fragrance, burdens become lighter and drudgery easy.'

Looking back, it would appear to have been inevitable. At the time, the news came as a bombshell. To George Railton and to Catherine Booth, both of whom had unquestioningly envisaged for Kate a life of total dedication, exercising what they called her special gifts, it was a disaster.

'I coveted to give to the world men and women who should have no other consideration, no other aim or object in life, but to win its inhabitants for Him,' said Mrs Booth. 'In carrying that out, God has led me a way I could not see.'

'Our husband is Jesus, *le beau Jésus*,' said the founding Salvationists. '*Nous vivrons un grand amour*: our lives will be one long love affair.' Even the Maréchale herself had been dubious where marriage was concerned. 'I don't agree with marriage,' she said once, wary and sceptical. 'I am frightened to death of it.' Much of her mistrust stemmed from personal observation, and she spoke of living among the rich and the poor in homes up and down the land, where, she said, 'I have observed.'

Marrying French and Swiss officers at improvised open-air ceremonies, she had spoken of marriage tersely as 'a more efficient instrument for the winning of souls', and often, after a couple of days away together, those she had married returned hungrily to the fight, leading corps many miles apart. 'Christ loved passionately,' she said, 'and He gives himself to those who love Him passionately.'

Between Arthur and Kate, however, divine and human passion were always to remain inextricably tangled, and she

150

9. Cartoon published in *John Bull*, 1905

10. Family portrait: *back row, l. to r.:* Augustin, Victoria, Evangeline, William; *front row, l. to r.:* Herbert, Frieda, Josephine, Theodore, Evelyn, Eric

11. The Maréchale in 1913

12. Arthur Booth-Clibborn

13. The Maréchale with her twenty-fifth grandchild

4. At the Metropolitan Hall with Theodore, Dublin, 1924

15. Arthur and Catherine Booth-Clibborn at Margate

spoke of the ecstacy, sweetness and joy of 'a pure betrothal', and of marriage as the perfect mingling of the hopes, sentiments and ideals of two beings. 'We women,' she said, 'are born with a picture in our souls of a companion.'

She had just finished a gruelling three-month tour of France and Switzerland. Arthur had been in Switzerland, preaching in a two-roomed roadside cabin hung with Indian corn and onions, the walls lined with *En Avant* to hide the cracks, opening a new Army hall in the poor quarter of Basle, situated alongside the prison, a cholera hospital and a slaughter-house: 'We like to begin low, as Jesus did.'

In England together, idyllic and idealistic, on the crest of a wave, they attended meetings where people crowded to catch sight of them, breaking into quaint, characteristic little choruses, weird incantations snatched from the air, Clibborn's soft baritone complimenting the Maréchale's clear soprano:

> 'All pure, all pure,
> As Thou Thyself art pure ...'

Arthur called himself 'one to whom an open heaven, a limitless sky, and an independent personal walk with Christ, had ever been the first principle of religion. A poet, writer, and singer of songs, composing hymns in French and translating Newman into German – 'one step enough for me' – he sought, as Kate had done, the presence of one like unto the Son of Man in what he called the furnace hours of life, referring to those who walked with him as brothers of the lowly Fourth.

A self-confessed salvation smuggler, his preoccupations were holiness, self-abandonment, and the sword of peace, which he preached with such persuasion that his cadets never forgot what he said. Claiming what he called out and out redemption (half measures had never appealed to him) for body as well as soul, he insisted that 'even now, the mightiest cures can be wrought and are being wrought for those who dare to go in for the full gospel.' Naïve to the point of obduracy, he believed the Bible implicitly, with all the unquestioning and dogmatic acceptance of a true fundamentalist, studying it untiringly, scouring it for signs and symbols, confirmation of the past, guidance for the future, and corroboration of those tenets particularly dear to him, drafting his calculations meticulously, though often untenably (a fact of which he was blissfully unaware), and dismissing those who

151

challenged his delighted discoveries with a firm 'this is no casuistry, this is simple logic.'

Charming, attractive, full of personality and magnetism, he was more restrained than Kate, but as passionate in the depths of his being, ready to ditch himself and anyone around him for the realisation of an ideal, neither counting nor always being wholly aware of the cost.

His faith was a simple one, as he never tired of saying; at times it was terrifyingly simple. Doubt, he condemned as one of the worst sins in the world, supporting his claim, as always, and quite illogically, with chapter and verse. 'This is His commandment, that ye should believe on the name of His only begotten Son,' he would quote, taking for granted the initial existence of God. 'God never commands us to do a thing we cannot do.' Those who did not share the same simplicity of faith were not so much wrong, as incomprehensible.

He was, as Kate had said, a mighty man for God, with all the discomforting intensity, intolerance, and occasional insensitivity that the phrase implies. He also had the instinctive courtesy, tenderness and lack of pride of the rugged immigrant Irish gentry which allowed him to stop a girl carrying the slop pail downstairs in the Booth household and insist on taking it himself. He could say, with sincere and blinding humility, 'thank God I have a clean heart and a peaceful mind,' and when overcome by the responsibility of marriage, falling on his knees and praying 'Lord, it is too great for me,' could find comfort for all time in the certainty that 'the Lord spoke to me and told me that he had called both myself and the Maréchale to this path.'

Where his passion was activated and prescribed by principle, Kate's relied more or less entirely on the promptings of love, that vibrant *force motrice* which she called the mainspring of her life. 'I would live my life all over again for love,' she was to say. 'Never for duty'. To her, Christianity was a love story, with all the agonies and ecstacies of a *grand amour*, the essence of which lay not so much in any pattern of virtue as in a constant manifestation of the miraculous intervention of God: the proof that God can do what man cannot. After less schooling than she would have wished, she called the Holy Spirit her professor; his baptism, the maker of personality. 'How can we save a dying world?' asked one of her most famous hymns. 'The only

152

way is love.'

To be Christian, so far as Kate was concerned, was to stand between life and death, time and eternity, dealing in the basic extremities of human currency, in sin and redemption, torment and peace. 'In such a situation, how can we be anything less than violent?' she asked, condemning 'our wretched palliating, apologising and compromising which always ends in defeat.' Her strategy was always to attack, since defence was negative. 'We are commanded,' she would say, 'to proclaim the Gospel, not to protect it or defend it or mutilate it.

'Nothing in the world matters but what you have done for Jesus,' she knew and taught. 'If you don't give Jesus, you give nothing.'

Unexpectedly widely read for one who appeared to have no time at all for reading, she nevertheless asserted that she had only two favourite books, the Bible and the heart of man 'which helps me with the first book better than any commentary.' Off-setting her faith in God with an utter and yet clear-sighted faith in the inherent potential for good in man, she called him three parts a god – 'I all but worship man! When he puts his life and example on the side of righteousness, he rises to the sublime' – and she never tired of the stories of David, Peter, Mary Magdalene, the giants of the Bible who 'fell deeply and were restored gloriously': 'I am a simple child and I must have a child's religion,' she said. Her Bible was thumbed at the book of Hosea, the prophet of unrewarded, unremitting love: 'I drew them with the cords of a man, with bands of love ... my heart is turned within me, how shall I give thee up? ... I will not execute the fierceness of my anger, I will heal their backsliding, I will love them freely ...'

'How did Hosea get this language?' she asked. 'He had an adulterous wife, and his grief over her made him understand. How could he have expressed the yearning love of God so perfectly except through his own heart's sorrow?

'It takes a broken heart to love as Jesus loved.'

Surviving on endurance and unshakable determination, she instituted for herself – and often for those around her – a spartan rule of physical exercise taken early in the morning, cold baths, and what she considered to be a healthy diet. Asked many years later to what she attributed her longevity, she replied without

153

hesitation, 'raw onions'. Since arriving in France, she had been blessed with an intuitive grasp of the language, having a quick ear if rather less instinctive grammar. After six years living among the French, she used the whole of her body when she talked, gesticulating with her hands, moving her eyes, which were lively and humorous, getting up, sitting down, walking round the room.

On the long, uncomfortable journeys in jolting wooden railway carriages, she read Pascal and Pere Didon, Lacordaire, Kingsley and Hugo – 'to conquer by brute force is stupid, but to conquer by conviction is great.' She read Madame Guyon, who spent seven years in the Bastille for her religious convictions, and of Archbishop Fenelon who supported her, with his contempt for professional talkers who used words as a quack used remedies. 'Salvation,' she said, in her practical way, 'is not a theory or a dogma nor a thing of the intellect; it is a change of heart.'

Thinking and speaking with swiftness and lucidity, she could be unnerving, shrewd, and at times, downright rude. Direct and intuitive herself, she could be irritated by slowness in others. Too much talk she described as the folly of the age: 'I defy an angel to talk too much without sinning.' Totally lacking in ambiguity, pouncing unerringly on the heart of a problem with a distinctness of expression and directness of purpose, she could be devastatingly and impulsively frank and endearing in her efforts to make amends. 'You are a fool,' she told her crestfallen secretary. 'Yes, you *are* a fool,' she repeated. 'And now let's have a cup of tea.'

Under her direction, in the Paris Training Home, they had made what they called a tomb for the spirit of criticism, promising to be more severe on themselves than on anyone else. Quite unable to dissemble, she spoke the truth in love, praying with her head as well as her heart, often with tears streaming down her face in desolation at sickness, sorrow and sin. Dispensing with notes when she preached, since she maintained that they stunted the spirit, her thin face lit up like a lamp as soon as she started to speak.

Love, she said, was the great dynamic of the universe, as superior to all other forces as the sun to a tallow candle. Marriage, she called the sublimest of all human ordinances. 'True love

154

cannot rest alone,' she said. 'True love runs to give and give and give, and to share all she has with her love.' This, she called the strongest incentive for marriage.

'It is one of the triumphs of the gospel,' she said, 'that it lifts and sanctifies the most intimate, fundamental relationship of life. How high God places it is revealed by the fact that it is the symbol through which He speaks to us of the relation between Christ and His Church.

'What manner of lovers then ought we to be!'

The wedding took place on a sunny Tuesday, 8 February 1887. It was held at the Congress Hall in Clacton, and it had much of the spirit of the barricades about it, with Arthur speaking of 'my beloved comrade' and Kate improvising a hymn of her own which she turned to Arthur and sang:

'After years of war together, comrade mine,
After fair and stormy weather, comrade mine,
We will fight and never tire, comrade mine.'

Tickets had been advertised in the *War Cry* for over a month, a shilling a meeting, or two shillings for the day, with half-a-crown extra for the wedding breakfast. One of the guests called it the largest wedding party ever gathered. 'Not even Her Majesty's daughters would have such a wedding party,' he said. 'And there certainly wouldn't be so many saints about, or so much prayer.'

French and Swiss soldiers had come to England for the occasion, and Kate and Arthur both wore the double badge of France and Switzerland. Kate, in her navy Salvation Army dress, surrounded by her sisters, wore a white sash of rejoicing across her shoulders, and looking back at reports of the ceremony, it seems a tribute to Arthur's tenacity, resilience and optimism that he survived it at all.

Five days earlier, like other Booth sons-in-law, he had changed his name by deed poll: 'I, Arthur Sydney Clibborn ... hereby give notice ... that I shall henceforth take and use the surname of Booth-Clibborn in lieu of the surname Clibborn ...' Now, since Kate was his senior officer in the Army, he had to promise to obey her.

'We must be most careful in forming this association,' read the General, performing the Salvation Army form of wedding service, 'that those to whom we are to be united shall be one with

155

us in purpose, one in consecration...' Catherine Booth wept openly throughout the ceremony – her family had only at the last minute prevailed upon her to attend at all – and Railton looked grim. 'Railton never forgave me for marrying,' Kate was to say later with sadness.

Mrs Booth spoke, reluctantly, of 'a side of life to which my child is as yet a stranger. Having experienced the weight of public work, and the weight of a large family continually hanging upon my heart,' she said, 'and having realised what a very hard struggle it has been, the mother's heart in me has shrunk from offering her to the same kind of warfare. But our ways are not God's ways,' she added. 'The consecration which I made on the morning of her birth and consummated on the day I gave her first to public work, I have finished this morning in laying her again on this altar.'

In spite of it all, Arthur's confidence in the Lord's call to matrimony saw him through. 'I am happy!' he exclaimed buoyantly. 'I am happy,' he persisted, 'because I believe we are pleasing God.

'I am not here to turn aside out of her path one whom God has so wonderfully blessed,' he said. 'I have not come in any way to lessen that glorious consecration to which her past life has borne testimony.

'I have often asked the Maréchale what was the secret of the wonderful power that God has given her. How often it has helped my soul when she has said: "It has been that always I have counted on the personal presence of God. In hours of greatest difficulty, I have stepped out upon God, trusted in Him, and the power of God has come."

'I have come here, I believe, to help her; to stand by her side and to give that help and cheer and comfort in those hours of darkness and trial which fall to the lot of every salvation soldier; to give her that help and cheer and comfort which I believe God will enable me to give.'

To the curiosity of those who watched, Kate held a collection of rough stones in her hand, which she laid on the table in front of her, one by one.

'Joshua felt the need to raise an altar to the Lord in commemoration of His goodness,' she said, 'and I, Catherine Booth, also feel a great need to raise an altar on the morning of the 8th

156

February, 1887, to commemmorate the goodness, the faithfulness, and the love of God, which has followed me all the days of my life, and brought me through many Red Seas and past many Jordans, through difficulties and storms, trials and conflicts, darknesses, tears, expulsions and imprisonments, onto dry land.

'Here are the stones I have brought to raise it with.'

Then, picking up the stones, she built her altar.

'This stone,' she said, 'is for the General and for my mother – and your mother – thanking God for such a man as General Booth, that he is little enough to serve, and little enough to rule.

'This stone is for the Army, an organisation which makes it impossible to belong to it without putting into practice the life of the Lord, the sacrifice, the love, the self-forgetfulness, which makes us run the race which is set before us.

'This stone I raise in thankfulness to God for having sent me to France.

'The fourth stone is for friends, and the fifth is for the women officers. When I get to heaven, the first thing I shall do will be to ask for an interview with the apostle Paul. I shall say to him, "You were in rather a hurry, but I understood you. There are many who have misinterpreted what you said, and their interpretation has done a lot of harm."

'I believe Paul will shout the loudest of anybody in paradise when the Hallelujah Lasses enter. We are as dead against putting forward such women as he described, as he was. I am sure he is glad for anybody to do anything to blot out sin and sorrow and to bring purity and holiness on earth. However, I am going to have a talk with him up yonder . . .

'This stone is for the men officers, and this sixth stone is for the saints, living saints here and now, the saints who have worked the longest like Commissioner Railton with his pen and ink, and Bramwell Booth, our dear Chief-of-Staff, with his grey hairs, Ballington Booth, and Saint Frederick Tucker.

'This stone is for the spirit of union in the Salvation Army. We are criticised, kicked, stoned, blacked in the newspapers, put into prison, misrepresented and misunderstood. The methods, the secret things, the springs which make the machine work, are taken out to public gaze. But inside, we love each other. Inside, there is home and there is sympathy. Inside, there is a family and a father and a mother.

'Many have tried to break that union. The devil knows we love each other. He has done his utmost to break the links which bind us together, but they are as strong today as ever they were, and all his forces put together cannot break them.

'The eighth stone is for what has been accomplished: our Training Homes full, two more corps opened today, making over fifty corps on the continent. So another stone for our prospects, and another for joy, because France is disgusted with a sad religion. Misery offends God: misery is selfishness, and all selfishness is sin, but this stone is for the happiness that wipes away tears and makes people dance for joy.'

The little heap of stones lay in front of her, a rough, tumbledown memorial. There was one stone left in her hand. 'This,' she said, 'this last stone, is for the Colonel. I have known him nearly six years now. Any hour of the day or night that the services of the war required him, I have found him ready. Fully saved, I believe him, saved from sin and from himself, and that is a full salvation: that is heaven, that is peace, that is joy and life.

'Compliments are not in our line, but facts are.'

She paused and looked around. 'Marrying,' she added frankly, 'is not in my line. I have been frightened for my people to marry, and they all know it. I have seen what a trap the devil can make of marriage, and how many men and women up to marrying are gloriously useful and godly, who in an instant lose their power and go down.

'It isn't necessarily so,' she said quietly. 'Marriage ought to bring us nearer to God. It ought to make us more beautiful and more consecrated inside, more prayerful, more holy, more useful, not less.

'Two ought to run faster than one on the road to Calvary.

'Now I have raised my altar to the Lord,' she ended abruptly. 'Remember what I did this morning. Everything that does not begin and end in God is a disappointment, bitter and cruel. But God is not disappointment, He is love and life and joy.'

Within a month, true to form, they were both back in France taking meetings together in Calais, where tall smoking chimneys at the foot of hills south of the town marked the start of the latest Channel Tunnel project which was going ahead in spite of a complete lack of co-operation on the part of the English, who feared invasion. Young men from the site left work early to attend meetings.

Kate was keeping a diary: '. . . glorious meetings . . . fighting with the devil . . . souls smashed . . . rows of young men on their knees . . . left for Paris where the girls sang like angels on their return at night.'

Paris was becoming an Art Nouveau fairyland, building in progress everywhere for the Great Exhibition to commemmorate the centenary of the Revolution. In the Champ de Mars, the foundations were being laid for Gustave Eiffel's new iron tower. Kate and Arthur worked from a small apartment, their first home together, three cramped rooms and a kitchen with American cloth on the tables. 'A man's worth does not consist in the abundance of the things he possesses,' Kate always quoted in favour of short engagements, (she considered long engagements, succinctly, a waste of time). They travelled a lot, sometimes apart, sometimes together, using two copies of *Daily Light* as a link, a book of daily Bible readings which both possessed, creating a sense of spiritual communion by reading the same texts morning and evening wherever they happened to be.

Kate's diary was an indication of the pace of the work she undertook:

'Friday, March 11th: Saw Colonel off by train at seven o'clock this morning for Audincourt, where he has meeting tonight. Lectured girls only on women's sins. Took meeting at night: God drew very near.

'Saturday, March 12th: Lectured lads and lasses on how to form a corps.

'Monday, March 14th: Lectured lads and lasses on treason versus loyalty. Letter from Colonel: "Victory is ours at Audincourt!"

'Tuesday, March 15th: Lectured men only on men's sins. Lectured on how to get at the masses to save them. Consecrated cadette for rescue work at Nîmes.

'Wednesday, March 16th: Colonel writes from Basle: "Glorious meetings all day Sunday. Gave 'S's to about 20 soldiers. You must come here later on. Oh, these dying cities! Oh, what a chance we have! Oh, for apostles!"

'Friday, March 18th: . . . half past one on Saturday morning, said goodbye to cadets. Rose at 5 o'clock to prepare for Niort, a

159

Catholic town with 25,000 inhabitants. The ground is very hard ...'

Swiss Salvationists had been sent first to Niort, just inland from the north-west coast of France, on the Sevre where the river splits and gives the region its name of Deux-Sevres. The Poitevins greeted them with cries of '*Ce sont des espions! À bas les Prusses!* Burn them and drink their blood!'

Arthur had arrived later with a follow-up contingent of French soldiers who fared rather better, selling *En Avant* at the weekday markets alongside gipsies telling fortunes, surrounded by poultry and cattle. 'Send me a lass who has some blood in her veins,' Arthur cabled to London. 'Somebody lively.'

'Sunday, March 20th: Niort – hand to hand with the devil in person,' wrote the Maréchale in her diary, after coming down from the stage of a hall in the Rue des Fosses-St Jean to stand on a bench in the middle of the hall, scolding the noisy, impolite crowd into grudging silence. 'Singing out of the question. Notwithstanding a bad cold, I succeeded in making them hear ... terrible fight to get them out, but second meeting went on till quarter past twelve, and two young men yielded.

'Monday, March 21st: ... another storm in the evening. Made my way over the forms to one of the worst disturbers, a grey-haired man, and holding him, spoke to the rest. *Hard* fighting. Held a long after-meeting and had five souls.

'Tuesday, March 22nd: Visited La Mothe.'

La Mothe was a pilgrimage: the hometown of Madame de la Mothe Guyon, whose life had so impressed Kate, thrown out of Geneva where, still in her twenties, she had tried to help the poor and needy, to wander through France in search of what she called 'holy living' until the French imprisoned her for heresy.

'Found a charming little hall in La Mothe holding 180, small house and garden, for £15 a year. It is between the church and the pastor's dwelling, but this does not hinder the hall being filled with just *our* class. Night meetings crowded, about 300 and more in the garden, on which we opened the windows to enable them to hear.

'Began at half past seven and held four meetings, the fourth in the kitchen, surrounded by 17 young soldiers, all kneeling and praying one after the other in their own simplest language. Very moving.'

160

Back at Niort, the town was on the alert. The theatre had been taken for Sunday evening, an ornate building with decorated dress circles and pillars, dominated by an enormous central chandelier. Two thousand people came, and Kate used one word to sum up the evening. 'Meeting,' she said, 'indescribable.' Hooligans yelled and shouted, made wolf-whistles and cat-calls and brayed like donkeys. They turned down the gas lamps, plunging the hall into darkness, and they threw dead rats at the officers. A stage hand asked whether to lower the curtain. *'Jamais!'* exclaimed the Maréchale indignantly. 'Never! We fight on! *Nous lutterons, tant que nous aurons le souffle.'*

'It reminded me of the Reformation Hall in Geneva,' she wrote. 'Those first, glorious days. At intervals, sometimes as long as five minutes, they listened and the truth went home. We watched our chance and gave short, telling sentences, choruses and solos – 39 centimes thrown up!'

Later in the year, while Arthur was in Switzerland, where they still talked, like David of old, of being hunted alive like partridges in the mountains, Kate toured the south of France, battling with exhaustion and sickness. '...left for Lyons on business with officers. Came on to St Étienne. Captain met me at station: "Two sous in the cash-box, Maréchale!" The little bed I slept on in the officers' quarters was borrowed, and the chair and the table. Poverty! poverty! but full of faith all the same. Too ill to take meeting.

'... I hear the fight is still hard at Niort – roughs stoning. Presented flag to Captain. Hall *packed*. Many rich people. Colonel writes: "War going ahead in Switzerland".

'... correspondence all day. The police here are won over. Inspector was very much against us at first, threatening to send the Captain back to Switzerland and shutting up the hall for a month. Meanwhile, the Captain prayed for the Inspector, and his heart is quite changed. He takes *En Avant* every week and protects us by policemen every night for nothing. The change surprises all except the little Captain.

'... consecrated Major Becquet's baby girl. Hall crowded. A number of gentlemen at the back appeared hugely amused. After the solemn promise of the parents, I took the baby and consecrated her. Opening my eyes, the whole assembly was in tears, even the gentlemen at the back using handkerchiefs. The audience rose to see better. Baby behaved superbly. Only four months old. I held her, sitting, standing, or walking, in my arms. She helped make the collection, and she helped me make an appeal that I feel many will never forget ...'

Together in Geneva, Kate and Arthur reviewed twenty-one corps with over 1200 soldiers, holding a march past in the mountains sitting on logs outside an old saw mill, waving their handkerchiefs as the files of soldiers passed them, the newest German corps with *Heilsarmee* glittering on their caps.

By the end of the year there were nearly 150 corps in France and Switzerland, where of the 250 officers only 40 were from England. Adelaide Cox was in the South of France and Kate Patrick in Gard. Blanche Young was working with Major Percy Clibborn, Arthur's tearaway young brother who had arrived in Paris one day from America and preceded to devote himself to the work with exuberance and energy; Blanche was soon to become Mrs Major Clibborn. Lucy Johns, working in Switzerland, was to marry a Swiss soldier, Staff Captain Cosandey: later they were to head work there and in Holland.

During the year, 102 cadets had been trained, 95 new officers appointed, and the majority of the Swiss corps were self-supporting. The most notorious music hall in Calais had been turned into a Salvation Army hall, where an ex-clown was the officer in charge. In Neuchâtel, a new hall was being built on ground bought by the Army. New German Swiss training homes had been opened in Zurich, and Kate and Arthur were planning a new venture, a House of Rest for sick officers where they could recover from the sultry summer heat before facing the long tramps across the mountains in the winter snow.

Back in Paris, Kate was out of funds: 'We are at the bottom of the cash-box,' she signalled urgently to London. 'We have nothing at all!' From Switzerland, Arthur wrote, whimsical and euphoric, of living in happy street opposite the river of life, with the tree of life growing before the door. 'God is a city of refuge,' he said, as he had once been unable to say. 'I have run there. I live there.'

Spending their first Christmas together in Paris, the Maréchale offered up a prayer of thanksgiving: 'Thank you, Lord, for Thy precious gift of 1887.'

Just after celebrating their first anniversary, they came to

England for the marriage of Kate's younger sister, Emma, to Frederick Tucker, the apostle of India, whose refined English voice, pale skin, twirled moustache and red Salvationist jacket contrasted strangely with his turban, shoulder cloth and dhoti. An Indian durbar replaced the more conventional wedding breakfast, and was accompanied by what the Army, in its quaint way, called oriental *conversazione* and extraordinary effects.

'I could not wish you more happiness than I have,' Kate said. 'The past year has been the happiest in my life.'

CHAPTER 12

Emma's marriage was precipitate and emotional, taking place
on William Booth's birthday, the day Catherine called their engagement day, when 'God flashed into our hearts that affection
which nothing has been able to efface.' Catherine was suffering
from cancer and had been given two years to live. 'We have
dragged through *hurricanes* of suffering together,' said the
General, baffled and uncomprehending, torn between faith and
resignation. Kate and Arthur returned to Paris printing sombre
calls to prayer in *En Avant*, and Emma and Eva took turns
nursing their mother, who still preached whenever she could,
unable to move from the reading-desk at the City Temple for an
hour after she had finished speaking.

'God lives,' wrote Eva, 'but, but . . . you know well enough all
the things one cannot admit in public which harshly try our
faith.'

Kate and Arthur toured Switzerland together taking eighty
meetings in seven weeks, many of them held in Neuchâtel and
Geneva in defiance of local decrees. Athur disguised himself in a
big Russian overcoat, and Kate, 'getting into towns as best I
could, putting up wherever I might, travelling at night,'
dressed, as she put it, *en civile*. At Chillon, the island prison on
Lake Geneva – 'thy prison is a holy place, and thy sad floor an
altar' wrote Byron – they were refused access to a gaoled Salvationist. Moved, as always by *'ce bête de mot impossible'*, they
hired a boat and rowed out over choppy water, bobbing around
beneath the barred windows shouting 'Hallelujah!' through a
speaking trumpet improvised from a cardboard hatbox.

Kate had undertaken to visit each of her corps in France and
Switzerland once a year, which meant travelling to the point of
exhaustion, often catching the third-class express in Paris at ten
o'clock at night, arriving in the south at 5.30 the next day, and
then taking a three- or four-hour coach ride into the mountains.
The time was spent dictating to her secretary, only breaking off

to greet and if possible convert passengers as they boarded the train. Not surprisingly, when her first baby was dedicated in London by the General – 'in the presence of the angels of God I give thee to Christ thy Saviour as an instrument of salvation' – named Catherine Evangeline after her mother and after Josephine Butler's only daughter who had died tragically, Kate was suffering from rheumatic fever and too ill to attend, and it was left to Arthur to give the required parental word of consent over two-month-old Evangeline, to see her 'maligned, despised, hated or put to death in the service of God.'

Paris in the spring of 1889 looked like a Seurat painting, the Eiffel Tower glowing russet in the sun. International fantasies made of plaster and stucco in preparation for the Great Exhibition sprang up along the banks of the Seine: a Jacobean house, a Belgian town hall, an Italian basilica and a Thai temple, a funfair, a food hall and a champagne pavilion dominated by the great glass and metal vault of the Grand Palais.

By way of a counter-attraction, a new Salvation Army hall was secured in the city centre near the Opéra, next door to the offices of Thomas Cook. With four storeys, two flats, a big hall and room for a printing-press, it also had electric light, the great innovation of the late 1800s, entwined like flowers round the tall grey pillars. The walls were painted apricot with a green dado and dark red texts, the flags of all the nations hanging from the ceiling and *VIVE JESUS CHRIST* proclaimed in silver letters above the stage.

Visitors – two million were expected, and fifty million came – entered Paris through a bizarre arch festooned with hundreds of twinkling coloured lights. They took the new elevated railway that cut across the city, or stood on the raised moving platform to view the sights. Asking directions to the Eden Theatre at the entrance to a small cul-de-sac called the Rue Auber on the corner of the Rue Scribe, they were directed politely to *'le vrai Eden'*, the Salle Auber of the Salvation Army, which was situated at the end of the cul de sac, opposite the Eden Theatre.

Railton, in Paris for the opening of the Salle Auber, spoke predictably, of love, furious love, not stopping to consider, but rushing to the rescue. The General, taking advantage of special cheap return tickets to Paris from London, issued for fifty shillings second class, spoke in English. 'You have come to Paris for your Exhibition,' he said. 'We have come to Paris for our exhibition. You say we are fools. We know you are. You scorn us. We bless you.'

As the Salvationists sang hymns to the accompaniment of drums, cornets, violins and a piano, the theatre company came out onto their balcony opposite and attempted to drown the noise by singing a rousing chorus from *Orpheus in the Underworld*, but the surprised audience of the Salle Auber were informed that it was nothing like the old days under the railway arch in Bethnal Green, with trains thundering overhead every ten minutes.

'*Nous, nous, marchons, marchons, marchons!*' chanted the Salvationists. '*Nous, nous marchons, vers le ciel!*'

In England at Clacton-on-Sea, lying in a big iron bed facing the window where she could see the sea and feel the breeze, Catherine read letters from her daughter and son-in-law which must have reminded her of the early days when she and William were preaching together, zealous and full of energy and hope. Kate wrote from Boulogne, one of her most natural letters, 'trembling from the emotions of a most thrilling incident that happened yesterday.' 'Arthur saved a man from drowning,' she exclaimed, underlining the fact heavily, adding proudly, 'at the risk of his own life,' and she went on to paint the picture for Catherine as she lay with her right hand useless and pain in her back, drinking life from her children and their deeds.

'We were sitting a good way from the sea when we heard cries for help,' wrote Kate. 'The bathing man went for a life-buoy, and I turned round to see Arthur flying down to the shore. Coat and trousers were off and he kicked off his shoes and in a few seconds he was in the sea . . .

'All eyes were fixed on him as he swam towards the black spot bobbing in the water. The man had lost consciousness, with his face down in the water. I tore up my handkerchief, though I felt and knew that God would look after him!

'When Arthur reached him and raised the head above water, there was a shout and he began to swim to land. The body looked awful – face bloated, black and blue, lips livid. He was a big stout man, and must have been a weight. Arthur laid the man on the sands and moved the limbs quickly to restore breathing. He put the body in different positions and held the feet up to let the water run out of his mouth. At last, the man opened his eyes and gave a groan, and I told a gentleman in white clothes who was looking on, to rub the poor fellow's feet, which he did, while another went for a carriage.

'All along the beach the people have been expressing their admiration of Arthur's courage, but he sees nothing extraordinary, and says, as usual, that he only did his duty.'

For years afterwards, Arthur wore on his uniform the silver medal awarded him by the President of France to honour the courage of an Englishman going to the rescue of a French life.

'It would take a long time to write down only half my reflections of that afternoon,' she finished. 'What a stir when a life is saved – and so little for a soul.'

A couple of months later, Arthur was writing to Catherine from gaol in Geneva: 'I was quite unexpectedly arrested last night after one of the most blessed meetings I ever was in.'

Only a man of Arthur's naïvety and cheerful pig-headedness could have expressed himself surprised, since he had gone to Geneva in answer to cables informing him of renewed persecutions and stricter, more repressive measures against Salvationists, many of whom had been shot in the legs and feet for attending meetings. 'It was a great cross to be away from Paris so long on account of precious K,' he wrote to Catherine, 'but the fight was getting hotter here and duty called me.' Put in a lockup cell at the local police station for the night – 'clean and sweet: I got some sleep on the wooden inclined plane which served for a bed' –he slipped his New Testament through a crack in the wall to a petty thief next door, 'talked to the gendarmes about their souls' and tore pages from his hymn book which he gave to a prostitute.

'You see I write to you from prison,' he began his letter to Catherine, spending a couple of nights in Geneva gaol before trial. 'I was taken here and searched and put in a bath. My clothes and a prison shirt were left me, and the cell is clean. I am sorry I am alone: I had hoped to be in with the thief. But all is well, I have such a lot to do and the gaol people are very nice. The Governor, a Protestant, has just been to see me and asked why I rebel. I had a good talk with him.'

Writing poetry that night, as he did whenever he had time alone, in a railway train or during a sleepless night, he, like Kate, composed a short hymn which became known as his prison song:

'My Saviour, I love Thee, I know Thou lovest me,' it began,
Alike are all times and all places when with Thee.
At rest in salvation, what can my peace destroy?
Whatever befall me, I've victory and joy.'

'When I came into Geneva again, on the seventh day of the week on the 7th of December,' he wrote, 'it was seven years from the time I came into Geneva first on my knees in the train.

'My prison number is 7, and I feel there are seven golden candlesticks lit in my soul.'

On his release – 'Colonel's defence magnificent: hearing in perfect silence for 20 minutes' ran a cable to London – he took the night train to Paris and the boat train to London, arriving at Clacton on a dark, stormy day, to find Catherine lying with an Army flag across the bed, determined, as she put it, to die under the flag as she had lived under it. She was in constant pain, suffering minor heart attacks and haemorrhages: 'Her life in the body was lived in a kind of warfare with it,' said Bramwell later. William was pale and distraught, hardly able to comprehend what was happening or to stem the tears until he was out of her sight.

They talked of trials of faith and the dark night of the soul when no signals are given and there is only faith to fall back on. 'I don't know what to ask, except that Jesus will do the very best He can, in His wisdom,' said Arthur, who had been praying intensely. 'My heart is so full of faith for you that I have no difficulty in believing that even now He could raise you up.' He paused, holding Catherine's hand and watching her intently. 'On the other hand,' he said, sensing what was in her heart, 'you may be deprived of any realisation of His presence at all. After such divine light and such high experiences, it would be natural for you to be exposed to a great trial of faith.'

Catherine smiled a little, because he was one of the few to read her fears and the darkness which was one of the most difficult of the pains she was having to endure. 'One of the hardest lessons I have learned in my life,' she said, 'and I have been learning it more and more the last few years, is to distinguish between faith and realisation. I have had to conquer all along by naked faith. Sometimes, afterwards, there has been blessed realisation. I

168

must have learned the lesson by now. How can it be any different?

'I ought to be willing to go down without any realisation at all, simply knowing that He is mine and I am His,' she said regretfully, but with a certain firmness. 'How else can I conquer in faith?'

Arthur knelt down to pray with her. 'Visible or not, He is with you,' he said. 'I feel it so,' replied Catherine, 'and I thank Him.'

Arthur returned to Paris with messages from Catherine to Kate, who was again too ill to travel: 'Tell her I cannot love her more than I do.' At the Rue Auber, young officers from St Cyr military school mixed with rank and file soldiers and Catholic students from the *École des Frères*. A Russian woman spoke of more than a dozen converts from Paris in St Petersburg, one of whom had spoken of the Maréchale to the Czar. When she was well enough, Kate made a three-month tour of Southern France, Arthur preceding her, booking halls – 'no footlights for Salvation work: God gave man eyebrows above his eyes, not beneath them' – and arranging publicity. Placards appeared on street corners advertising La Maréchale, and handbills were distributed in hotels and cafés. Wherever they went, poverty was extreme.

At the Salvation Army post in St Étienne there was a simplicity which they called '*tout apostolique*', living on a diet of black coffee and bread with the occasional luxury of sheep's milk. Out of four chairs, three had no seats and one had only three legs. At Toulouse, candlesticks were made from potatoes with holes in and the only cutlery was a handful of knives with thin blades and broken handles. At St Hippolye-de-Fort in the Cevennes, the officer in charge still wore his soldier's uniform, mended where roughs had slashed it, '*Mon chemin, c'est la croix*' embroidered across his jersey.

In Bordeaux, the culmination of a week in south-west France, they held meetings in a dirty garret. In Rochefort, they held meetings in the town Stock Exchange, the *Salle de la Bourse*, where the Commander in Chief of the West Coast of France attended. Anarchists joined most audiences, violent but informed, and the Maréchale was called '*une type de Bernhardt.*' '*Elle avait plus que personne les cordes pathétiques,*' they said.

In the southern ports they held midnight suppers for '*les filles*

169

perdues', cards left in the most notorious brothels: 'A lady devoted to the cause of women desires to speak to them on subjects which deeply interest them.' At twelve o'clock, added the invitation, there would be supper, music and singing.

The tables were laid with damask tablecloths and vases of flowers and one evening, as a meal of boiled beef, vegetables, fruit and coffee was being prepared, a grotesquely ugly old woman walked through the door.

'Come and have some supper,' said the Maréchale.

'You don't want me,' said the woman.

'I do want you,' insisted Kate, but the moment her back was turned to welcome more arrivals, the old woman had gone again. As the tables filled up, there was a buzz of conversation against the background of piano playing. Some girls were well dressed; others wore rags. Many were very hungry indeed. As the Maréchale rose to speak, unaccountably heavy-hearted, the old woman burst into the hall again, bringing two attractive girls with her. 'It's these you want!' she exclaimed with joy, bringing them up to the Maréchale. 'It's too late for me,' she said, 'but they are young and pretty with all life before them. Show them the other side,' she begged, *'le revers de la medaille.* I spent a long time looking for them: *maintenant je suis contente.'*

Refusing, in Catholic or in Protestant towns, to make any public statement aligning herself with one denomination or another, Kate claimed always 'to give the truth as I see it.' Booklets entitled 'Mary the Mother of God,' 'Confession,' 'The Pater Noster' and 'My Credo' endeared her to Roman Catholics. On the last day in the south, she travelled back to Paris with a thank-offering of 5000 francs tucked inside her coat, wide awake and vigilant in a train full of workmen. The next month, she and Arthur took little Catherine Evangeline to England where they showed her to Mrs Booth. 'It wasn't their good points which called out my affection for my children,' she said, watching the child. 'It was their weak points. It was for their defects that I loved them.'

The Salvation Army was celebrating its 25th anniversary with services at the Crystal Palace, and Catherine, who could not be present, sent messages. 'I regret not having got more happiness out of my life,' she said to Florrie one sleepless night. 'I should have done. No one should be such a slave to any work as to have no time to love one another and make one another as happy as possible.' When she was dying a few months later, towards sunset in October on the Feast of Saint Francis, she asked those of the family who were with her to sing her favourite hymn, which was one Kate had written:

> 'We shall walk through the valley in peace
> For Jesus shall be our Leader.'

It was said that there had not been such a funeral in London since the funeral of Wellington. 'Only soldiers win such honours,' said a reporter. Detractors said it smacked of a royal occasion. Crowds watched the procession of carriages, headed by William Booth, standing, gaunt and bowed. At the service, he led the children in a heartfelt vow which they repeated fervently: 'Blessed Lord, we do solemnly promise that we will be true to our cause ... till we meet our beloved mother in the morning.'

Kate walked with Emma behind Bramwell and Herbert. Both wore sashes decorated with a cross and a crown. Eva and Ballington were there, and Maud, who had married Ballington the previous September, three days after her twenty-first birthday and against her father's wishes. Florrie was there, and the Bramwell-Booth children. 'My mother was an overcomer,' said Kate at the graveside. 'She overcame: her own timid nature, her physical sufferings, her mother's natural feelings when she sent her children north, south, east and west for her God. I remember that day when she kissed me goodbye for France. How she overcame then!'

General Booth's book, *In Darkest England*, had not long been published, heralded as a blueprint for social reform. As a result, the Salvation Army was to experience a shift of emphasis from spiritual to social warfare. Railton disapproved, and said so. Arthur and Kate, for whom the salvation of the soul was paramount, chose, as far as they were able, to do their own work in their own way. For William, it was a bewildering and troublesome time: in many ways, a crossroads in his life, just when he was least equipped to cope with it.

'If you had a counsellor who, in continually occurring hours of perplexity, had ever advised you, and seldom advised wrong,' he said in an address which few forgot, 'and the counsellor, while you were in the same intricate maze of your existence, had

171

passed away, you would miss that counsellor.

'If you had a mother for your children who had cradled and nursed and trained them for the service of the living God in which you most delighted, and that darling mother had been taken from your side, you would feel it a sorrow.

'If you had a wife, a sweet love of a wife, who for forty years had never given you cause for grief; a wife who stood with you side by side in the battle's front, who had been a comrade to you, ever willing to interpose herself between you and the enemy, ever strongest when the battle was fiercest, and your beloved had fallen before your eyes, I am sure there would be some excuse for your sorrow.'

Catherine Booth had kept her temperamental family together, binding them with cords of love and unquenchable determination. Without her, they needed an interpreter. The administration of the Army passed into Bramwell's hands, meticulous and careful, while remaining nominally with the General, who toured from town to town and continent to continent, a lonely figurehead, preaching the old gospel of blood and fire while the central life of his Army progressed without him.

It was a troubled time in Paris, with violent crime and little police protection. Suicides were rising, women throwing themselves from the high rocks in the Buttes-Chaumont Park or inhaling charcoal fumes and choking to death. Revolutionaries threw bombs in the streets in a campaign of terror which was to last until the assassination of President Carnot by an anarchist in Lyons in the summer of 1894. Talking with anarchists, Kate provoked an unexpected response. 'You have suffered: I too have suffered. Some of you have been in prison: I have been in prison. You have been exiled: so have I. You have wept over injustice and cruelty: so have I wept, so do I weep. You fling your bombs to destroy life, but how can people be converted when their heads are gone? Christ shed his *own* blood.'

At the Quai Valmy, urchins let fly a swarm of cockchafers in the middle of a meeting, but when one of the women officers was ill, they visited her in her room, bringing a lamp to cook food on, and delicacies which they would never have considered affording for themselves.

The winter of 1890–91 was bitterly cold, with no workhouses in Paris and a record number of unemployed. Salvation Army

172

halls throughout the country were opened at night as shelters, accommodating 2000 in Paris alone, where 18,000 were given soup for a few centimes a bowl. Out-of-work clerks, labourers and craftsmen walked across Paris to wait in a huddled queue for admittance, and when her halls were crowded out, the Maréchale rented a huge building called the Diorama, filling it with rows of seaweed mattresses and giving away free soup. A temporary workshop was opened so that men paid a sou for lodging, or else worked for it. Many came to the Army meetings, and some became soldiers. Soon after that, the new Salvation Army car, *La Petroleuse, 'ce phaeton automobile'*, became famous, with its hood with a flag pole at each corner holding banners with texts written on them. Country people called it a fairy coach pulled by invisible horses, as it spluttered and backfired, filled to the brim, scattering literature at fairs and markets, offering soup, soap and salvation.

An orphanage had been opened in Paris for the children of those the Maréchale called *'parents illégitimes'*, and there were now *Phares* or Rescue Homes in Neuilly, Lyons and Zurich, as well as the original one in Nîmes. Fired by Josephine Butler's example – 'If you and I could only stand up together!' Josephine had said to her – she spoke to meetings of hostile and influential men. 'You say "It is only a girl,"' she said to them, giving examples of child prostitutes not yet in their teens. 'Your mothers were once only girls, and what are your daughters? Where is the difference?

'I am told that things have always been so and will always be so. I hear it said on every hand that vice is a necessity, and that it is inevitable that some women, the daughters of the poor, should be sacrificed. All I can say is, if it is for the public good, let us not despise them and call them lost, fallen prostitutes, let us be honest and acknowledge them. Let us allow them to stand at least on the same level as our soldiers who sacrifice themselves for their country . . .'

'If the Lord in you isn't strong enough to cast the devil out of a twelve-year old child, you should go and not the child,' she cabled a frantic house-mother who complained that the girl's language was disrupting the home.

Officers had to be supported, the rents of houses, halls and training homes paid, as well as the Rescue Homes, the orphanage and the House of Rest. At times Kate was forced to go begging from door to door, from one rich acquaintance to another, kneeling to pray on the floor of the fiacre without the money for the fare in her pocket. 'Though the fig tree shall not blossom, neither shall fruit be in the vines, though the flock shall be cut from the fold and there shall be no herd in the stalls – yet will I rejoice in the Lord!' was her text when they met to pray together, calling on God to defend His honour.

In the autumn of 1891, she decided to go on a fund-raising tour of America, taking with her her secretary, Blanche Roussell, who had married Albin Peyron. They sailed on the Columbia to New York where they were met by Maud and Ballington, who had over a thousand American officers under their command, and they visited twenty-eight cities in America and Canada, travelling from one to the other in third-class pullman cars, thirty- or forty-hour journeys with a twelve hour hold-up in the snow.

'From her long acquaintance with the lower classes and the socialists and free-thinkers of France, she has acquired a fiery directness and ease and attractiveness in her speaking which is fascinating to Americans,' said the students of Yale.

They went to a tiny chapel in Niagara, praying until midnight and then marching through the village afterwards. They sang in Toronto among the tall pine trees in the snow, reminding the Maréchale of the Swiss scenery she loved so much, and then travelled across the snowy plains to be welcomed in the strange Canadian-French of Montreal. Wherever they went reporters were waiting to talk to them, handing them down from the train doors and queueing to talk to them late at night. Blanche called the Maréchale *'une routière endurcie'*: a seasoned traveller. They held meetings in theatres and factories, music halls and churches, sometimes climbing up into high pulpits to address the people: an experience as strange to them as to the Americans, who had never seen a woman in a pulpit before.

'Do you need all those beautiful golden rings on your fingers?' asked the Maréchale bluntly, surveying the wealthy women listening to her. 'When I arrived, I saw the statue of Liberty in the bay. France gave you that. A Frenchman, Lafayette, helped you to gain your independence. Now give us the money to save France.'

174

A millionaire lent them his luxury apartment and then gave them 150 francs, and Blanche talked incredulously of *'ces grand bourgeois'*. Nevertheless, they returned to Paris with $60,000.

By 1894, there were five children, Evangeline, Vicky, (consecrated Victoire by Kate, which was French for victory, but renamed Victoria by the General who demanded testily, 'Can't you speak English?'), Herbert, Augustin and William. Kate and Arthur lived a chaotic family life, travelling incessantly, 'always,' said Kate, 'with an inside or an outside passenger'. They employed Adele, a sixteen-year old Salvation Army peasant girl who had toured in the cafés with Kate as a nurse at the Paris flat, but when she was home, Kate loved to watch the children, struck by 'the entirety of their consecration, the simplicity of their faith, and the way they obtain their petitions and experience the fullness of the spirit.'

One man gave several thousand pounds each year to the Army work. 'It is a branch,' he said. 'They broke off branches from the palm trees and strewed them in the way and shouted Hosanna, and so do I.' When he wanted to give £10,000 for the upbringing of the family so that the Maréchale could be free of care, she refused, determined to rely on the little she and Arthur received as their Army pay. Missions in France, Belgium and Switzerland were preceded by tearful farewells, faces pressed against the window, and cries of *'Ne pars pas, Maman. Rest avec nous . . .'*

In Rouen, they took the Casino on the corner of the square, and 400 met with Kate privately afterwards. One man, an engineer in the French army, was in despair over his personal life and the wrong he had done. 'One day these hands of yours which you hate so much will bring blessing in places I can never go,' she told him, and years later he wrote of his work among criminals, and of the orphanage he had opened in the Ardèche for the children of prisoners.

At Le Havre there were rowdy meetings at the Lyre Havrais and the Sailors' Rest. Night after night jeering crowds fought their way in, refusing to let her speak even when she came down from the stage and walked among them undeterred. A cable arrived to say that two-year old Augustin was seriously ill and she longed to take the next train back to Paris, but after praying all the afternoon, she decided to stay one more night, because

175

she knew that if she battled with them long enough, they would listen.

That night, for the first time, the whistling and the cat-calls ceased and the people sat in silence to hear what she had to say. The meeting went on until past midnight, and eighteen hundred remained for prayers together afterwards. The next morning, another cable came to say that Augustin was better.

Kate went and sat on the beach alone. The life she had chosen demanded strange sacrifices: sacrifices which sometimes neither she nor Arthur understood. At times, though rarely, it caused dissension between them. Occasionally, there were rewards. As she sat on the shingle, the sound of the sea in her ears and her heart full of love for her children, and for the souls of those to whom she believed she could bring peace and light after so much battling in the dark, she wrote a hymn:

> *'Qui quitte famille et terre*
> *Pour mon nom, pour suivre mes pas;*
> *Qui quitte enfants, père ou mère,*
> *Reçoit centuple ici-bas.'*

'I never felt more free and regardless of man's opinion,' she wrote at that time. 'I am stronger with the rough element alone in my weakness, so much stronger, as I throw myself on them. This hour may never come again. My soul is on full stretch ...

'Do you know what the "centuple" is for me?' she asked. 'It is that my children shall become apostles. I claim that of God.'

CHAPTER 13

At the beginning of 1896 orders came through from the International Headquarters of the Salvation Army in London that Kate and Arthur were to leave France and Switzerland to take command in Holland or Germany. To Kate, the choice was immaterial since she understood neither the language nor the temperament of the Germans or the Dutch.

'The French have no soul,' said a princess to her once.

'How dare you say such a thing?'

'. . . but you have found the soul of France.'

It had been a search conducted through counselling at its deepest level, through subtlety and insight, intuition and heartfelt confidences, impossible through an interpreter and without that extra dimension of instinctive intimacy. 'It is natural,' they had always said of her. 'She has the French temperament. *Elle aime la France.* She has bought us at the price of tears and sacrifice.'

'I love France' she said, echoing their words in letters written, sometimes on consecutive days, pleading with Bramwell and the General to let her remain in France or at least to go to one of the Gallic countries. 'I love its people as much as my own. I have become familiar with its peasants in the provinces. I have sat down with the French women who clatter about in sabots, I have shared their chestnuts with them and heard their sorrows and their joys.' At times, when she was in London, her English deserted her, so accustomed had she become to thinking and speaking in French, and she would pause, searching for a phrase.

Many of her letters received no reply. When replies did come, they were terse or wordy and evasive, written with Bramwell's brain and education but typewritten, and signed by the General: always in the past, he had written by hand, full of love and enthusiasm.

Kate and Arthur were not the only Booths ordered to farewell, a policy deriving from the far off and not strictly parallel days of

177

Wesley, who believed that no man had more than 150 good sermons in him, and consequently moved his ministers from place to place every three years. Herbert was to go from Canada to Australia; Eva from England to Canada. Ballington and Maud were to leave America, and Emma and Frederick were to take over. Lucy and her Swedish husband, Emmanuel Hellberg, described as cold as the North Sea, were to take command in France and Switzerland.

The orders, issued from International Headquarters in London, where Bramwell was in charge, were immediately, rightly or wrongly, laid at his door: the General was away on a tour at the time. Inevitably they were interpreted as jealousy and a misuse of power, by Territorial Commanders already irritated with the constant stream of administrative additions to Army Rules and Regulations.

It was now fifteen years since Arthur sent up his cry of thanks for primitive Quakerism, primitive Methodism, primitive Christianity. The Army was successfully established throughout the world, in over seventy countries. In Britain, it was tolerated, welcomed even, as a powerful force for social change. Inevitably doctrines were becoming formalised and customs institutionalised, and as William and Catherine in their day had gone out in disillusion and blind faith from the confines of the Methodist New Connexion, so there were those now, who hankered after the first fiery days of blessed unpopularity, when leaders were given – and used – authority as well as responsibility without being hampered by central bureaucracy.

'I was Territorial Commander of France, and I couldn't make a corporal a sergeant without permission from London,' Kate was to say later. International Headquarters dictated where she held campaigns and what buildings she used.

'No book could be published unless it was revised by London,' was among Ballington's list of grievances, the greatest of which was the cry for American autonomy and freedom from London's apron strings.

'It is not in the wit of man to devise a stricter code of laws than are those which relate to a Commissioner's expenditure of funds,' said Herbert, complaining of what he called Bramwell's dominance, while striving to maintain the old ardent affection which had always characterised their correspondence.

178

For the Army, and especially for the family which had founded it, it was a time of disturbance and disillusion. Before Catherine's death, family feuds would have been unthinkable. Within twelve years of it, three of her most brilliant children were to have left its ranks for ever, with William, bewildered and disappointed, obstinately reiterating his claim, 'I have no children outside the Salvation Army.'

'They must conform to Orders and Regulations as other officers,' he wrote in his Journal for 1893, unable, without Catherine, to cope with his unruly children. 'I am a General first and a father afterwards,' he added, as he so often did. 'Alas, that was the fatal blunder,' Herbert was to write later in the margin.

'Who taught us so well the autocratic principle?' he asked his father. 'Are we not as familiar with discussions at home concerning the importance of leaving your hands untied and your will unfettered as we are with our alphabet?'

As far back as 1891, Arthur had written to the General requesting freedom to preach what he called the full, plain Gospel of the Sermon on the Mount. Based on the doctrine of the atonement, the idea which had so captivated Kate when she was eleven years old, it departed from official Army lines on three main issues, pacifism, faith healing, and the second coming of Christ, all of which he supported with a string of Biblical references.

Pacifism ('If my kingdom were of this world,' said Jesus, 'then would my servants fight') had been a political hot potato since the first signs of unrest in the Transvaal. Faith-healing ('Himself took our infirmities and bear our sicknesses') he called the natural antidote to war, not only preaching and practising it himself, but sending sick soldiers to homes and healers outside the Army. Anticipating the second coming of Christ much like the apostles of the early church, the call 'Repent and be converted that your sins may be blotted out when the time for refreshing shall come' was a call given added edge since, in his eager, eccentric way, he had calculated that the millennium was to end in forty years' time.

'This liberty is a right and a duty,' he wrote to the General. 'I have never asked, and would not ask you, to make any compromise with what you esteem to be essential to military or Army principles. I would not, and will not myself, make any compromises as regards what I esteem to be fundamental principles concerning truths which I hold to be vital parts of the Word of God.'

'He did intimate very often that he must be faithful to his convictions,' Kate was to tell her father later, and more gently, after he had constantly – and in many ways understandably – refused to allow Arthur any such freedom. 'As I have often told you, he would die for principle.'

Railton, living on sauerkraut and potatoes in Germany, sleeping on the floor, holding forbidden services for the sick during an outbreak of cholera and sticking tenaciously to the tenet that 'all this social doesn't save', tended to ignore the majority of directives issued from London. In 1894, at the Jubilee International Congress to mark the 50th anniversary of the General's conversion, he denounced the newly launched Salvation Army Assurance Society from the stage of the Queen's Hall in the Strand, tearing up and trampling on what he called the dirty piece of paper 'inviting officers to pay 20 shillings of the Lord's money and offering them 33 farthings, a farthing for each year of Christ's life on earth, in return.'

Unjustly towards one who had always lived blatantly and rigorously according to the creed that 'everyone that has forsaken houses, or brethren, or lands, for my name's sake, shall receive an hundredfold,' Railton's outburst was put down to mental strain and he was sent to America.

In the autumn of 1894, the General visited the United States, ignored Railton, and thoroughly upset Maud and Ballington, who had been fighting a long and arduous battle against the residue of resentment still retained against the British. Dyspeptic and ill-tempered, he criticised the number of American officers heading the American Army – he had always been wary of too much British delegation – and showed marked distaste at the sight of the American flag paraded side by side with the flag of the Salvation Army, which, to his indignation, flaunted an eagle in place of the crown, which had seemed, to Americans, to smack of colonialism. He questioned the involvement of American churchmen (ever since leaving the New Connexion he had prided himself on being outside organised religion), showed little interest in Maud's work in the American prisons – she had been inside the New York City prison, Sing Sing, and San

Quentin, overlooking the waters of San Francisco Bay – and when a crowded meeting asked to hear her speak, he said, 'Let her. I'll go to Canada.'

Ballington, dangerously ill in Chicago with appendicitis, received nothing but a cursory query and no visit – William had always been plagued by illness, and tended to ignore it in others as an everyday occurrence – and when Maud asked if he was pleased with the enormous crowd they had mustered for him at Carnegie Hall, he barked, 'You get it? It's my name that brought them.'

'Are you going to forgive me?' he asked Maud as he boarded the ship for England, overcome for the moment by honesty and a slight unease.

'I can forgive you, General,' she replied. 'I can never forgive how you have treated Ballington.'

Towards the end of 1895, Ballington was ordered to mortgage all the American property so carefully saved up for and bought by American Salvationists, and to forward the money to International Headquarters, registering the properties in the General's name. When he refused, the General maintained an angry silence for the next six months. In January 1896, along with all the others, Ballington and Maud received orders to leave America within nine weeks. They were not told where they were to be sent.

'Recall of the Booths,' read American newspaper headlines. 'General Booth thinks they have made the Salvation Army too American, and wants to anglicise it again.'

In typical Booth style, Herbert rushed from Canada to New York under an assumed name, and Eva sailed from England dressed as a lady's maid to evade reporters. At a stormy meeting during which Ballington refused to take his case before a Salvation Army Court of Inquiry, calling it nothing more than a Court Martial which he had done nothing to deserve, Herbert shouted that insubordination meant dismissal. 'If you won't go to London, you are to turn over your keys and offices by ten o'clock tomorrow morning.'

The following morning they left while it was still dark, to stay with friends in New York. 'The thorns in my path are not sharper than composed His crown for me,' wrote Ballington. 'The cup that I drink not more bitter than He drank in Gethsamene.' They had nothing but their children and their personal possessions. The General had long ago made it clear that none of his children would receive a penny from him if they left the Army.

'I can never go to another country and build confidence in the Army when I have lost it myself,' said Maud, while Ballington talked bitterly of 'a system of governing the work in this country from a foreign centre by laws made by those unaware of the needs and conditions of the country.'

'This is perhaps the saddest of all tidings which have ever reached the General,' commented Bramwell, reporting their resignation in the *War Cry*. 'I have no words to speak of his sorrow.'

'Dear, darling Katie, I don't like to hear you say the year has been a sad one,' wrote Eva recalling memories 'when I made you laugh and gave you baked potatoes.' 'The years pass, but then what matters? Every day brings us nearer our Eternal home, does it not, and then we will live and love together for ever and ever, *all of us.*'

After fifteen years on the Continent, there were over 200 Salvation Army stations in France alone, over 400 officers, headquarters in five French cities, and four weekly Army newspapers. Refusing the choice between Holland and Germany, in spite of the fact that he could speak German, Arthur agreed that he and Kate should leave Paris for Amsterdam. Choice, he said, only increased the trials; safety was to be found in simplicity and straight lines.

'I left France,' Kate was to say later, 'in simple obedience without conviction. I have made to the organisation the highest sacrifices it was possible to make.

'There is all the difference in the world between working from devotion and working from a sense of duty,' she wrote in an article. 'Love beareth all things, believeth all things, hopeth all things. Love,' she ended, writing the words in capital letters, 'ENDURETH ALL THINGS. Love never faileth.'

'I am nearly grown up now, Maman,' said seven-year-old Eva, seeing her mother in tears one evening. 'I am old enough to share your tears. Don't ever cry again without telling me why and letting me help you.'

'I am commanded,' Kate said sadly, after further passionate

exchanges of letters between herself, the General and Bramwell Booth.

'If the Angel Gabriel descended from heaven himself and bade you go, you ought not to leave France,' said the French.

'*Te quitter, c'est mourir,*' was the quotation most often on her lips and in the heaviness of her heart, echoing the sentiments of Mary Queen of Scots, as she packed up to go.

'You came to us as strangers,' wrote the German Swiss. 'Our people misjudged you. Prejudice, misrepresentation, hatred and persecution awaited your first efforts on our land, proud of its liberty and renowned Christianity. Your persevering and enduring patience, your immovable meekness, overcame us at last, and humbled and put to shame our narrow, self-conscious Christianity.

'Through your far-seeing hopefulness, your deep sympathy, you made our cold and narrow hearts larger, warmer, and more tender. As an example of courageous faith and fearless obedience, you condemned our formalism and led us back face to face with primitive Christianity.

'You have bound us and thousands in German Switzerland to you with indestructible bonds of eternal gratitude and of heart-fellowship through that love which is your power, your light, your life, your all. Those who go forth weeping, bearing precious seed, shall return with joy bringing their sheaves with them.'

'Even before your arrival you had become naturalised in these two countries by the love which God put in your heart for us,' wrote Salvation Army Officers from the Paris Headquarters. 'But you became doubly naturalised in the course of time, by your struggles. Could you, the spiritual father and mother of thousands of French and Swiss be other than French and Swiss yourselves?

'Like the Galatians who would have torn out their eyes to give them to the apostle Paul, we also would give all to show our gratitude to you.

'We will not forget that we have been born in the midst of privation; that someone suffered for us; someone passed the night vigils for us; someone interceded for us on bended knee. Our continued march forward will be the most glorious testimony that you have not laboured in vain.'

Before the end of the year, French officers mutinied against

Lucy and Emmanuel Booth-Hellberg, who could not, with the best will in the world, take over where the Maréchale had left off, and peace only began to return at the turn of the century, when Railton arrived to take charge, carrying the two battered suitcases he had taken round the world, to the Zulus, the Russians and the South Americans, preaching *l'amour furieux* as the only force strong enough to snatch souls from hell, and calling it a baptism for his work in France when a man in a bar poured a large glass of liqueur over him.

'Explain our position,' Lucy had begged in vain; 'make Katie believe that there is no personal feeling against her.'

Kate and Arthur arrived at their quarters in the Weesperzijde in Amsterdam with their seven children and Adele. They were welcomed graciously by Queen Wilhelmina: occasionally Dutch cabinet ministers were to be seen at meetings. Before long, Eva and Vicky were gathering local children together in the kitchen and preaching to them in Dutch. Arthur, who viewed any new language as a challenge, invaded a notorious café in the city centre and held an impromptu meeting on his knees. 'My comrades think I am learning Dutch well,' he wrote enthusiastically. Kate found it impossible, speaking in French or in English, and using an interpreter, which was frustrating and a barrier. She could not communicate with those in trouble through an interpreter. She could not counsel through an interpreter. She could preach through an interpreter, but that was only an initial, surface ministry.

They converted the ground floor of a shelter for men called the poor man's Metropole, into a meeting hall, and on Christmas night, five thousand came to a midnight supper. Earlier in the day, they served dinner for a thousand in the Verde, the Whitechapel district of Amsterdam. Brigades were started to take the *War Cry* to the lowest pubs by the canals, and in January, the Maréchale went to take a three-week campaign in Brussels, where she was to have the luxury of speaking in French.

It was an apt debut for the woman known throughout the continent as a second Bernhardt. 'I am going to live these three weeks as if they were the last on earth,' she told her officers. 'I am going to exist for this town.'

On the first night, 800 people turned up in the brilliantly lit Salle de la Grande Harmonie, deputies of the Belgian parliament among them, sitting in the room where men and women had once danced on the eve of the Battle of Waterloo. The Maréchale stepped onto the stage wearing a sackcloth robe of coarse brown cloth, a rope girdle and ashes on her head.

There was a long startled silence until she spoke. 'He was despised and rejected of men. He was a man of sorrows and acquainted with grief. We esteemed Him not and we still do not esteem Him.

'I come to you in mourning,' she said, 'I come to you mourning for your sins, for your selfishness, for your rejection of God. It fills me with sorrow, and unless you forsake it it will bring upon you the judgement of God.'

Then she went on to speak emotively of the return of the prodigal son, and to tell the story of the city in the book of Revelations, where there were no tears because God was there. The three-week tour went on for two months, and a Belgian senator called it the most astonishing thing he had seen. Returning to Holland, she went on to the Hague, Gouda, Rotterdam, and Liège, preaching mourning and repentance in sackcloth and ashes.

In the summer, the General visited, holding hands with his grandchildren while women in lace caps and men in broad-brimmed brown straw hats crowded into the orangery to hear him speak. He was strangely ambivalent, embarrassed and yet delighted at his own fame, sending his hosts scuttling for extra comforts and dietary necessities, and leaving them nervously exhausted. He no longer had to fight for recognition, either in England or abroad. 'It is a curious piece of comfort,' he had written to Frederick and Emma when they arrived to take on the difficult task of the American command, 'that anything is better than stagnation and being left alone. That is the condition we seem to be rapidly approaching in England.'

Travelling to London to attend a meeting of the China Inland Mission, against specific orders issued three times by International Headquarters, Kate and Arthur talked of the privilege of associating with missionaries who were soon to become martyrs: 'the Christian cannot renounce the right to mingle with fellow Christians,' they said. At the annual Salvation Army field day, Arthur refused to attend a music festival which seemed to him to cater more for those he regarded as pagan onlookers than for Salvationists. He had already been given a disciplinary reproof from the Chief Secretary of the Army in Holland for refusing to stage similar events in Holland. Instead, he toured the pubs and cafés with his auto-harp which he played like a zither on his knee, plucking it with a plectrum and singing hymns, while Kate visited the miners and iron workers who were on strike. By autumn, exhausted and unhappy, she was in Haarlem suffering from Dutch malarial fever.

Looking back, Arthur was to call it an hour of intense perplexity.

In 1881, the year Kate was sent from England to France, the Battle of Majuba had heralded the first war of the Boers in South Africa. Since then, gold had been found in the Transvaal, and priorities had changed. In the January of 1896, the year she and Arthur arrived in Holland, Jameson and his impetuous raiders were overpowered by the Boers. 'Will there be war?' asked a headline in the *War Cry*, and as the General reinforced his establishment image by holding what he called a fireside chat with Mr Gladstone at the statesman's home in Hawarden Castle, it came as no comfort to learn that his Quaker son-in-law was still persistently advocating pacifism as the true Christian path, talking passionately of the inverted communion taken over broken bodies as men met to bury their dead: 'this ignorance of one's fellow across man-made frontiers is the very life of wars.'

In conflict with official Salvation Army policy, he and Kate refused to take sides in the emotive issue of the American-Spanish war, which was fought the same year, since war, whatever the principle, was un-Christian, and when members of the Hague Peace Conference drafted a congratulatory address to the Czar, applauding his propositions for peace, Arthur refused to sign. 'Christians,' he insisted, 'have nothing to do with the false peace or the real wars of the world and the worldly.'

In 1898, conscription was introduced in Holland. 'Stay in the Army to renew it,' said Arthur, when he encountered disillusion or complaint, giving his unstinted support to conscientious objectors. 'The Army is still made of by far the best people in the world. The hour of the spiritual people is coming,' he said confidently, 'and then there will be a complete change in the depths of the Army . . .'

Together he and Kate visited the General and asked, again, for freedom to preach the Gospel as they saw it. Kate called it

186

daring salvation work: the work she had been sent to France to do and for which she had been jeered at and gaoled. Nothing is known of what passed, except that the request was refused.

'What else could I be but a Salvationist?' Kate wrote repeatedly afterwards. Behind her words lay the unthinkable and yet the only possible solution.

CHAPTER 14

Just after his seventieth birthday, the General visited Herbert in Australia. When he left, Herbert spoke of tears of disappointment. 'The result of your visit,' he said, 'was to leave us utterly dispirited and broken-hearted.' At Adelaide, the General had handed him a bound copy of the new Army Rules and Regulations, with a peremptory warning of the disciplinary measures following any attempt at evasion. Herbert called them unworkable, a mixture of autocracy and democracy, arbitrary, ill-omened, and ill-informed. They had been drawn up and issued without his seeing them or being asked for advice.

'I felt most keenly the miss of old-time confidence,' he said. 'Of recent years, my place in the family has by no means been what it used to be.'

The General hurtled through the continent like a cyclone, causing much the same consternation he had caused in America. He left with the same feeling of unease.

'All through the moments of a wakeful night, the things I ought to have said or might have said or wanted to have said, have in rapid succession been progressing through my brain,' he wrote from the ship as he left.

'I appear to have lost a part of myself.

'I was a good deal disappointed that there was no little note for me to read when your launch and waving hat and handkerchief had faded from my view. A note would have helped to drive the trifling mists more completely away from my heart and kept them away forever.

'However, I will regard it as written, and read into it what I wish, and will rest in hope and faith that we are one, not only in purpose but in practice for ever and for ever.'

It was no wonder that he returned with gratitude to Bramwell in London, whose careful spirit was as willing and energetic as his brothers and sisters, but less obstinately independent.

With war officially forecast in South Africa, Arthur was

writing books which he was not free to publish. Talking angrily of authority without responsibility, he and Kate read the wording of the perpetual vow to be enforced on new candidates to the Army – to obey a General or any succeeding General, and regulations 'now in force or hereafter to be enforced . . . and to be a true soldier of the Army till I die' – and decided to ignore them. They also stopped dedicating their children into the ranks of the Army at birth.

Arthur, in his indignation, called it idolatry. 'Wherever the human vow to a fallible institution is introduced it at once weakens the obligations of man towards God,' he said. 'This is common to all systems of idolatry. The perpetual vow to an institution or a nation always has something in it of idolatry.'

Writing jointly and separately to the General in protest, they called themselves outlaws, ceasing to accept any official responsibility, and signing letters and reports 'pp. the Chief Secretary.'

'Re Holland,' the General wrote to Bramwell. 'Let us be straight and plain and firm as a rock. Make them understand that we shall be so.'

In July, Kate and Arthur were again absent from the Army Exhibition, which was one of the grandest ever to be held. Billed as a Spectacle Beyond Description, it sounded much like a nineteenth-century Ideal Home Exhibition, with stands for bonnet-making, wringers, mangles and bassinettes, underclothing, drapery, boots and shoes, watches, texts, Bibles, and a tea-weighing machine. 'Exhibition Zulus' danced in native dress before astonished spectators who had come on special railway excursions to London from all over the country, there were exhibits from Mashonaland and Zimbabwe, and newspapers commented on the 'interesting kaffir men and women' who 'seem perfectly happy erecting their round grass covered kraaals on the floor of the hall.'

'I suggest arbitration,' said Chamberlain, pictured with his wing collar and monocle in a *War Cry* cartoon.

'Where and when?' asked Kruger with his forked beard.

'Any day during the Salvation Army Exhibition.'

'All right, I'll come,' replied Kruger. 'The Exhibition alone is worth the journey, and Rhodes admires the General and so do I. Why not ask him to be arbitrator?'

On 10 October, the Boer War began. Salvationist Uitlanders

were expelled, Salvationist Boers called up to fight. 'I am like a father with a divided household,' cried the old General. 'My children are on both sides. Whoever wins, I lose.' He talked in a bewildered way of just wars, unavoidable wars, wars approved in the Providence of God: 'whether this African conflict can be regarded as belonging to this class is not for me to say. I know not.' Resolving the situation as best he could, he ordered teams of Salvationists to the front to give 'counsel, comfort and practical aid to men of both armies,' and Bramwell's children wrote letters and sent copies of the *War Cry* to Salvationists fighting at the front.

In 1900, Kate and Arthur began writing publicly in defence of Christian pacifism and appealing to the Dutch government on behalf of pacifists in prison. When Kate came to England, she stayed with the General and with Bramwell and Florrie, sitting up late at night, arguing.

'I didn't know a lot about it, but mother cried so much,' says Catherine Bramwell-Booth, who calls her Auntie Katie a woman she greatly honoured and admired. 'I was thirteen or so when she came into our schoolroom and began talking to us and trying to convince us that you couldn't be a Christian – be saved, as we say in the Army – if you were involved in war.

'She had such influence. Usually when she came to stay, she never stopped talking – laughing and talking and seeing the funny side of things. She carried you along with her, she was a master of crowds, self-confident, determined, successsful. This time, she talked so earnestly and she quoted the Bible, and she said she felt we ought to be openly opposed to war, and I remember the perplexed feeling it gave me, because our parents had encouraged us. I knew she was wonderful, and yet I knew that you couldn't say of any of those men that they couln't be saved. We were in correspondence with them. They were heroes, British soldiers at the front, showing their colours. We knew they were saved, and I had the feeling that for the first time, I was separated from someone I loved.

'It was a curious mental disturbance to me to find that she thought so differently.'

Impressed by 'this awful climax of contradictions,' Arthur wrote a poem and pinned it to the wall of his Amsterdam office.

'For Christian war to have fair play,' ran the second verse,

'The Christ must quit the field.
For just revenge to win the day
His grace to guns must yield.
Dare any Christian raise a song
Or stop a soul to save,
'Twould be to death a deadly wrong,
High treason to the grave.'

'What would happen if in London's Queen's Hall, in the Paris Trocadero or in the Unter den Linden some extreme preacher were to stride across modern Christianity and say that Christian war with worldly weapons was a ghastly crime against Christ?' he asked realistically. 'If he were to add that the price for which Christ was sold was exactly the price of a modern gun, and if to give emphasis to his protest and to show that he was not going in his own name, but was treading on holy ground, he were to take off his shoes?

'What would happen? You know. He would be called mad.'

Continental opponents to war were, in the main, opponents of the churches, agnostics, anarchists, free-thinkers and atheists, who likened the behaviour of the Dutch government, forcing conscientious objectors back to barracks after imprisoning them, to a second Spanish Inquisition, making men kiss the crucifix and abjure their faith. Arthur declared that 'my views are not anti-military, they are simply pro-Christian,' and was horrified to find that a political cartoonist and artist to whom he had gone for a head of Christ to illustrate a book he was writing on pacifism, had used the same head on the shoulders of de Wet, adding a slouch hat and beard.

In England in October, the Cape Imperial Volunteers were given a triumphant welcome home after a tour of duty in South Africa. Every station en route from Southampton to London was packed with cheering crowds, and after a thanksgiving service in St Paul's, they marched through the crowded streets to Guildhall where they were given a banquet and told that 'London is proud of you.'

Arthur was in England delivering religous tracts to boys in their teens leaving on troop ships. The service at St Paul's was postponed for a day because of fog in the Solent, and an American faith healer, Dr John Alexander Dowie, stole some momentary limelight by arriving in London, where he encountered a display of unadulterated hatred and venom, people pelting him in the London streets while he laid hands on those who came to him, many of whom went away saying that they were healed.

Inevitably, the contrast impressed itself on Arthur. 'This soldier of Christ was received in London with a passion of hatred only equalled by the passion of approval which met the soldiers of the CIV,' he said. 'They had crossed the world on a mission of wounding and death. He had crossed on one of healing and life.'

On Christmas Day, 1900 – Arthur, in his pedantic way, called it the last Christmas of the old century – he and Kate wrote yet another joint letter to the General. It was more of an ultimatum than a suggestion, asking once more for liberty to preach divine healing, pacifism, and the Second Coming of Christ, in the degree in which they were held 'by one or the other of us, or by both. This liberty,' they said, 'has become a necessity to us. The full Gospel would have rescued the Salvation Army by compromising it more deeply and creating again the gulf between it and the world. As it is, the Salvation Army is something of the past century. Let every spiritually twentieth-century man and woman in the Army be careful not to grieve the Spirit...'

The answer was again one of stubborn re-affirmation: it is hard to know what else it could have been. It could however, have been given differently and with more tenderness and tact, as it undoubtedly would if Catherine had been alive, with her overwhelming confidence in the love that binds and conquers every obstacle. Arthur, in his dogmatic way, persistently asserted that she would have been a pacifist.

Disillusioned and frustrated, he contacted Dr Dowie, and arranged to meet him in Paris at St Cloud.

The American evangelist founded his faith on godliness, love, and the primitive New Testament teaching of healing. He was a resounding, prophetic, old-time preacher, who seemed to galvanise those who heard him into instant hatred or adoration. His most controversial claim was to being a second Elijah, the forerunner of Christ, and he was building a city called Zion in Chicago, which bore uncanny resemblance to Arthur's childhood temperance home at Bessbrook. Salvationists circulated stories about Dowie, and rumoured that he wore wings. The French, systematically begging for the return of their leaders, shook their heads sadly and said 'Clibborn *dérailla!*'

192

'I looked upon Dr Dowie as a mighty man raised up,' he was to say later. 'The fact that he never preached healing apart from conversion, and put the latter first, also impressed me. But I looked upon his declaration as the Elijah of Malachi, the Baptist of the Lord's Second Coming, as a woeful error and fanaticism. I went to see him at St Cloud. He did not convince me. I did not convince him. But I was deeply impressed by the spiritual experiences he related to me, and by the utter absence of any pressure or effort to win me to his cause.

'He said he would ask God to make the truth known to me, but long experience as a minister of the Society of Friends and as a Colonel and Commander in the Salvation Army had created habits of great caution in such matters . . .' He had followed one fanatic when he gave all his money to the Salvation Army and offered himself to William Booth; impressionable, frustrated and sick at heart, he was ready to follow another. While beginning to send sick comrades to Dowie for healing, he studied the Bible afresh to see whether the claims of the man who called himself a prophet could be substantiated.

Kate was staying alone by the sea. Carefully she drew up a statement of her convictions, and of those points where they differed from those held officially by the Army. When she returned to Amsterdam, she read it to Arthur, and they knew there was little possibility of remaining within the Army.

A few months later, a Salvationist officer in the Dutch army said that his conscience told him to lay down his arms and refuse to fight. 'I told him I would befriend him and publicly defend his action although it would mean my suspension or dismissal from the Salvation Army,' said Arthur. 'I respect the General for his faithfulness to the limitations he considers to be imposed on him by the Army's Foundation Deed enrolled in Chancery,' he added, pointing out, nevertheless, that the Deed was based on the word of God, and as his own ancestor, Robert Barclay, had said, 'it is as easy to obscure the sun at midday as to deny that the primitive Christian renounced all revenge and war.'

'When we sang, 'No nation owns my soul' I took it to signify that no nation owns us at all, body, soul, or spirit. I knew where the national Churches stood on this question, but I considered the Army a great advance on them in fearless war. Yet I have realised that the more the Army comes into favour with the unconverted wealthy, and with statesmen and politicians, the conservatism which this entails makes it very difficult if not impossible for it to preach the whole Gospel.

'That very fact seems to make this daring advance the Army's one plank of refuge in the growing flood of deadly popularity.'

Kate was expecting her tenth child in February 1902. Torn between the intransigence of her husband and her father, she was facing the most difficult time of her life. In correspondence with her father, both of them baffled and incomprehending, she accused him of trying to break up her marriage. 'How can you write to me like this?' she asked, quoting Biblical texts supporting the indissolubility of marriage. 'How can you demand that I turn my back on my husband? I love him with all my heart and all my soul. What is there in the rules of the Salvation Army that takes precedence over the conviction between a man and his wife, and demands the renunciation of the vows and faithfulness of marriage?'

Arthur spoke of the Hebrews who were those who had crossed over, and the Church as an assembly of those who have been called out. 'The pangs of separation from friends or family for the Gospel's sake cannot be allowed to weaken faithfulness to God,' he said. 'The Gospel forbids it. No one can more truly honour father, mother, or friends, than by going out in their day and generation to follow Christ.' After facing death time and again for his faith and knowing that his name was on the black list of those condemned to death by the Paris Nihilists, he had never been prone to compromise. He had also long ago sacrificed friends and family, a family just as clannish, though less close-knit than Kate's.

In July, another Commissioner was sent to take over the government of Army work in Holland and Belgium, and Arthur and Kate visited the General's home at Hadley Wood for what they were to describe later as a painful three-day interview. 'You make a great mistake when you assume that Arthur puts faith in divine healing and the Second Coming before salvation from sin,' Kate said angrily. 'He has too much sense for that.' Compromising letters from Arthur to his fellow officers, containing his views on Dr Dowie were in the hands of those at International Headquarters. 'I have told you often enough that he would die for principle,' Kate told her father wearily. 'He has intimated often enough that he must be faithful to his convictions. How else can he act?'

As they parted, William hesitated before kissing Arthur, and Arthur, in his honest, provocative way, said 'Please don't kiss me if it means that I surrender anything of my faithfulness to my convictions about the Word of God.' In September, proceedings began against him at the Salvation Army Court of Inquiry in London: the court martial which Ballington had refused with such contempt.

Personal letters from Kate to her father were used at the Inquiry. Writing eight times for their return or for copies of them, she received no reply. A decision was reached during the last days of the month, but although they waited daily to hear the result, no news came. In the end, word leaked out that the judgement had been to 'dismiss immediately.' Arthur's commission, as new regulations permitted, had been officially withdrawn separately from that of the Maréchale, but because it was evident to everyone in London that immediately her husband was dismissed, Kate would follow him, nothing more had been done.

'The Army set aside its rules in not dismissing me,' Arthur said bitterly, 'and having thus declared my resignation to have no value apart from that of my wife, liberated me from all moral responsibility.' From then on, living in what he believed to be the Saturday night of the world, he felt free to preach the urgent Gospel not only of Christ the Saviour, but Christ the healer and Christ the Prince of peace.

Because of her health – and perhaps, too, because he couldn't bear to lose her – the General gave Kate until February to resolve her own position with the Army, while at the same time suggesting that Arthur should say nothing of his beliefs until then. Kate wrote back hotly renouncing favouritism at the expense of Arthur's principles. 'Katie, let's give that unborn child a chance,' said her father. Arthur talked of founding a new mission, but the memory of Dr Dowie and his hypnotic black eyes nagged at the back of his mind. On 3 November, he discovered a series of Biblical coincidences which appeared to substantiate the Doctor's extraordinary claims.

He spent the rest of the month in study and intense prayer, agonising into the night with Kate who mistrusted Dowie and his methods. On the last day of the month, he wrote 'Thank God for Zion! I have decided to offer myself to you, dear Doctor, and do so firmly believing it to be the will of God and his great gift to me in answer to years of prayer . . .' Apparently insensitive to the tussle still going on in Kate's mind, or perhaps relieved at having at last allowed his own conviction to eclipse the awareness of her love and loyalty towards her father which had tempered his actions before, his unadulterated delight echoed that with which he had once offered himself with such abandon to the Salvation Army. 'I recognised in this God-given man and his message, a voice, a cry, a trumpet blast, an epoch-making advent, which summoned me personally to a spiritual fellowship with him in his warfare and crosses,' he said. 'From that day, I became fully and finally convinced.'

It was a conviction which was to lead to the years Kate was to look back on as 'my years in hell.' It was also to lead to his own disillusion and near loss of faith. With the exercise of tact, perception and charity on both sides, instead of obstinate pigheadedness, it need never have happened.

Years later, he was to write 'Dowie helped to destroy my true faith. He was a good man – at one time. So was the devil.

'*Que je souffre,*' he wrote to Albin Peyron, the old French judge he called Papa. '*Que je souffre pour tant de braves et devoués Chrétiens qui ont fait la même erreur que moi – et beaucoup par mon exemple . . .*'

In Australia, isolated and ignored, mail taking months to arrive, which meant that a conversation in any constructive sense was impossible, Herbert took a year's leave. Spending a night wrestling like Jacob, kneeling on an island fording the Collie River, 'pleading full stretch on the shingle, searching by a lighted candle for illumination in the Bible,' he made up his mind to resign his commission.

'I thought of dear Mother and remembered the many promises of faithfulness to conscience and duty I had given her,' he wrote to the General. 'I thought of you, dear father, and wept bitterly.

'Next to my conversion and my marriage, it was the event of my life. It was like going from abundance into a blank.'

In Amsterdam, Kate and Arthur attended, as they had promised to attend, a Council of Salvation Army Officers. As soon as they left, the remaining officers were asked to promise to stand by the Army and its principles to death. 'We have for a long time believed that such vows can only be made to God, or between husband and wife,' commented Arthur later. One officer refused to raise his hand, and was immediately disciplined. When Kate heard what had happened, she sent in her resignation to her father without waiting for the baby to be born.

'My dear Father,' read the brief letter from the Weesperzijde. 'Desiring as you know for years past a greater, fuller liberty for Arthur (whom I look upon as a mighty man of God especially called and remarkably qualified) and for myself, I now after much thought, prayer and intense suffering of heart, decide to cease to be under the government of the Salvation Army. I hope by this step to get nearer to you as your daughter – to my brothers and sisters and to be a better comrade for every Salvationist and all true children of God – but above all, to be a greater blessing to this poor lost world for which I have felt that my life could have been better spent for many years past.

'Your ever loving daughter, Catherine Booth-Clibborn.'

'The reason which our late comrades have stated in their letters of resignation for leaving the Army is that they may obtain liberty to preach what they speak of as "a full Gospel,"' commented Bramwell, unfairly and with more than a shade of sarcasm. 'A painful explanation of what they mean is afforded by the announcement that the Commissioner has accepted the teaching of a person called Dowie, who is the leader of a small American society called Zionites . . .

'The General is responsible for maintaining inviolate the purity of Salvation Army doctrine according to the word of God and in harmony with those principles of the Army which are now so well understood. He has been compelled, therefore, to refuse that liberty to teach false and dangerous error which both the Commissioner and Mrs Booth-Clibborn have been demanding.'

'Mr Bramwell Booth,' Arthur was to point out later, when he and Kate wrote at length on their resignation from the Army and the years of wrangling, desperation and heart-searching that had led to it, 'reduces the whole of our protest and appeal of years, to the question of one man, and the whole of our correspondence to one moment.

'Those who seek to replace the rigidity of the machine with the flexibility of life, must necessarily sooner or later arrive at being considered by the heads of the Army as holding "false and dangerous error." '

Bramwell tortured himself with memories of childhood days when he and Kate had stood shoulder to shoulder on the East End corners preaching salvation in all its simplicity: 'Put on Katie,' he could hear the General say, 'she's my trump-card!' To the 72-year old General, writing of his darkest hour and asking those who supported him to win 100,000 souls for Christ in 1902, it must also have brought back memories: memories of the days when he and Catherine had gone out from the security of an established movement to face the world like Abraham, all faith and fire and principle; memories of the beginning of the Army, standing on an orange-box waving an umbrella and a Bible, convinced of revolution and the movement of the Spirit; memories of his Blucher, his favourite child, marching beside him through Whitechapel, whose instincts had so impressed him that he had told her to follow them and she would never go wrong.

'I cling to it that Katie is ours at bottom,' wrote Bramwell to his father. 'I suffer twice over everything, first for you, and then for myself. I feel God must deliver us.

'It is awful. I feel the wickedness of it so intensely, and the ruin it brings to souls.'

'I don't worry so much about harm coming to the Army,' wrote Eva. 'What distresses me is our losing Katie and the General's nine beautiful grandchildren, and the terrible anticipation that presses in upon me of the poor girl's desolate future all full of delusion and disappointment.'

'She was perfectly marvellous,' says Catherine Bramwell-Booth. 'Think of it: her husband, her babies. What could she have done? In spite of all the strain of breaking with her family, in spite of the loss of her position in the Army, with officers under her command and against all the persuasions and prayers and tears of the Booths, she had the courage to do what she felt was right. Who is going to quarrel with that?'

Within weeks Herbert's formal resignation followed, speaking of a movement built on family principles and founded and fostered in the midst of a family, 'a family once as happy and united as ever God made one. We go with our three children,' he said, 'to start life afresh, supported only by God and a good conscience.'

At the end of February, a baby girl was born, Kate's tenth child, called Joséphine after Josephine Butler. In a letter headed 'Springtide, Amsterdam' the Maréchale attempted to clarify her position to her colleagues and friends. Throughout England and the Continent there were rumours and gossip, much of it false, and most of it malicious, and close friends were writing in hurt and bewilderment.

'For many years I have been at variance with some things in the Army principles and system of government as they now exist,' she said. 'I have had strong views as to the best lines for work on the Continent.

'My leaving the Army has nothing whatever to do with Dr Dowie.

'I left England for France before many of the present developments of the Army system came into existence. My judgement and my deepest spiritual convictions could not accept some of them. My husband and I have never been able to impose them on officers. Owing to these differences International Headquarters has not felt free to permit me to hold a meeting in England for many years.

'I believe in right government and discipline. Lawlessness is godlessness. There is a right, a voluntary, sacrifice of some liberty in the interests of united work. But it cannot be indefinitely prolonged into new things in which there is no agreement and extended to new regulations in which the governed have neither voice nor choice . . .

'In the first seven years of work in France and Switzerland, when regulations were few and of the simplest kind, divine love, daring war, and an open Bible, were sufficient to do a mighty apostolic work which neither persecutions, imprisonments, nor expulsions could crush, and which will live throughout eternity. Never were Officers better disciplined . . .

'We are, and ever will remain, Salvationists; and in order to do so and to move forward in our day, as my father and mother did in their day, we have moved out of the Army as they moved out of the Methodist Church.

'I have the deepest conviction that no one rejoices over the step we have taken more than does my mother in heaven.

'My husband is led of God, and I shall always support him in his faithfulness to his religious convictions. I have never known him leave plain Scripture ground or deviate from the straight line of truth and principle. Christ and his apostles constantly did saving and healing work independently of custom and tradition.

'This step has cost me more than words can express, but my deepest conviction is that the united and freed lives of the Commander and myself will do far more for the poor lost world than they have been able to accomplish for many years past.

'There never was a time in my life when I so hungered that Jesus as He is, the same yesterday, and forever, should be lifted up, and that the simple, pure, entire Gospel should be given to people.

'Here is the great attraction!' she ended, unconsciously echoing the words her father had used more than twenty-five years ago, surveying the Mile End wilderness. 'Here is the greatest power in the universe.'

Writing to those close to her, she used fewer words. *'Voilà ce que cela m'a coûte,'* she said of the decision. 'See what it has cost me. My life's blood: *le sang de mon coeur.'*

CHAPTER 15

'Qui quitte famille, père ou mère, pour mon nom': whoever leaves father or mother for my sake ...

Submissive to the point of apathy, Kate put her name with Arthur's to the founding of what was called a Christian Mission of the Friends of Zion. The date, 8 February, coincided with their fifteenth wedding anniversary, and the evening portion in the *Daily Light* was apt, if in this case inaccurate: 'Praise waiteth for Thee, O God, in Zion.'

'On July 12th, we went into Zion City,' reads her diary for 1902. 'I cannot write here all the anguish of heart and mind I went through. All my days were nights.'

Years later, Arthur issued a statement. 'The Maréchale would never have had anything to do with Dr Dowie but for me,' he said. 'When she came near him, it was on every occasion unwillingly. She suffered unutterable anguish, pain and grief, from the fact that from the first, all her instincts as well as the consciousness of her true religious interests, were against Dr Dowie's spiritual personality, his ways, his claims, his style of government.

'If in a kind of despair she went with me into it, though she was in it, she was not of it. It was never sought, it was endured. The only comfort in the enduring was the possibility of doing a little good meanwhile to the people in it, and of ultimately helping in the opening of my eyes.'

John Alexander Dowie, a Scot by birth, was a stern man with straight, piercing eyes, given to thundering rhetoric. As long ago as 1896 he had voiced his hopes of building a city called Zion where he could stand on the dome of a temple holding twenty thousand people and see multitudes coming to be saved and healed and cleansed. His vision began in an old wooden hut in Chicago. In 1901, the foundations of Zion City were laid on a six and a half thousand acre plot of land forty miles north of Chicago, bought through a debenture scheme backed by fol-

201

lowers and founded on a small community of lace-makers. Early in 1902, about the same time he was calling Islam a shocking blot on humanity and prophesying that all Muslims would be destroyed unless they bowed before the cross, Zion City was opened, with Dr Dowie as General Overseer.

It was the springtime of a brand new vision. Like Bessbrook, which had no public houses, pawnshops or policemen, Zion City was founded on principles of abstinence from drink and drugs. Even its geographical appearance was similar, built on the same system of straight lines and intersecting roads. Arthur called it a commonsense town because it was a clean town. 'If there were bullets flying, I would bare my breast to receive them,' he told delighted audiences of thousands, so formidable was his certainty that he had found his true spiritual home at last.

'I should think Katie's and Arthur's eyes will be opened while over here,' Eva wrote to the General. 'I shall be very surprised if Katie's are not. Dowie's greatest means of getting converts for Zion is by making people believe that the Church to which they already belong is a cesspool of filth and hypocrisy.'

Before they had been in Zion a week, Kate had openly defied Dowie twice. When an audience of thousands rose to testify their faith in him as a prophet and forerunner of Christ, she was the only one to remain seated, and when he began vilifying the Salvation Army, and condemned William Booth as a man who had failed to reprove the sins of the rich, she leaped to her feet, pointing her long finger at him and shouting, 'That's a lie! No man ever reproved the rich more faithfully than my father.' After listening to him denigrate the Old Testament heroes – that dirty dog David, the coward Elijah and the murderous old fool Abraham – she preached for more than an hour to five thousand people on David the man after God's own heart, blinded by passion when he fell, but deep in penitence, and she was never asked to preach in Zion again.

'I have not felt one breath of the Holy Spirit since I came into this place,' she said, calling it Christianity without Christ, and Dowie an exceptionally clever businessman. 'That heavenly dove cannot rest here. This man has gone back to the bondage of the Law. There is no love in his religion; nothing but terror. Under his influence people are forced to think and speak and act

202

as they would never think or speak or act if they were away from him. It is terrorising. He is to be obeyed, he says a thousand times, and they follow him out of fear.

'As for the people,' she commented, 'they are nice as far as I can gather, but flat. Mrs Dowie could be no companion for me.' Looking askance at an expensive lace dress which the Doctor's wife wore, she called it irreconcilable with the Gospel. 'When I compare her with my mother or any of my sisters or with many of the leading women in the Salvation Army, she is nowhere..'

Publicly, Dowie warned her, as he had warned others, that he had prayed many a wife dead, and his words began to weigh on her mind to such an extent that she was frightened to cross the road or travel in a tram-car, especially when she had baby Josephine with her, or the two elder girls, Evangeline and Vicky, who had accompanied their parents. 'I feel I am in danger and all alone,' she wrote in a letter. Privately, Dowie offered her his cheque book, telling her she should be rich instead of poor.

'My Master was poor,' she said. 'My conscience is not for sale.'

'He, being rich, for our sakes became poor, that we through Him might become rich,' argued Dowie.

'Why don't you take my husband and ordain him?' she asked wearily. 'He believes in you and is ready to serve you. Let me darn stockings or dig potatoes. I will be a wife and a mother to my children.'

'It is you I want,' he said to her. 'I will not ordain him without you.'

'I cannot give my ten beautiful children to this man, I can't,' she wrote to Josephine Butler, calling her position one to make the angels weep, and signing her letters 'broken-hearted but not in despair.' 'I have felt here as I have never felt in my life,' she wrote to a close Swiss friend. 'I never was so unutterably unhappy. I cannot bring myself to accept Dowie. So much in him revolts me and violates the highest spiritual instincts I have. He thunders! He struts around the platform and literally thunders. You have to have pretty good nerves to stand it.

'I have yielded all along the line, and now here I am. I have looked it in the face more than once – for me to join and bear – but I should be as miserable as a creature could be out of purgatory. Think of me in such a position. It would be intolerable. It would be annihilation: moral suicide.

'Dowie will begin to thunder at me because of his conception of wifehood, but I cannot go further in this direction. I cannot follow him. I have too much of my mother's blood in me.'

The reply to her letter offered convention rather than comfort, and made her feel more isolated than ever. 'He couldn't understand,' she wrote sadly in her diary. 'He said I was a wife, and the responsibility was on my husband, and I must stand by him even if he was in error, and God would forgive me if it was a mistake. I was so taken aback that I turned the key of my heart. I felt God had a lesson to teach me. Now I shall go alone with Him.'

It was four months before she persuaded Arthur, against his will, to leave Zion City. On a salary from Dowie – unknown to Kate, Arthur had resigned his Army salary immediately he heard of his dismissal – they began touring together. Arthur preached with enthusiasm, provoking riots and uproars, recapturing the sense of excitement which had accompanied the persecutions of the early days in the Army. Kate travelled restlessly, hardly knowing what she was doing or why. Baby Josephine – José – was taken to seven countries before she was ten months old, sleeping in drawers and makeshift cots, Kate feeding her all the time: not surprisingly, years later, it was discovered that she had suffered from ricketts. Salvationism, the shared cause which had once brought Arthur and Kate together, now became an invisible barrier of resentment heightened by their inability to agree over Dowie, but it was an unacknowledged barrier, less strong than the intensity of the impetuous passion which had always sustained them in the past: during this time, Kate suffered a miscarriage.

In New York, they stayed with Herbert and his wife Annie at their home in Yonkers. 'She sat for hours gazing into vacancy,' remembers Vicky, who was to be with her mother and preach with her for the next twenty years, and at over ninety years old is still an evangelist in America today. 'For the time being, her sorrow quenched the flame of her individuality.' 'Stop drenching that baby with tears, Katie,' said Annie. Ballington and Maud had started a group called the Volunteers who were fighting hand to hand and chorus to chorus with Salvationists in the streets. Maud wrote to Kate begging her not to weaken and

204

return to the Army. 'I beg you on my knees,' she said. At the end of 1903, Emma, Frederick Tucker's wife and Kate's closest sister, was killed suddenly in a railway accident. Ballington held a prayer meeting before the funeral which none of the family attended, and Herbert was turned away from the platform.

'*Il faut plus que jamais aller à la recherche des perdus,*' said the General, on a broken-hearted tour of France.

Kate, counting illogically on old friends, found Salvation Army halls closed to her wherever she went. Salvationists, many of whom had known and worked with her since the first days in France, were awkward and hostile, bewildered and uncomprehending, and because she refused to say anything which could be construed as condemning the Salvation Army, the mystery and the misunderstandings remained. After living for a while in Brussels, they moved to a borrowed house in St Cloud, on the Bois de Boulogne, with chestnut trees at the bottom of the steep garden where a single track railway line ran which used to take Napoleon the Third from his château into Paris. From the top attic windows it was possible to see the green trees and the crowds walking to the races on a Saturday afternoon.

Kate resigned herself to believing that she would never speak in public again. To do so, she felt, would appear to be preaching in opposition to the Army. She read the letters of Père Didon on heroic acceptance, and wrote in her diary, 'When I compare myself with what I was in the past, it seems as if that person was dead. Depression, *timidity,* fear, and sadness, mark my character today. I stop at difficulties and seem unable to rise above occasions as I used to do.' The word timidity was underlined disbelievingly.

'Loss of reputation and the misunderstanding of family and friends. No. Impossible to accept': the words on the slate in the prison cell at Neuchâtel and signed at last with such reluctance. Letters came rarely, and when they did, although beginning with an outpouring of genuine affection – 'My darling Maréchale...' – they were stilted and ill-at-ease, addressed pointedly to 'Mrs Clibborn.' French newspapers reported that the Maréchale had burned her principles.

'It is terrible to allow oneself to be turned aside,' she said, calling it her grievous sin. 'I was sent to the masses as a child, and my greatest and deepest spiritual blessings and lessons have come in following that calling. This is not my calling, nor have I ever once been blessed on the road. I have lost ground spiritually, and darkness has followed.'

Battling against this new and uncharacteristic timidity, she took the train one day to Paris and climbed to the fifth floor of a house in the Villette, hesitating opposite a familiar door and then knocking on it. It was opened by Eugenie, the girl who had tried to commit suicide. At the sight of her, the Maréchale burst into tears, and Eugenie comforted her, putting her arms round her and making her lie down on the bed while she cooked some food which they ate together.

'To the God-fearing person, suffering is nothing compared with the loss of the light of His face,' say those who knew her. 'She felt she was separated from Him, rejected by Him, and it was an agony and a crucifixion.'

'Hast Thou forgotten me?' ran one of her hymns, written at that time. 'Why go I in mourning, my Lord? Mine enemies say I am forsaken of Thee. Look up, look up, my soul...' Another returned to the theme of her childhood, and the promise she had hung onto then, during what had seemed to be years of incomprehension and darkness: 'The Lord whom you seek will suddenly come to His temple.' 'For Thee I watch, as for the morning,' she wrote. 'Come quickly to Thy temple.'

One spring morning she sat beneath the chestnut tree listening to the birds and the sounds of the open air. 'The past, whoever was right or wrong, shall be buried,' she wrote. 'Let the dead bury their dead. I will not be dragged into it. Leave it, and this beautiful springtide let us begin again. The crocuses and snowdrops in this lovely garden all say the new life of the resurrection.

'And now for the children,' she went on, as if stirring herself to hear their voices around her for the first time in months. 'They must all see some salvation work and feel the glow of the heavenly fire. It will warm them far more than all the Bible lessons in the world.'

Tentatively she began to preach again, not to thousands this time, but to twenty or thirty people in small church halls in Marseilles, Lyons, Cannes, testing herself on other people and finding, unimpaired, the old springs of faith and certainty.

'Has Christ saved *you*, father?' she asked an old priest, as they walked beneath the trees talking, and he turned away sighing sadly and replying after a long pause, 'all the days of my life I sin, and I expect I shall sin to my last breath.'

'Then Calvary is the greatest fiasco the world has ever seen.'

'Don't say that, madame...' he stretched out his hand to her. 'Please don't say that. It is blasphemy.'

'But father, you have left what men prize, and you say you have found torment instead of rest, conflict instead of assurance, bondage instead of deliverance? Jesus didn't come to increase our burdens, but to relieve them. How can you show others the way if you have not found it yourself? How can you unbind if you are not unbound? How can you heal if you are not healed? Is it all from the head and none of it from life or from the heart?'

'I try. Oh my God, I try.'

'It does not come by struggling ' she said to him. 'He says "abide in me and ask what you will and it shall be done for you." Saint Paul said "I can do all things through Christ who strengthens me." He is able to save. Put Him to the test. You have a right to salvation.'

While she was away, Adele looked after the children. Salvationists had tried to persuade her to leave her post with the family, but she was adamant: 'In serving them, I serve the Lord.' She scrubbed the floors and laundered the clothes and walked long distances to the market and back for cheap food. *'Quand je dis "non", c'est non,'* she would tell the boys firmly when they were naughty, *'et quand je dis "oui", c'est oui.'* Her decisiveness and her gentleness, her round face and beaming eyes, were green pastures and still waters to the volatile children, and her advice to them never changed: 'Be natural; just be natural.'

'You are so sweet, Adele,' they told her, remembering years afterwards the way she would always turn aside a compliment into a song: 'So sweet, things so sweet, just to know His precious promises: things so sweet!'

The Maréchale called the children angels, which proved effective blackmail. The girls were older and more responsible than the boys, Vicky and Evangeline already helping their mother by speaking for her if she was ill, Evelyn playing the piano and Willie the violin. Clothes were secondhand and food spartan, with the hope of gifts on the doorstep. In the winter, the local children made snowballs with stones in them and threw them at the boys shouting '*À bas les Anglais!*'

The children who were too young for school had a Russian governess who spoke to them in Russian, French or German. The boys went to French schools. A tutor came to teach English and was plagued by bells tied to his mattress which rang every time he turned in bed, and strings which pulled his chairs mysteriously across the floor. Villagers came to their doors to watch him chasing the boys down the street when they were due for a hiding.

Willie amused himself by making enormous kites with long tails of string and paper and attaching a basket into which he put the baby, cooing and chuckling as the kite rose into the air. Saying his prayers at night, he refused to tell the Lord how bad he had been. '*Jamais,*' he said firmly, shaking his golden curls. '*Jamais. Cela le découragé:* that would only discourage Him. I shall tell Him how good I have been tomorrow.'

'*O, Jésu,*' he would pray then. '*Tu es la plus belle des femmes.* Of course Jesus is a woman,' he explained. 'He is so tender to us.'

Arthur took the two oldest boys, Willie and Augustin, to see Napoleon's magnificent tomb with its massive gates made from the cannon captured at Austerlitz, and Napoleon's words inscribed above them: 'I desire that my ashes shall repose on the banks of the Seine, in the midst of the French people I have loved so much.' The last time Arthur had been there was with his own father on his way to school in Switzerland in 1868, the day after Napoleon the Third had ridden in state through the city.

Inside the museum of Les Invalides, there were steel suits of crusader armour made for boys the same age as Willie and Augustin, and bloodstained flags hanging in the church. 'Napoleon so loved France that he took millions of her sons and made them believe that whosoever followed him to death might spread endless death throughout Europe,' Arthur said to them. His wars cost eleven million lives: two million were the lives of his own people.

'God so loved the world that He gave His only Son that whosoever believed on Him should not perish but have everlasting life.'

At home in the evenings, he and Kate told the children stories of the battles they had fought in France and Switzerland, and of the times they had been gaoled and wounded, stories of excitement, and adventure. Often, like William Booth in the old Whitechapel days, Arthur came home from the Paris streets with his face cut or his clothes torn because of the obstinate, provocative way he persisted in preaching what he believed in.

One day in 1905, he was viciously attacked with an iron bar which pierced his leg. The wound failed to heal – probably because he refused to rest, though he attributed his inability to overcome sickness to the prevalent lack of faith in Paris – and when he caught influenza, blood poisoning spread and the leg became gangrenous. To call a doctor would have been to violate the strictest principle of the Catholic Church in Zion. Kate cabled Dowie, who refused to permit any medical aid whatever. After praying for a long time and watching Arthur grow steadily weaker until he was unable to speak to her, she called in a man she had known for years, one of the most influential doctors in Paris, who said there was little that could be done because it had been left too late.

Four operations were performed on Arthur's leg – Kate refused to allow it to be amputated – and his life was saved, although he was always to be crippled, unable to bend his leg or move it properly. 'It is the least we can do in return for all you have done for France,' said one of the surgeons who performed the operations, refusing to take any payment. Nevertheless, Kate had spent her last penny, and unable to bring herself to write directly to her father, she wrote to Bramwell in June 1905. Bramwell informed the General in comments which he headed 'The Clibborns':

'Katie writes to me today that although the doctors say he is not yet out of danger, he is certainly improving and able to take more nourishment and get more natural sleep. The wounds have still to be dressed under chloroform, but the discharge is more vigorous and healthy, and although he still lies in a frame and can do little for himself, he begins to take more interest in what is going on, and to speak.

'In her letter, Katie again speaks of the heavy expenses which she is under, and the financial difficulties she is placed in, but I cannot see how we can help her. She informs me she has not yet heard any more from Dowie. I should think the fact that he has not made any sign rather indicates that he does not intend to take any extreme measures. Clibborn himself, so far as he has expressed any opinions seems to remain just as surely convinced.

'Katie has made no further sign to me as to any readjustment of her relations to us. The fact of the matter is, I do not think she knows what she is going to do, or what she wants to do.'

As it turned out, the lack of communication from Dowie signified nothing more than his preoccupation with a new scheme, forging ahead into Mexico, where he was raising debentures for 100,000 acres of land, with an option on 250,000 more. Before Arthur had recovered sufficiently to understand what was going on, two emissaries arrived from Chicago with a document announcing his dismissal as 'Overseer Clibborn', which they went into his bedroom and gave to him.

'I enclose you my latest from Katie,' wrote Bramwell to the General. 'I understand that as the truth is gradually being revealed to Clibborn – he has not yet been allowed to see his wounds – he feels the position more and more acutely. When he comes entirely from under the influence of the chloroform – he has never yet been really free from it since the operations – no doubt this will increase.

'The doctors now seem to think that he will recover and that his leg will be saved,' he added, making plans for the General's proposed visit to France to review the French troops. 'Of course, this disposes of all question as to your delaying in Paris. I do not think you need concern yourself any further about stopping in Paris. There is no necessity.'

Arthur's salary stopped from the moment of his dismissal, and Kate was faced with ten children to care for, a sick husband, and doctors' bills. A few friends came to her immediate aid, and as soon as she could leave home, she began mission work again, exhausting, thankless campaigns for very little money, starting from the bottom to build up a new following. In his satirical magazine, *John Bull*, Horatio Bottomley printed a cartoon showing John Bull and General Booth playing football together, relentlessly kicking the Maréchale backwards and forwards between them – with over sixty writs filed against him, he could afford to sail close to the wind. As a result, Bramwell and the General broke their tour of Paris to visit the house in St Cloud: 'I don't want them to be able to say that I refuse to meet my daughter,' he had said once before, anxious to avoid adverse publicity.

The interview was brief. No one knew what passed during it, and Kate never spoke of it afterwards. She was not to see her father again until he was dying.

The same year, 1905, Dr Dowie had a stroke in America from which he never really recovered. The following year, he ran into severe financial trouble, and he died in 1907, still convinced – or apparently so – of the truth of his message and identity. Mirza Ahmed, the self-styled Promised Messiah of India, had challenged him on the issue of Islam, to 'pray to God that of us two, whoever is the liar may perish first.'

As for Arthur, the fire and the impetus had left him. He was bedridden for sixteen months, and when at last the silver tubes draining the pus from his leg were extracted and he could be wheeled around in a bath-chair or walk a little on crutches, much of the fighting spirit had gone, and with it that naïve and impressionable enthusiasm prepared to trust life and limb to the cause of someone else. He was still an impressive figure reminiscent of the prophets of old, with his greying beard, quietly penetrating eyes and massive frame, a Moses who had fought with Pharaohs and striven in the wilderness, glimpsed God on the mountain top, but had been cheated by the perfidy of man from setting foot in the promised land, and if he suffered a long time from a shell-shocked lack of faith in humanity, he continued, as St Paul said of Moses, to hold to his purpose like a man who sees the invisible, still hanging on to the fundamental truths which he fervently believed.

The years to come were known as the years of obscurity, but 'if obscurity is to stand for unpopular truth in the comparatively lonely outpost,' said a pastor who knew him later in his life, 'then he was like the man who went down and slew a lion on a snowy day. He was no longer the warrior in the sense that he was in the forefront of the battle, but he was still the man who had made the warrior.'

For much of the rest of his life, he was content to remain at home, writing poetry and playing his auto-harp, studying the Bible he loved so dearly, telling the children stories and composing and singing hymns: 'My soul keep up thy singing, turn thy sorrows into song!' But it was not until 1927, more than twenty years later, on the occasion of their fortieth wedding anniver-

211

sary, that the Maréchale was able to write, 'for the first time in long, long years, I notice how bravely he is ceasing to talk of the past and of the negative. But I dare not look back . . .'

CHAPTER 16

In 1908 they returned to England. Kate spoke the language like a foreigner; the children spoke it hardly at all. Evelyn consoled herself with the sight of a bank covered in primroses which she had never seen before. Moving into two small houses by the sea at Westcliffe on the mouth of the Thames, the children lived in one house with Adele, the other turned into offices, guest rooms, and a home for Arthur and Kate. Instead of shouts of '*À bas les Anglais!*' they were referred to disparagingly and with a certain astonishment as 'those foreigners.'

Arthur remained secure in the certainty that the Lord would provide. That He did was due for the most part to the fact that Kate summoned up what little courage she had, and began preaching in England. Every Salvation Army hall was closed to her as it had been on the Continent, and many churchmen were suspicious or openly antagonistic: 'there are none so cruel as Christians' it was said later. For many years there was not so much as a Christmas card from the Booths, and Arthur's family had severed relations a long time ago.

'When I began work alone on this side of the Channel,' Kate was to write later, 'I experienced the desolation of David.' For comfort, almost obsessively, she read Psalm 42 over and over to herself: 'Why do my enemies reproach me? Why art thou so cast down my soul? Why art thou disquieted within me? Hope thou in God!'

When Evangeline married soon after they arrived in England, Kate scoured the shops until she found several yards of cheap spotted muslin which she made into bridesmaids dresses for the girls, and newspapers reported that William Booth's 'destitute' daughter had spent hundreds of pounds on pretty dresses for her children.

'I lost my reputation years ago,' she said. 'I have fought hell's legions and learned to ignore them. We can ignore this.' To a certain extent, it was a defensive reaction, disguising the fact that such calumnies still had power to wound. Calling on a friend in Chelsea, he sensed her bewilderment and gave her a book of Browning's poetry to read, opening it at the ballad of Rabbi ben Ezra:

'Earth changes, but thy soul and God stand sure:
What entered into thee,
That was, is, and shall be . . .'

The final verses she called a Sursum Corda which lifted her heart. 'He sees his heaven beyond,' was her only proviso. 'I want mine down here in the salvation of souls.'

Walking one evening with Theo, the youngest boy, in Southend after it had been raining, a rainbow suddenly appeared in the sky through the thin sunshine.

'Look!' she said to him. 'Isn't it lovely?'

Theo was eight years old. 'I can't see anything,' he said.

'Come over here.'

He came and stood beside her. 'How wonderful!'

'If we are in the wrong position, with the wrong attitude towards God and the truth,' she said, looking back on the incident afterwards, and taking it to herself, 'we know nothing and can do nothing. The solution is to walk with God. The road to this blessed experience is not by the intellect but by abandonment of ourselves to the will of God. Then our intellect, our gifts, our talents, rise to their highest and are far more effective than ever they were before.'

Since the anxiety of Arthur's long illness, her hair had begun to fall out, and she cut it short and spiky, making her look bold and boyish like a latter day Joan of Arc. She began taking small missions anywhere in the country that would have her, wearing a long navy dress with a white sash across her shoulder reminiscent of the Salvation Army sash of rejoicing. The burden of feeding, clothing, and taking care of Arthur and the ten children fell entirely on her shoulders, and at times it was a burden she resented.

'I've had a lonely road to travel,' she was to write several years later. 'It is easy for evangelists who are alone or with only two or three children, but I know that faith in God can rise to all possibilities . . .' Later, when the children were married, she wrote more tersely, 'Father says he will not take any responsibility for anything, nor does he.'

214

'My husband never cared for money,' she said, in a studied understatement after his death. 'Indeed, in many ways, he did not care enough, for material burdens are very real, especially when obligations are ever increasing. They must be carried by someone.

'And yet . . . and yet . . . if he was extreme on the one side, are not many of God's children extreme on the other? Does not the material often take the first place in their plans and decisions? Are they not often so obsessed by it that they lose their spiritual vision? They forget that we are only pilgrims here and the journey is so soon ended.'

With the impetus that had beset her since the earliest days in France – 'nothing matters but the souls' – and with the added obligation to earn money – 'send them all to board schools' said Arthur, when she spoke of tutors for the children and sending the boys for cheap schooling in the States – she began undertaking three- and four-week missions, travelling to Liverpool and Sunderland, south to the sea, and north to Scotland where a dour Presbyterian minister produced a five pound note at the end of three weeks. 'Maréchale,' he said, 'we are just, but we are not generous.'

'Isn't it wonderful, brother,' she replied, 'that God is just but He is also generous.'

Bishop Moule supported her stoically, often inviting her to preach at Durham. 'Will sleep with you stop have glorious time!' ran her telegram when he asked if she wished for hotel accommodation or a room in the Bishop's Palace. Meeting her personally off the train, he informed her it was the most beautiful telegram he had ever received, already framed on his study wall.

Often she returned home exhausted to a riotous welcome. Usually she brought with her drunks and beggars and girls off the street, people she had met casually in the train or drinking in a café. With thirteen to every meal, there was little to go round, and groans from the boys at the sight of bowls of beans on the table again: 'If you want more, then go upstairs and pray for it.' Sometimes she came home triumphantly from the market with a bag full of fish heads which the fishmonger had given her with the assurance that they were full of goodness. 'Fishes' eyes have saved many a poor child yet,' she was fond of telling them.

The Russian governess arrived at six o'clock every morning,

turned on the cold tap in the bath, and called to the children in German to be out of bed and into the bath before the water overflowed. Most days began with gym. To catch cold was considered a sin: it was indicative that most of the children were ill only when they went away to school. Meals were washed down with a spoonful of Scott's Emulsion, and when bills came with no money to pay them there was an urgent call to prayer, the whole family kneeling round the bed in their parents' room.

Accustomed to secondhand clothes and bare boards with no linoleum, there were twinges of envy when they visited the homes of friends and saw the blazing fires, shining silver and carpets. José, the youngest, had her first new dress when she was ten years old: 'I can still remember the smell of the material.' Unable to speak any English when she first went to school, she threw a French fit when other children laughed at her, and learned what she calls one of the great spiritual experiences of her life: 'I hated them, until I realised that love and hate cannot live in the same heart.'

Three of the boys played the violin, Willie played the clarinet as well, and Evangeline played the cello. Three of the girls played the piano, and Kate and Arthur sang their French hymns together. Passers-by gathered outside the window to listen, and the neighbours in the front begged to have the piano moved to the back of the house, and the neighbours in the back begged them to move it to the front again. On Saturday evenings, Arthur laboured up the stairs to 'discipline' the children. 'Arthur, stop spanking that boy!' Kate would call from her desk as wails thundered round the house. 'Katie, I haven't reached him yet ...'

Arthur had discarded his bath-chair and was walking slowly on crutches, and the children piled the chair to overflowing with tents and towels and ran downhill to the sea where there were Punch and Judy shows and a Christian beach mission. Willie buried the girls under tunnels of sand and Kate went out early when she was at home, doing her gym energetically on the beach. 'Why don't you do it too?' she asked a stout Presbyterian minister one morning. 'It would do you good to bend.' Her humour was often questionably double-edged.

When she was at home, she rested as much as she could, the youngest children allowed, as a treat, to sleep in her bed with her

216

at night and share breakfast in bed with her in the morning, or to lie down on the chaise longue with her in the afternoon telling her everything that had happened while she was away until they realised that she had dropped off to sleep. Later there remained impressed on their minds her constant insistence on sacrifice: 'To win, you must sacrifice and you must sacrifice and you must sacrifice.' Sometimes Herbert helped her with her papers. One night, he hummed a tune to himself, 'For I feel like going on, I feel like going on . . .'

'It's not according to feelings at all,' she interrupted him. 'If I had gone according to my feelings, you wouldn't be here at all.'

In the summer of 1912 she snatched a rare holiday with Evelyn in Devon: 'Kicking your heels in the air,' as she called it. It was quiet and idyllic and they ate clotted cream teas and talked. Then Kate read that the General was dying, and she left for his home in Hadley Wood, north of London, determined to see him for the last time.

It was the same house where she and Arthur had spent the 'painful three-day interview' before leaving the Army. As a boy in Nottingham, the General had promised to give to God everything that there was of William Booth. 'His secret was that he never took back the promise,' Eva was to say later. He had sacrificed himself, everything and everyone around him to the Army. Now, after a fall and an unsuccessful operation on his eyes, he was blind and semi-conscious.

When Kate arrived and asked to see him, the request was refused. It was thought that the shock would be too much for him. 'I must go to him,' she insisted, and eventually she was allowed in to his room on condition that she would not say who she was.

The General was lying in bed, his hair white, his fingers moving constantly: the gesture she remembered so well as he had counted the numbers coming forward to the old Whitechapel penitent benches. As she bent over him, he stirred and asked, 'Who is it?' but she looked at him for a long time and then, keeping her promise, came away without answering. Augustin had accompanied her. Their features, as she bent towards her father's white face, had seemed almost indistinguishable. As she left the room, Augustin noticed she was trembling.

People lined the streets for the General's funeral, sitting on

217

top of the walls, hanging from window ledges and climbing up lamp posts to see the procession go by. Salvation Army bands played and crowds waited outside the burial ground and refused to leave. Arthur, Kate and the children went to the funeral and ate in a restaurant nearby. During the meal, Arthur flung open the windows and called down to the people gathered outside: 'What shall it profit a man if he gain the whole world and lose his own soul?' He called it a time of appalling trial, visiting Germany for one of his rare preaching and teaching tours, quickly tired and walking with a stick. He was still preaching pacifism and the healing of nations, and everywhere he went he sensed the inevitability of war.

When war broke out, he went to Alexandra Palace and spoke in French to small bands of refugees who had escaped to England. Many of them, he brought home with him. Often the courts called on him to assist them when conscientious objectors were petitioning against call-up. Kate continued taking missions all over the country, and the girls, usually with little to eat and not much in the way of bed linen, would open the door to strangers – a family of Flemish refugees, a Belgian woman who taught them to sew, a Russian count with a pointed beard– 'Your mother told us to come and you would look after us and feed us . . .'

During the first year of the war they moved to a big old house with a rambling back garden on Highbury Hill in London, between Highbury Barn and Highbury Fields. At the end of the road a sign forbidding street cries still hung from the lamp post, and there was a small summerhouse in the garden beneath the trees at the back where Kate sat and worked. Arthur's room was in the middle of the house, and the safest when the air-raids came. Exhausted with travelling or writing, Kate was usually asleep on his bed with her good ear muffled in the pillows when the boys cycled through the streets shouting, 'Take cover!' At the first distant hum of the Zeppelin, she stirred. 'Pa, do stop making that noise.'

'Yes, darling. I won't make any noise.'

Brrrm, brrrm, brrrm. 'Pa – you are not kind to me. I can't sleep. Stop shaking the furniture.

'Yes, darling. I will try to be quiet.'

Adele hurried about the house turning on all the taps and

filling the baths and basins in case of fire, the Russian governess complained of stomach-ache, and Arthur walked round solemnly with a pillow on his head. At first he was anxious and agitated, and then he became more calm. One day he stopped dead, thrust his clenched fist into the air with a gesture of excitement, and sang out in joy, 'I see it, I see it! It's not our faith at all. It's His faithfulness!'

Walking through the streets, tall and distinguished, with his stick in his hand and a big black hat on his head, jotting down thoughts as they came to him in a notebook which he carried everywhere (before he died he had written over 300 hymns), he came home one day accompanied by two policemen who suspected him of being a spy.

'Play us a hymn while we talk, Evelyn,' he said, offering them a seat. Evelyn sat down at the piano and began to play while he sang. 'I'm not in this little war,' he told them. 'This will soon be over. I'm in the great war that goes on year after year. The war between light and darkness; the war between life and death.'

When the war ended, young men went back to university to continue their education. Many had been wounded, some seriously. Many were shell-shocked and disillusioned, forced into re-thinking their values and priorities. Some turned to communism, some to atheism, others turned to the evangelistic revival which centred on the great Keswick Conventions which had been held in the little town on the shores of Lake Derwentwater in the Cumberland Hills since 1875. In the summer of 1919, a Methodist minister invited the Maréchale to hold an open-air meeting in the Keswick market square.

'I couldn't tear myself away from that market square,' said a young Scottish minister afterwards. 'I never heard such speaking in my life. I never knew the English language was such a magnificent weapon.'

The following Sunday, Kate preached in the Methodist chapel. Two hours before the service was due to begin, the little church was full, undergraduates sitting on the windowsills and up the pulpit steps and many of the Keswick speakers themselves sitting on the floor to listen. Platforms made from rough boards were put up outside the church windows so that those who were unable to get inside could stand and see as well as hear.

They called her the heavenly witch. 'Her eyes glowed when

219

she was inspired,' they said. 'They bored into us. We were bewitched.' 'I couldn't sleep,' wrote one man. 'All through the night I saw her index finger pointing directly at me.'

Hungry for truth after the harsh realities of war, she presented them with a new, spiritual reality. 'People may walk over your heart. People may trample on your heart,' she told them. 'Whatever happens, go on. The Holy Ghost was given to make a barren Church bear children.'

Sometimes her meetings provoked resentment. They drew crowds away from the organised and conventional tent meetings, and there were those among the invited speakers with a Brethren background, who disapproved of the ministry of women. José and Evelyn went with her to play the piano and sing hymns. One day they found her standing outside the church looking up at the green hills, tears running down her cheeks.

There had been a long discussion with strict evangelicals about Roman Catholic doctrine. 'They are so rigid,' she said. 'You must love people first. You must understand them, be alongside them, be very close to them, before you can talk of doctrine.'

Often though, it was her sense of humour that prevailed and endeared her to those who sat at her feet. 'Call on me whenever you need to discuss a problem,' she told them. 'I live in Hell . . . I live in Hell . . .' the name of the Keswick road defeated her – or was it the eternal delight in dramatic effect? 'I live in Hellvellen Street!' At night, sharing what they called potato beds, full of uncomfortable lumps, the girls were kept awake by the merriment of their mother, looking back over the events of the day and rocking the bed with her laughter.

Noel Palmer, a handsome six-foot-eight-inch giant of a man, had been badly wounded in the Battle of the Somme, and had returned to university with a new vision of life to study for the ministry. Taken a little reluctantly to Keswick, he went with everyone else to hear the Maréchale. José was seventeen, Evelyn twenty and they sang one of their mother's choruses, Evelyn singing contralto and José singing the melody.

'How can we save a dying world?
That problem has been solved above.
The key is found on Calvary:
The only way is love.'

'That is what the Maréchale understood by the word love,' Noel was to say later. 'She loved God in Christ as a child loves a mother, or as an artist loves beauty. She saw in Him the answer to every problem, the perfect harmony of all the virtues, and the harmony, too, of opposites, a harmony which escapes the shallow, selfish mind.

'She wasn't bookish. She was different from all the rather stodgy preachers we normally heard. When she sang, she sang with her eyes shut and her face alight and I thought of Stephen when he was being martyred and his face was like the face of an angel. She had an amazing dramatic power: a blend of humour and tragedy, spiritual depths, tender understanding, and humanity. She spoke 'with authority, and not as the scribes'.

'Bishop Taylor Smith took me aside one lovely summer evening and walked towards the lake and questioned me. 'Why do all you chaps flood to hear the Maréchale?' I told him we had never heard anyone who made Jesus so real before. She brought Him right to us. He was there. He was speaking to you. You were touching Him, and His love was enveloping you. His purity and His power seemed to burn through you. It was preaching such as we had never heard in our lives before.'

One summer evening when over 1500 people tried to crowd into the little chapel, a farmer invited them into his field and brought out one of the old-fashioned harvest carts for the Maréchale to stand on. 'Stand here, Tiny,' she said to Noel. 'Let me lean on your shoulder.' It was more a risk than an honour, for she had been know to grab onto a head of hair for emphasis; once she had picked up a trouble-maker by his hair and thrown him out of a hall.

'We clustered round her like bees round a honey-pot, eager to catch the last drop of honey as it flowed,' says Noel, likening, 'this slender little woman with her aquiline features and glowing eyes,' to Wesley and the great crowds who collected to hear him in the open. 'She looked round at us all, and put out her hand with her unique air of authority. "You can speak the word that unbinds," she said. "Off you go: flame number one," she pointed at each of us in turn, "flame number two, flame number three, flame number four . . ."'

Five years later Noel and José were married. The wedding took place at the nearby home of the Booth-Tuckers, Frederick

221

there in his Indian robe and sandals. 'Go to your Aunt Minnie's' the Maréchale had said, full of enthusiasm and excitement but with very little time to spare, except on the wedding day itself, when, incapable, like her father, of not taking advantage of a captive audience, she preached a long and not entirely suitable sermon.

She was an unnerving mother-in-law, lavish beyond her means and devastatingly direct. When Noel had written to her of his intentions to marry José, he received a telegram by return: 'Hallelujah! Have faith in God.' The first time the three of them met after the engagement had been announced, bathing on the beach at Eastbourne, Noel prepared nervously to talk to her. 'She'll give you beautiful children,' was all she said, looking him straight in the eye.

CHAPTER 17

Early in the 1920s began what was later to be called the Irish revival. Homes were being burned down and men shot and killed and the Maréchale said that the place was calling her. Cabling the children to help her, she embarked on a series of campaigns, beginning in outlying areas and moving in to Belfast, Portadown, Dublin and Armagh. The night before they arrived in Armagh, the bodies of seven men, brutally murdered, were laid on the steps leading up to the door of the church where the Maréchale was to preach. As people began to arrive, there were those still on their hands and knees trying to scrub the bloodstains off the stone.

By the time the Maréchale left Ireland, the Prime Minister of the north, Sir James Craig, said her ministry there had helped to save Ulster from revolution.

Men and women drank gin and raw methylated spirits, while children in rags with their bottoms through their trousers and no shoes on their feet warmed themselves in the market places. Women lay in the gutters with their hair dishevelled. 'I've known women take the shoes off their feet and pawn them and come back to buy drink,' said a publican. 'I'm sick of it.' Although Theodore organised the main campaigns, he and Evelyn preaching and singing with their mother, José helped with those at the beginning, held in outlying towns. Nineteen years old and just out of school, her knowledge of Ireland was so limited that she had to look up each place they visited on the map before she knew where it was. Young and idealistic, she dreamed of spectacular revolution, and when the first mission was a total failure, she went down to the sea, bewildered and discouraged, wrestling inside herself with God, trying to understand what it meant. When she returned, the Maréchale was writing. Looking up from her letters, she asked, 'What's the matter?'

'Why are things going so badly? I don't understand.'

Kate put down her pen and looked at José for a moment.

'You'd have been no use to me in France,' she said. 'You're not a soldier. A soldier goes on whether things go badly or well. Whatever happens, a soldier just goes on.' Then she went back to her letters. The next mission was a success.

When the gates were shut, people tried to climb over them. A girl lost the sleeve of her coat in the crush. Thousands came, and three or four hundred attended the prayer meetings held beforehand, which meant that Kate was working four hours at a stretch before they hurried home to beat the eleven o'clock curfew. One young man, on his way home, was astonished to see the Maréchale in her long flowing dress doing physical exercises on the deserted pavement outside her guest house. The publican turned his public house into a grocer's shop, and asked the Maréchale to bless it, and at the end of one long series of meetings, traffic was held up by people marching, four or five abreast, singing hymns, and José called it heaven on earth. Kate spoke at the Presbyterian church in Great Victoria Street, at the downtown church in May Street, and in the enormous Assembly Hall. with its difficult acoustics, where she scorned the use of a microphone. Archibald Irwin of the Central Presbyterian Association gave a graphic description of her addressing the audiences of 5000 who attended every meeting during the ten-day period: the most continuous crowds seen in the hall since it was erected.

'As she takes her place on the platform and faces one of the largest audiences ever crammed into that spacious auditorium, she looks frail and weak and showing evident signs of bodily fatigue,' he said. 'A tall, slight, erect woman, very simply dressed, apparently past life's meridian, you wonder whether she will have strength to carry on to the end; will her voice reach the upper gallery?

'A few minutes afterwards, she rises to speak. No sign of weariness now. With ringing voice and dramatic gesture, she dominates and controls the whole assembly. On her face is the flush of youth; her look and gestures are those of a girl of twenty-five. What command she has over her voice: it is always audible, sometimes appealing, at others, defiant; every inflection means a change of attitude of mind.

'She lives for her arguments and aspirations on the platform. Her emotions are communicated to her audience. What an orator she is, never at a loss for a word to express her exact

224

meaning. Her logic is of the law court, keen, close-jointed, and convincing; no loose-thinking with this most accomplished and convincing speaker, just a trace of humour, more than a trace of pathos, and all seasoned with grace.

'The Cross is the centre of all her preaching. It is to put the Cross in its rightful place in the hearts and lives of the people that she undertook the present campaign. And how wonderfully she has succeeded.'

Leaving Belfast and travelling through the towns and villages of Northern Ireland, men came to listen, went away spellbound, and sent their wives who turned up asking 'to be converted because my husband told me to' without the slightest notion of what the word meant. A commanding officer garrisoned nearby called to ask whether, since the soldiers in his battalion had been so moved and revolutionised by what she said, she might consider preaching on the bearing of religion on obedience within the camp. A casual invitation to anyone 'hungry for the Lord' brought over a hundred young people crowding into two small rooms behind a local country village church, and a young man who had joined the Sinn Fein and murdered a man in cold blood in his bed, became persuaded that the love of Christ extended even to murderers.

Because of their hard-line 'to Hell with the Pope' attitude, many Protestant evangelists in Northern Ireland had been banned from the South. The Maréchale had worked with Roman Catholics in France and Belgium and Switzerland, refused to align herself with any specific denomination, and had written books which Catholic clergymen had not only praised, but preached. Theo travelled on to arrange a campaign in Dublin, and a bomb blast blew him out of bed the night he arrived. Clergy in the North questioned the wisdom of sending a woman in her sixties into evident danger, but the Maréchale was determined to go under any terms, even if no one came to hear her.

Before she arrived in Dublin, the hall she was to speak in was blown up. Instead, she accepted an invitation from a clergyman at Ormond Quay Presbyterian Church in the suburbs, and from there, she gradually moved in to larger churches, until she spoke in the Metropolitan Hall, the largest hall in the centre of Dublin.

'The most remarkable feature of the mission was the attendance of so many Roman Catholics,' said the Rev. Fred Gibson, who had been instrumental in inviting the Maréchale to Dublin in the first place. 'Never in the experience of Christian workers in Dublin has this feature been so prominent, and it is indicative of the growing spirit of independence evident in Ireland today, as well as the spiritual hunger which a merely formal religion has failed to satisfy. It is just here that the Maréchale, with her positive gospel untrammelled by dogma or sectarianism, appeals to the minds and hearts of men and women of all classes and every religious opinion.'

'What is it about your mother?' a clergyman asked José. 'She has had more confessions in three weeks than I have had in the whole of my ministry.'

'The secret,' says José now, 'was in her prayer meetings before the missions. Many a time we would arrive in a place, and Mother would tell the Vicar that we were going to have a prayer meeting for an hour before the service. 'Impossible!', he'd say. 'No one will come. They'll be eating their supper.'

'She said, 'Never mind if there are only two people and a cat. I'll be there,' and she would announce it at once. If the meeting began at eight, the prayer meeting would begin at seven. If the meeting began at seven-thirty, the prayer meeting would begin at six-thirty. Time and time again there would be two or three to begin with and I would see with my own eyes those prayer meetings grow to three or four hundred people.

'Whenever anyone was blessed, or if they had problems, broken marriages, heartaches, distresses of all kinds, she would say to them, "I'll meet you at the prayer meeting tomorrow night", and time and again divorces were avoided because they found it wasn't divorce they needed, it was love. Distressed people broke down, and she allowed them to break down, because that meant that the terrible reserve which kept them locked into themselves was broken down.

'All she did was pray. The clergyman said "you won't get anyone," and she said, "Never mind – we'll pray". She had it perfectly under control. If a man prayed too long, she'd say "We'll sing a chorus while our dear brother is finishing his prayer." She would walk among them, and she'd say to a woman "Now pray," and the woman would say "I couldn't pray, I'd faint," and she'd say "That doesn't matter. Faint, but pray."

'She had to break through the shell of timidity and self-consciousness. General Booth knew that principle. She knew it. Express what is on your mind to God. Speak out to God. This was new. It was a revolution, and the release came when they opened their lips like the day of Pentecost.

'This was her secret: her total dedication from the time, as a child, when she gave herself to God. And what impressed me so much was the depths of that dedication; the willingness to sacrifice at every turn and corner. "To win, you must sacrifice," she said. "And again you must sacrifice, and again you must sacrifice."'

Before going to Ireland, Theo had arranged a tour of Canada and America, accompanying his mother, singing, leading the choruses, and playing the violin. Invitations had been coming in from Keswick men scattered abroad, from nostalgic Salvationists, through Maud and Ballington with their Volunteers in New York, and Herbert in Chicago, and through the influence of the Booth-Clibborn sons, Willie the clergyman with his booming voice, nervous energy and tempestuous nature, Augustin, artistic and introvert, and Eric engaged to be married, on his way to Africa as a missionary.

'To the masses I was sent, and my greatest blessings have come in following that calling...'

José travelled across the Atlantic with her, discovering her up at first light on the top deck doing her gym, the deckhands lined up, their wash buckets to one side, copying her. In spite of rarely being persuaded to leave off a life jacket, she revelled in the novelty of life at sea, breathing in the squally air and walking round the deck every day.

At Calgary, the Methodist church was packed full with people sitting on the windowsills. Men's meetings were attended by over 2000. 'She is the most wonderful woman preacher in the world,' they said. In Toronto, people who had called a woman in a pulpit a disturbing innovation, stood night after night to hear what she had to say. In Columbia, they called it a mission to make men and angels rejoice, reminiscent of the acts of the apostles. In Edmonton, they said she possessed the flaming spirit of her father. 'She has one theme,' said the minister. 'Christ, and the complete abandonment to God.'

227

She travelled into the Rockies where it was 30 degrees below zero, walking up to seven miles a day and revelling in the air and the brilliance of the snow, and insisting on bathing in the sulphur lakes bubbling with steam, from a tiny cabin hung with icicles, 'Is it safe at her age?' a query treated with total disregard as her children struggled to persuade her out and into her clothes again before the hot water froze on her.

In America, Pennsylvanian families travelled sixty miles several times a week to hear her preach. She spoke to 2000 men on Easter Sunday morning in the United Federal Penitentiary at Georgia, and to 2000 young people in the Academy of Music at Philadelphia where they called her 'this remarkable lady with a voice of thunder and sweet pathos, who denounces hypocrisy and describes the sublimity of eternal life.'

'The good, the bad, and the indifferent come to Atlantic City,' they said after her campaign there, when for three weeks she filled one of the largest churches in the city. 'Ten million people visit us annually from all over the world, but there has been no one quite like La Maréchale.'

'We have been deluged in this country with freak evangelists who could do certain tricks which catch the passing attention of the crowds,' they said in Chicago. 'Maréchale, God bless *you*.'

Theo helped his mother on each mission. Sometimes they were joined by José and another sister, Frieda. Eric met them in Seattle and came home one night shocked by a nearby cinema where girls were parading the streets in nothing but fur coats advertising a strip-show with admittance for men only.

Kate went to the ticket office and demanded a ticket.

'I'm sorry, Madame. Only men allowed.'

'You mean you are going to stop me, the mother of ten children, from coming inside? If you don't allow me in, I shall make a scene.'

The ticket officer sent for the Manager, who led her inside, where she sat down, the only woman in an auditorium full of men.

A small man with a baton appeared on the stage. The first girl was called in, taking off her coat and standing naked on the stage while the man touched the contours of her body with his stick. Kate stood up and pointed at the man with her long finger. 'You will be judged for this!' she cried out to him, her voice ringing through the auditorium. 'You will be judged and not the girls,' she went on, as he stood transfixed, his stick poised in mid-air. 'I myself,' she said, her voice strong with indignation, 'I shall be there to see that you are judged.'

Still with her eyes fixed on the unfortunate man, she began addressing the audience much as she had spoken years ago to the manager of Bon Marché: 'Why don't you pay your girls a fair wage?' And his reply: 'Let them do what the other girls do.'

'You call yourselves men?' she asked them. 'You sit here taking pleasure in the degradation of women – women who support you with their charity, their courage and their love? Would you like to see your own wives and your own daughters standing there?'

At last she took her eyes off the man and turned to those sitting around her. 'If there are any among you who have any honour or respect for women, get up and follow me outside.' Almost everyone in the big cinema hall got up and followed her sheepishly out into the daylight, where she stood up in the middle of them and talked of Christ and His purity and His gentle love of women.

'She reminds us of her father,' said the people of Tacoma in Washington – a compliment which touched her more deeply than any other. 'She is more like him than any of her brothers and sisters.'

'We have heard four members of the Booth family speak – the father, one son, and two of the daughters,' said audiences in Pittsburgh, who saw in her voice, gestures and attitude what they called the flash and energy of the old General. 'The Maréchale is by far the most impressive and effective speaker of them all.'

Emerging at last from what she was always to call her dark, dark time, Kate was realising again, as she had realised so long ago, the potential of the gift she had been given, and the sin of allowing it to stagnate. Encouraged by Theo, she began working from now until she was ninety years old, almost obsessively, as if trying to make up for lost time. Theo organised and planned her campaigns, making all the contacts, booking halls and churches and theatres, going on before her to prepare the way, rehearsing the choirs – as time went on, there were as many as 750 people in them – and then preaching and playing the violin until the audience was prepared for his mother's entrance. Then he remained with her throughout the evening until the last enquirer had gone home: often they were up until two o'clock in the morning. At many of the campaigns, Evelyn and José came too, playing the piano and singing. Kate was already nearing seventy and many called it the start of big-time campaigning on a scale she had never imagined before.

Back in England, she visited Southampton during the dock strike. The Southampton Coliseum had been booked for three weeks, but the dockers wanted to use it for meetings, and they asked angrily who was this Maréchale, and why an evangelist wanted the largest hall in Southampton for three weeks on end.

'Tell them they can have the hall in the afternoons and I will have it in the evenings,' said the Maréchale after giving it some thought. 'On one condition. I shall have the first few minutes of their afternoon meetings.'

On the first afternoon, the hall filled with dock strikers. José played the piano: well-known hymns, 'Abide with me' and 'O God our help in ages past'. 'She would come walking in by herself onto the stage,' she remembers. '"Good afternoon, gentlemen. It's lovely to see you here. I know you are here for your meeting, but your committee has kindly agreed that I can give you a few minutes first. Then I shall be speaking again this evening, and you can come again – won't that be splendid? Now we are going to have a hymn. Mind you sing it now."

'Was this a religious meeting or not? Some took off their caps, others looked round to see what everyone else was doing. Gradually all the caps came off, and they began to sing a bit sheepishly. Then she talked.

'"I know all about strikes. I dealt with anarchists in Paris. Oh yes – the real thing! Real anarchists! They didn't just have strikes, they threw bombs, but what good did it do? The heart of the matter is who you belong to, and who really runs your lives. We can't live on negatives all the time. We must have positives. We must have joy and love in our lives. The love of Christ constrains me, Paul said. Do you know what happened to Paul? He said he was turned inside out, and that's what should happen to you. You should be turned inside out too."

'She kept to her side of the bargain: she only spoke for ten minutes. But in the evening, they came back for more.'

Towards the end of 1925, when Kate was in London at Highbury Hill, Frederick Tucker burst in waving a book in his hand. Published in France under the auspices of the Salvation Army, it was a history of the Army in France. Frederick was uncharacteristically angry. 'What right have they?' he stormed. 'What moral or Christian right have they to extinguish your place in the history of that heroic age?' He showed Kate the book. Throughout it, she was referred to conscientiously as 'Miss B . . .' Written by someone she knew and trusted, produced and perhaps censored by the Army Headquarters it came as a jolt, renewing all the old resentment and isolation.

'If only you were here,' she wrote to José, who was in America with Noel, speaking of the longing to be understood. 'You understand me, which means you can leave yourself and think of me and care for my cares – not that I want you to, but you have the willingness. Oh José, I so ache. To be understood is to be thrice loved . . .'

Herbert wrote to Bramwell: 'How you could permit such a publication to go forth with your endorsement passes my understanding,' he said, likening it to petty persecution and Jesuitical excommunication. 'I have again and again entreated you to modify your revengeful attitude towards Catherine, which seems to me utterly unjustifiable as a Christian. Far better print in the preface your disapproval of her retirement from the Army than treat her as if her name was beneath mention.'

In 1924 Eric had died from dysentery and malaria in French West Africa leaving a young widow, Lucille, with a baby daughter and another baby on the way, all of whom were, at least for the time being, reliant on her. 'Jesus said I am the resurrection and the life,' she had said to the children when she told them the news, but she was awake more than usual during the night and sometimes she was crying. In 1926, Herbert died too, the split with his family still on his mind: 'As if any Salvation Army bond could be greater than the God-ordained family bond,' he had written to Kate a few months previously.

'Separations are hard,' she wrote. 'Sometimes far harder than words can express. I have suffered many deaths in my life through them.'

Three years later, in the summer of 1929 Bramwell died, weak, ill, and disillusioned. Deposed less than a year earlier after a General Council had been called and pronounced him unfit to hold the position of General, the shock had killed him. One of the instigators in his removal had been his sister Eva, who he had ill-advisedly ordered to leave America. Under the new democratic method of election, Eva was eventually to become General herself.

'*Aimez toujours et malgré tout*': Kate was the only one of Bramwell's generation of the Booth family to speak at her brother's funeral, and the *War Cry* reported the occasion with more than a twinge of nostalgia. 'Mrs Booth-Clibborn spoke, as the eldest sister of early campaigning, breaking into song in the good old-fashioned way to illustrate her words. She recalled the departed General's assiduous attachment to his work, his courage, his devotion to his father, and she depicted the meeting in heaven: "My mother, my father, Herbert and Emma! What a meeting! Because I live, ye shall live also!" she thundered. "It's the truth, Hallelujah!" echoed and re-echoed across the hall.'

As far back as 1924, Kate had been hankering after a return to the continent. Staying with friends in Switzerland, where the children serenaded her in her bedroom on her sixty-sixth birthday – 'It was so sweet and reminded me of long, long ago, and do as I would, I could not help weeping' – she went on picnics by the lake in the mountains – 'we did gym: they say I have resurrected gym here!' – and began, tentatively, to speak at a few small meetings arranged for her, coming away jubilant.

'The meetings were a wonderful success,' she wrote. 'Now comes a surprise. My French!' the words ringed round in ink. 'What has really frightened me was that I could never preach in French again, and that is exploded,' she went on, her grammar suffering as it always did when she was excited.

'Three public meetings in the tent and two crowded drawing-room meetings wonderfully successful, and all in French. People in tears, and my spiritual children all coming round me, tears and smiles and invitations pouring in from Vevey, Lausanne, Neuchâtel, Zurich, Berne. Now, I am booked up for England, but in the future...'

Theo was twenty-six years old, bold and ambitious for his mother. He had formed a committee to guide the Maréchale's financial's affairs in England. A tour of the continent would have to finance itself, and the tour he envisaged was on a far grander scale than meetings in tents and drawing-rooms. Kate had first gone to Paris as a girl of twenty-one; Switzerland when she was twenty-three. Now she was nearly seventy. It was a calculated risk: was it possible that they could still remember?

She started quietly in the north of France, in Lille and St Quentin and the little mining town of Bruay-des-Mines where she spoke to a thousand miners. Three hundred remained behind to pray with her, and her approach had not changed.

'Going up to one man to make sure he was sincere, I said "Will you pray with me?"'

'"No," he replied. "I haven't told you who I am."'

'"Who are you?"'

'"A drunk. I swear. I beat my wife. I am immoral. Will you still pray with me?" he asked.

'"Oh yes," I said, and drew him aside, and we knelt down and he put his hands together like a child.'

Within three hours of her arrival in Paris, she had been interviewed by most of the leading newspapers, who printed long articles about her work and her past association with France. Theo had booked the Salle Gaveau in the centre of Paris, on the Rue la Boetie, one of the finest concert halls in Europe, holding 1800 people. At the Maréchale's expense he had also booked half the public 'colonnes' in Paris and plastered them with posters of her with her old Salvation Army bonnet. He had taken the Salle Gaveau for two and a half weeks. 'You will fill the hall for one night with Salvationists,' he was told. 'That is all.' On the first night, he left the flat where he and his mother were staying, murmuring 'God forgive me, what have I committed us to?' When he reached the hall it was surrounded by police. 'C'est fou!' said one of them. 'They are going mad! The place is full and no one can get near.'

It was thirty years since Kate had addressed a Paris audience, and she called her French a gift from God. 'What pen or tongue can describe what I suffered on leaving France for Holland,' she had written in letters. 'I dare not commit to paper my anguish at that time.'

'I love Paris as I have never loved any other city,' she told them. 'Perhaps I love it so much because I have suffered so much for it. Today I bring the same message I brought then, almost as if the years have not passed: the message of the miracle-working grace of God. We need it now as we have never needed it before.'

'*Notre Maréchale,*' said Albin Peyron from the platform. '*Notre Maréchale!*' he said again, to cheers and clapping. '*Nous vous avons suivie. Nous vous avons imité. Et si nous sommes quelque chose pour Dieu et l'Armée du Salut, c'est en grande partie à vous que nous le devons.*'

When the meeting ended, Pastor Durrleman of Paris sent the collection plate round a second time, asking that no one should leave until the costs of the campaign had been covered. It was an unprecedented gesture towards one he described as speaking with authority and not as the scribes and the pharisees. 'In this Paris,' he said, 'this Paris in which it was once stated that such an effort could not succeed, she has proclaimed the Gospel without a single interruption.'

In the collecting plates were gold rings, gold bracelets and diamond necklaces. More than five hundred people remained behind after each meeting, all of which were full, and there was always a queue of people outside her dressing-room and at the hotel, asking to see her.

When she left France, three pastors sent a message: 'In France, messengers of God are rare. You have the ear of our people, and the secret to their hearts. Will you not be the messenger for resurrection, you who love France? You make people believe in God and in love, and you make them want to be Christian.'

A year later, still officially an exile, the Maréchale returned to Switzerland.

In Geneva, Theo booked the Salle de la Reformation for nearly a month, and the *Journal de Génève* reported that it had never been so full even during the sittings of the League of Nations. Nearly four thousand people attended each meeting, many of them standing all the time. Often the Maréchale addressed 12,000 people in a day. Police had to be called in, not this time to stop people from throwing stones or to arrest the evangelists, but to control the crowds who struggled to gain admittance. A leading modern ecclesiastic, Pastor Dubois, said that in his estimation, the liveliest spiritual work going on in Geneva could be traced directly back to the Maréchale, with her Bible reading which 'threw a flame over the old texts' and her theme of tragedy and everlasting hope.

'We of that generation could not envisage the visit of our old leader without profound emotion,' said old Pastor Lenoir. 'I emphasise the word "our", for this frail girl, as she was then, filled with divine boldness and divine love, was a leader for many who never joined the organisation she then represented, but who were one, intensely one, with its early spirit, simplicity and fire. Nor can we think of her or her husband without remembering that wherever they could, they bore the brunt of the attack.

'Now again it is to the Reformation Hall, and to proud and prudent Geneva, to which the Maréchale has returned. Once more people are moved to hear her, people from every district and every class, but this time it is is with reverent attention, with admiration, and with affection.

'As I listened to the straight, tender, passionate plea, and as I observed the eagerness to catch every word, I praised God for once again visiting our city.'

At Neuchâtel, meetings were held in the big Temple du Bas, the front rows reserved for the *'Vieille Garde'* who had tramped out with her into the mountains during what they now called the historic days of '83. Afterwards, they went together on a kind of pilgrimage, to the forest at Prise Imer, to the prison, where she preached to the prisoners and gave them flowers, and to the President's château, where instead of being put under arrest, she was officially received and presented with a state apology for the treatment she had received over forty years previously.

'I am touched by your visit,' said the President. 'We are touched. I regret the events of other times: we have made progress since then.'

Every night the Temple du Bas was crowded, with people from miles around standing in the aisles, sitting on the wall brackets and on the stairways leading to the roof. When she left, it was impossible to reach her car until the police cleared a way through the crowds. 'The Maréchale comes, and all are joyful,' they said. 'She goes, and it is with a sad heart that we see her go. After her visit, it is more than memories which remain.' Among those who stayed behind at one of her meetings was the daughter of the Prefect who had arrested her.

'How can you or Theo understand,' she wrote to José, baffled by such a response. 'You are young, and it is impossible. There are such terrible, dark experiences when for years there was no light and I was a slave. Yet *God is love!'* she could never write the words without underlining them and rounding them off with a triumphant exclamation mark. 'He allowed it. But when I see what He enables me to do in one hour, and I know what I could have accomplished during that terrible time when humanly speaking I was wasting my life, it is mysterious.'

Back in England, she went on six-monthly tours, sleeping badly and waking up at night to make tea on a spirit stove, to pray, and to write letters to those who had asked for her help, to her children and her children-in-law (Arthur called them children-in-love), interspersing reports of campaigns with domestic advice. When Willie was ill in America she had to be restrained from packing her bags and boarding the first boat to be with him: 'It is wicked for him to preach three times a day and preach as he preaches, but he is so like me and cannot put the brake on when preaching for souls.'

At Christmas, a circular letter sent across the world – 'Should any who read these lines find themselves in special trial or sorrow, do not hesitate to write to me' – had scribbled on the back to one of the children, 'When do you expect? Stick to green stuff, salads, no *meat* and *no* starchy food.'

'I am in the middle of my first campaign here, to be followed by seven more,' she wrote from Chatham and Rochester. 'Such terribly hard ground. Oh how I dread new people around me. They don't and can't understand me. But I must be brave for the work's sake. There is a cure for nervous headaches,' she added. 'Take an egg beaten up in orange every day – a raw, new-laid egg and the juice of a whole orange – and fill one cup with water. Also eat marmite on bread and butter.'

Many letters, when they did not end with 'Love, strong and unchanging, from Arthur, and love deeper than the sea from the Maréchale', tailed off in exhaustion and frustration: 'Too tired to write tonight as I would, my back hurts me so ... Can't sit up any longer, too tired – these meetings take a great deal out of me ... I am so tired I fear you cannot read what I write, and neither can I.'

'These nights sleep forsakes me, so I can write to you – all is quiet, it is ten to one,' begins a letter from Bournemouth enclosing £3 for José to buy liveroids. 'I had begun a heart to heart letter, but I feel it would be misunderstood. No, not that, but *selfish* at Christmas, to pass on any sad thoughts – and you cannot guess how sad they are.

'The meetings here are very hard. It is a place reeking with modernism and pleasure. No one can know the fight to go on. But now the crowds come, and the spirit of the Lord is working mightily. There is a tremendous opposition on the part of the clergy. The mountains shall fall, and *what* mountains: of pride and selfishness and pharisaism. I wish you were here to help.'

In her mid-seventies, she was as busy as she had ever been in her life, dictating to three secretaries at once, campaigning in England and abroad, visiting the continent again and seeing the magnificent new Salvation Army hostel in Paris designed by le Corbusier, the six-storey Palais de la Femme with its single rooms and dormitories and sun lounge not far from the first hall on the Rue d'Angoulême, the Maison de la Mère et de l'Enfant, and the Maison du Jeune Homme dominating the area round the notorious Rue Oberkampf. Celebrating the fiftieth anniversaryof the day in June 1883 when she first went to Nîmes, old memories were resurrected: *'Maréchale, vous tentez l'impossible. Allez! Retournez donc en Angleterre!'*

'J'aime la France, moi. Je pourrai toujours mourir pour la France.'

In New York, thousands were unemployed – 'Give me information re the National Debt,' she wrote. 'Thousands and thousands of pounds shut up in the banks and yet there are people starving. 800,000 unemployed!' she added in ink. Hitler's Third Reich was a year old; Mussolini was hankering after Abyssinia. Speaking at universities, she was besieged by students echoing Arthur's urgent call to spiritual arms. 'British Israelites say, and so do many more students, that a great crisis is on the way. All agree there is nothing more to come after 1934 . . .'

She had been working obsessively on a book of memoirs – 'the time is short and my work and responsibilities are ever increasing.' Called *They Endured* it was a characteristic rag-bag of muddled memories and catchpenny conversions which only scratched the surface of the depths of her life. Published by Marshall, Morgan and Scott, Campbell Morgan wrote an introduction to what he called a volcanic story, likening the Maréchale, in the words of a popular song, to the blackbird of life's storms. 'Her life has been a tempestuous one,' he said, 'but through all the storms she has been a singer of songs.'

In the final chapter, she looked to the future like a woman in

237

the prime of life. Whatever she foresaw at the close of 1934, it was not the end of the world, though perhaps the beginning of a new reality, and a new chance for religion.

'The adherents of communism and fascism are alive and in deadly earnest, while the majority of professional Christians sleep,' she said. 'The cry on every side is: 'We need a man, a leader!' God makes much of man. The command 'Go ye into all the world and preach the Gospel to every creature' was not given to angels, it was given to man. So I go forward in faith, believing for greater things done in His name than we have yet seen.'

CHAPTER 18

In April 1936, when she was seventy-seven years old, the Maréchale left Southampton for a year's tour of Australia and New Zealand. 'You come and listen to me,' her brother Herbert used to say after his retirement there. 'But you should hear my sister Katie.' In Melbourne, they said that to leave England for Australia at her age to be a messenger of the Cross reminded them of Abraham.

It was an unobtrusive departure travelling uncomfortably in the emigrants' section of the train from London to Southampton because there was more room to work. The fare to Australia had been paid by Dame Violet Wills, a member of the tobacco family, a staunch supporter of the Maréchale, and, ironically, a campaigner against smoking. The Australian end of the venture had been organised by Bill Bradley, a Christian businessman in Sydney, through the Mildmay Movement at Stoke Newington, near the Maréchale's Highbury home. Theo suffered a coronary breakdown – it was an ironical tribute to the Maréchale's stamina that one by one those around her fell out exhausted while she soldiered on with apparently invincible energy. Her new organiser and secretary was Clifford Ross, 'my friendly gaoler', a young man from the Southampton docks who had heard her preach on David: 'Joab was in the field with the army, but David stayed in Jerusalem; backsliders always get into trouble.'

'I was at one with her in what she was doing,' he says. 'So when she asked me, I gave up my job and joined her. It was a big decision. Ships were lined up at anchor with no trade, but I was lucky – I had a job. Not much of a job, but a job nonetheless, at a time when the foreman would go out to the yard gate where there were four or five hundred men wanting a day's work and call out ten or twelve names and that was it.'

They sailed first on the USS *Washington* for New York, the harbour lights coming into sight at eleven o'clock at night, with

239

Willie's voice resounding across the water from the pier-head two hundred yards away where he was waiting with Evelyn. Kate stayed with them in New York, and then went on to Toronto to see José and Noel and their children, travelling 2000 miles by train across Canada, past places with evocative names, Moose Jaw, Medicine Hat, the Great Divide and Kicking Horse Pass, through fur-trapping and nickel-mining country, lakes and wooded hillsides which reminded her of Switzerland – they counted twenty-nine snow-capped peaks at once – and the flat prairies of waving wheat to Vancouver, where she broadcast for the first time before taking the boat for Australia.

Stopping en route at Honolulu, she walked along Waikiki beach in a summer dress wearing a wavy-brimmed straw hat which Clifford bought for her, and then they sailed on through squally rain clouds to Fiji, arriving eventually at Sydney where the Maréchale declared decisively 'God has a mighty work for us to do.'

In Sydney, the church where she spoke was so full that the canon who had invited her had to sit on the floor. In Melbourne, meetings began in a large church with seating for a thousand, but soon it was too small, and she preached instead to 2000 in Melbourne Town Hall, where the Melbourne Municipality gave a party to celebrate her seventy-eighth birthday. She held special afternoon meetings for old people, spent over an hour with 200 mental patients, and visited a state reformatory for boys, telling them of her imprisonment in Switzerland. In Hobart, where everything closed down at nine o'clock in the evening – 'we got quite out of the habit during the Maréchale's campaign' – they called her a preacher, an orator, an artist, a musician, a hundred women wrapped in one.

Up early every morning, she wrote an average of twenty letters a day. Sometimes she called Clifford in to pray with her for someone she was worried about: 'I fear he is having a struggle.' She preached twice daily, gave private interviews once a week, held gospel meetings in the evenings, women's meetings in the afternoons, and meetings for ministers only. 'You have confirmed in us, regardless of denominational distinction, our sense of being bound together,' they said. 'You have reassured us of the possibilities that are ours through prayer.' When she preached it, it was often for an hour or more, with energy and vigour, and many of the Sunday services were broadcast or printed verbatim in the press.

'If this was oratory, it was oratory unconscious of itself,' said a Jewish businessman. 'I have never heard a broadcast like it.'

'After hearing you say you begin work at six a.m. writing letters, I too now rise at six and give God the first hour of a new day,' wrote a housewife.

Wherever she went, there were Salvationists in the audience – a sight which moved her, and moved them – and as soon as she spotted them, she called them out: 'Come up here and help me to sing . . .' A woman came to her who had been converted at the meeting at Exeter Hall in 1883 to celebrate the release from Neuchâtel gaol. There were many who had been in the little Keswick chapel, and a man from the famous Brussels campaign when she wore her robe of sackcloth and ashes.

An ex-Salvationist heard her on the radio: 'I felt your message was all for me. I knelt alone and made my vows to God again. I told Him I would fight to the end. If it means back to a corps or back to the kitchen, I will go.'

After a rest in the Dandenong Hills, they sailed for New Zealand with its glaciers and ice fields and towering mountains and waterfalls, travelling from the most southerly point of South Island to the most northerly point of North Island, journeys which often took all day, arriving late into the night. Two were made by air, the Maréchale revelling in her first experience of flying. At a convention in Ngaruawahia, a Maori word meaning the meeting of the waters, flowing water described not only the geographical location, but the spirit of the people, of the meetings, of the Maréchale's sermons on living water, and the weather, which was so wet that a hot water bottle had to be placed inside the piano before it would work.

Returning via South Africa, with its Cape Dutch houses reminiscent of Amsterdam, a South African minister called her a fresh breeze in the land, and then they left, with albatross circling overhead and shoals of flying fish, for Las Palmas, under Franco, with martial law and soldiers with guns in their belts, and the docks at Liverpool.

At home there was news from Maud in America to say that Ballington was gravely ill. 'Oh, the anguish the separations in our family have caused,' wrote Kate. 'But I must *not* go on in this strain. I must not look back, but forward, and must believe the precious promises more ... if we truly desire God's will first, then even should we make a mistake, I have learned, it is not counted to us a mistake, it turns to His glory. We are so mio ... myo ...' caught up in the gist of what she was trying to say, spelling as well as grammar eluded her. ' ... short-sighted.'

The following year she went to Scandinavia where King Haakon and Queen Maud of Norway unexpectedly attended one of her meetings in Oslo. Invited to dinner at the palace the following evening, seated on the right of the Queen, she returned home having made nothing but polite conversation, and felt she had missed an opportunity. Against all the rules of court etiquette, she sent a note to the palace the following day asking to be allowed to see the Queen again, and in return, received a bouquet of flowers and a second invitation. At the end of the meal, summoning her courage to make what she knew to be an impertinent request, she asked to speak with the Queen alone, and when they were together, she put her hand on the Queen's knee, looked into her eyes, and asked 'May I pray with you?'

Kate never revealed what passed between them, except that the Queen's tears fell on her hand while she was praying, and that after they prayed together, the Queen confided in her. 'I can never thank God enough for your visit with my darling wife; joy and peace came over her,' wrote the King, while within the court, it was noticed that a remarkable change had come over the troubled Queen. Before war broke out, she was to visit England for a major operation from which she never recovered; later, the tussle Norway had faced with Hitler was known throughout the world.

Kate returned to tour England through her eightieth birthday. In Glasgow they called her a Celtic Duse, and in Swansea it was said that her preaching displayed all the virility of the most robust male. 'Yet the Maréchale is not that undesirable kind of person, a masculine woman,' they hastened to add. 'She is a gentle, tender-hearted lady.'

Her tongue was still as sharp and as bitterly regretted: 'Will the lady who prayed that extraordinary prayer stay behind to talk to me?' 'I forgot all your sermon except for one thing,' a man said to her. 'You called us glorious humbugs, and I was awake all night, because that is just what I am.' And her humour was as eccentric still, and as devilish. 'She had a heavenly smile of pure joy,' says Noel Palmer, 'and the merriment and the mischievous smile of a child.' Names were a source of unfathomable concern to her. Mr Curry became Mr Powder, and Mr Herring, the Keswick janitor, was summoned imperiously as 'Haddock!' ('I knew it was the name of a fish . . .'). For the most part, mistakes arose from genuine confusion; at times, from obstinacy.

'How do you do, Dr Dyer,' she said, extending a hand to Dr Divine, a Presbyterian minister.

'Mother, it's Dr Divine.'

'No. He's not divine. How do you do, Dr Dyer.'

'Mother, Divine.'

'No. Never.'

'I don't mind what my daughter does so long as she doesn't make herself remarked,' said a mother at a drawing-room meeting.

'Then she cannot be a disciple of Jesus. It is absurd to think that you can follow Jesus and not be remarked. And you will be more and more remarked if you are obedient to the heavenly vision.'

'We must be very prudent,' commented a minister.

'You will never win souls if you are. Cry aloud! Warn, persuade – persuade with tears.'

'Maréchale, I want the power that you speak of,' said a young man. 'Please pray for me.'

'Where is the cross in your life?' she asked him. 'What does your Christianity cost? Renouncement and power are married, and you cannot divorce them.'

'England is pagan,' she wrote in a letter. 'Churches deserted – thirty sold in Islington within a few years. Modernism takes the field and has nothing to show but criticism and death – spiritual death. The Bible is openly pulled to pieces in the churches and on the radio. The Atonement is cut out.

'What an opportunity for the violent, for the kingdom of Heaven suffereth violence, and the violent take it by force. What a chance we have now!'

John Palmer, the Maréchale's grandson and now a journalist in Canada, watched at the Sun Hall in Liverpool with the candid appraisal of a fourteen-year-old. 'There was an immense audience of some 5000 people, and I spent the time wondering

243

just how this grandma of mine could control them in the way she did,' he says.

'The meeting made so much of an impression on me that I have never really been able to take any other evangelist seriously. I have never seen in my life anyone hold an audience in her palm in the way she did at that meeting. Her only props were a microphone – which if I remember correctly, she hardly used – and a pianist. It seemed as if the audience laughed, cried, prayed, sang, or came to the penitent bench at the movement of her finger. It was the most amazing example of audience control I have ever seen, and I have seen a lot of people speak in front of a lot of audiences.

'I cannot remember a word she actually said – although I can guess – but what stands out is the aura which she presented, the way she did it, the dynamite of her presence, her way with words, her incredible charm, and above all, her complete absorption and dedication to her subject.'

A letter from her at that time was begun at three in the morning and finished at five, a careful, paragraph by paragraph analysis of someone else's problem and the possible solutions to it, the only time left in which to write after a busy day, and a practical way of passing the sleepless nights, comforted by tea, a rug, and a hot water bottle.

In 1939, when he was eighty-four years old, Arthur fell downstairs into the garden, and the shock of the fall affected his heart. Four days after their wedding anniversary, on 12 February, he died. They had been married fifty-two years. Anniversaries had inevitably been times of renewal, of hope, and often of regret. 'Pa wrote a sweet note, and I wrote one,' Kate had said on their fortieth anniversary. 'Whatever has happened, I want to make his last years as happy as I can.' And now, when the time came, she was with him, holding his hand, singing his songs to him, and whispering 'You fought the good fight. You are ready.'

Evelyn had come home, giving up her career as a concert pianist in America to 'do what God wanted me to do' and be with her mother – she was to remain with her until the end. 'They had fought so many battles together,' she said. 'It was difficult, because they had to be so often apart, but it was her calling, and God never let her leave that calling. In many ways she grew quicker and quicker while he grew slower, and there were tears, bitter tears, but the fire never went out.'

In a letter to Kate afterwards, Brigadier Wycliffe Booth, Bramwell's son, wrote from the continent. 'Wherever I go in this dear land of Switzerland,' he said, 'the people speak about you, and especially of him. He lit in those brave days of real warfare, a fire which has never died down, and again and again when your songs are sung and when the prayer meetings come to fever heat, the old comrades recall "those days" and speak of his example, and fervour.'

England in 1939 was unsettled, with people trying on gas masks and the constant threat of war. When war broke out, a landmine fell a quarter of a mile away from the house on Highbury Hill, blowing out all the windows, and Kate went to live in a cottage called The Haven on Dame Violet Wills' estate at Hay Tor in Devon. The Haven was two cottages knocked into one, with crazy paving and a rockery and roses growing round the door. There was a pool in the garden with fish swimming in it, and bluebell woods falling away 1400 feet down to Torbay and the sea.

Kate talked a little at local meetings and spent much time in bed because her back was troublesome, writing letters – she had started what she called her Pen Mission, corresponding across the world – and reading Peppini's *Life of Christ*. On the radio Lord Haw-Haw said that the Germans were coming to Newton Abbott, eight miles away, and one night the sky glowed red after a raid on Plymouth. To fend off frustration, she took brisk exercise walking several times daily round the tennis court. Sometimes, without thinking, she said 'I don't like my life.'

Immediately the war ended, she began a campaign in Dublin, where Eva Stuart-Watt had modelled her work in the slums on the Maréchale's work in Paris. Relieved to be active again, letters were written in large, sprawling hand-writing, three or four words to a line, often including Americanisms picked up from her children and grandchildren: 'You are a sermon to me every day, and how!'

'Meetings splendid here,' she wrote from Dublin. 'Crowds overwhelming. We break the laws all the time, packing 2500 in a hall for 2000. I never preached better in my life. Sunday night was marvellous, not only for the crowds, but for the power. I must rest now, as I have a drawing-room meeting tomorrow and

245

Sunday – 2500. I speak in faith, for am very low today and feel utterly unfit . . .'

Since Arthur's death, the old regrets were worrying her: the visions of what might have been. 'I have been greatly perplexed and am tortured all the time regarding the *past*,' she wrote. 'It appears to me I did wrong to leave my father . . .' but more and more frequently her letters were ending with the fiery exuberance of long ago: 'Courage, comrade – en avant! Yours for victory, La Maréchale.'

Although it went against the grain to admit it, big campaigns were more exhausting now, not only physically, but mentally. Arriving back home in Devon during the early hours of the morning, she sat down and wrote to José. 'Darling, I missed your birthday. Been very, very low – through deepest waters God has been more wonderfully kind than I can understand. Ireland was a great big spiritual success, but it is the inner side of me that has suffered. The heart.' Around the edge in the margin of the letter she had scribbled, 'travelled all day – arrived 4 a.m.' At that time, she was eighty-eight.

As she grew older, she began wearing coloured dresses: 'All my life I've worn navy. Now I shall wear pink!' Unable to resist a bargain, even if it was something she had no need of – 'I have a good coat,' she wrote once, ' a *fur* coat – cost £30 and I got it for £16!' – she sported riotous silk bonnets and secondhand dresses which she wore with all the innocent enthusiasm of a child. Given dresses by her daughters, she would wear them until they were threadbare because they had spots on, or flowers, or were a delicate shade of blue: 'This is my *pretty* dress.' Wherever she went, she instinctively sensed need, holding an assistant's hand and sobbing with her among the stockings in Selfridge's, or discovered with her arm round an old man forced to sell his house, praying that God would comfort him in his loneliness and fill his life when the house with its memories of married bliss was gone. By the time she was ninety, her blood pressure was normal for the first time in her life, and her doctor told her that she had the blood and the pulse of a young woman.

Before her ninetieth birthday, she asked Theo to arrange one last meeting where she could meet her old comrades in the Army and talk to them. 'I am still a Salvationist at heart,' she said. Theo met the Chief of Staff of the Salvation Army – the General was away – and told him of his mother's request. A fortnight later, he received a letter saying that it would be impossible for 'Mrs Clibborn' to address a meeting of the Salvation Army. When Kate saw the letter, she wept.

'I shall always remember that,' says Theo. 'She didn't say anything. She just wept. So I said, "Look, darling, be damned to the Chief of Staff, you'll *have* a meeting in London, and you'll *meet* your old comrades," and I went to the Central Hall Westminster and said to Dr Sangster who was there then, 'The Maréchale is ninety this year, and she'd dearly like to have one more meeting in London", and he said "But of course – let her have the Central Hall."'

On her birthday, which fell on a Saturday, she was interviewed on *In Town Tonight*, confounding her interviewer with tales of Whitechapel rats and fighting on the continent.

'It's her ninetieth birthday today. Better known as the Maréchale, she is the eldest daughter of General William Booth, founder of the Salvation Army. Congratulations and many happy returns, Mrs Booth-Clibborn. How have you been celebrating your ninetieth birthday?'

'The big event is tomorrow evening, when I'll address a great meeting in the Westminster Central Hall, but yesterday we did have a family party. I have had ten children you know. I have over twenty grandchildren and twelve great-grandchildren.'

'When all the excitement's over, you'll be taking things easily, won't you?'

'Certainly not. Next Thursday I am flying to the continent for a tour of five weeks . . .'

The next day, Sunday, Salvationists in uniform packed the Central Hall while two or three thousand people unable to gain admittance waited in Parliament Square outside. Congratulatory messages and telegrams from all over the world were read out, and the Maréchale shared the platform with Dr Sangster. For the first time, her memory faltered, the stories muddled, the memories confused, but the message of sacrifice which she had preached all her life came through, and Augustin, the artist and Bohemian agnostic, sat in his seat and wept. The next week she flew to Switzerland for what Evelyn calls the great sunset of her life.

It was dusk when they arrived at Contrin airport in Geneva,

247

with coloured lights twinkling on the lake. Salvationists were waiting to greet her, waving their handkerchiefs in the air as they had done during the big march-pasts in the mountains. Wherever she went to speak, audiences rose and stood in silent tribute as she came onto the stage.

In Lausanne in the church of St Francois, shaped like a cross, with impossibly difficult acoustics, she sang, 'All things are possible if you only believe!' In Neuchâtel, every seat in the Salle de Conference was filled, with many standing in the galleries. 'Neuchâtel has a special place in my heart,' she said to them. 'I have had precious moments here. Now, Neuchâtel, adieu!' The final meeting was held in the Salle de la Réformation in Geneva – 'What can these children teach the city of Calvin?'

'*Nous sommes des lâches,*' she said vehemently to the leaders and the churchmen gathered once more to hear her, the words coming out like a whip. 'We are cowards: *nous sommes des lâches.*'

Evelyn had accompanied her, playing the piano for her, stopping at times to allow her mother's pure high notes to be heard. On the way home, they went to Paris, to the Salvation Army Hall. Evelyn played the piano and Willie had come from America to play his violin. An audience full of French Salvationists stood and cheered and banged tambourines as they had done in the early days, and Wycliffe Booth, Salvation Army Commander in France, who had suggested and arranged the occasion, laid the Salvation Army flag in his aunt's hands.

'Mother's face was indescribable,' says Evelyn. 'Perhaps glory was the word. Her face was full of glory.'

It was the last tour she made. Returning to the Haven in Devon, she spent the fine days walking among the flowers in the garden singing her songs: '*Aimez toujours et malgré tout*: whatever happens, never stop loving.' In 1950, a newspaper reporter asking to what she attributed her vitality received the imperturbable reply, 'Raw onions', but although she repeated the encounter with glee, there were days when she sat in the kitchen and wept: 'I am doing so little for the Lord.' Much of her time was spent in bed in her blue bedroom, facing the big bow window, the brass cowbell from Neuchâtel beside her, writing letters to her family and friends and the people who still sought her advice, filling the pages with her large, round, exuberant hand-writing, spilling over into the margins and writing down the side of the page, ending with a flourish: 'Yours in love and fire, La Maréchale.'

'Oh for Fire from Heaven,' she said, asking to go down and stand on the car and preach to the people. 'Nothing else will meet the need but the Fire!' The Church of England she loved longingly and despairingly, dismissing it in her darkest moments as dead and past recovery: 'It makes me sad to see fine young lives going into a church-yard cemetery.'

Catherine Bramwell-Booth, her niece, compiling a biography of Catherine Booth, the Army mother, came to visit, and found her sitting up in bed with a sheaf of letters in her hand. 'Oh darling Catherine, I've been reading the letters,' she said. 'Such lovely letters.' And then she began to cry. 'Grandma seemed to be rather strict and serious,' said Catherine, and the Maréchale rose up in her bed. 'Of course she was!' she said. 'She took life seriously. Life is serious.'

Her letters indicated a growing frustration. 'My sight has gone dim since I am here. It is the lamps, the eye doctor says. They flare all the time,' she said, speaking irritably of 'this isolated, forsaken spot.' When anyone tried to indulge her, she was indignant. 'I am a warrior,' she said.

'Oh help me by praying for me sometimes,' she begged José. 'I feel often I've failed in *every way*, but I must not listen to the Enemy or my own heart. I feel I should not have left my father . . .'

When Theo asked if she had ever wanted to go back to the Army, she thought long and deeply before replying. 'No,' she said. 'It was marvellous. But it was losing its spiritual impetus. It was all social, social, social work, and necessary as that was in those days of desperate poverty, the Salvation Army wasn't destined to become a soup kitchen.' Another time she spoke of remaining within its ranks, which might have saved it from becoming what she called 'organised to death'. 'There were things I could not agree with,' she said, 'yet could I not have saved it?'

'I was more like him than all the others,' she would say, suddenly interrupting a conversation with her own thoughts. 'I ought not to have left him. How I long to work with him now.'

When she was ninety-five, Billy Graham held a campaign in London at Harringay. 'What are they doing in London?' she asked. 'Thousands are coming to Jesus,' Evelyn told her, and her face filled with delight. 'Souls,' she said. 'I want souls. I want souls for Christ. If you live to be my age,' she would say, sitting up suddenly in her bed and fixing her eye on a visitor, 'you will know that nothing in this world matters but what you have done for Jesus.'

When she died, in May 1955, from double pneumonia, she was ninety-six years old. On her birthday, coming downstairs for lunch as she did every day, she had lectured the assembled family on her philosophy of life. 'Always go on,' she said to them, wagging her long bony index finger. 'My father said that something always happens if you only go on.' José and Evelyn were with her when she died, singing to her until, as José remembers now, 'her familiar heavenly smile came over her face and realising we were drawing her back, we stopped singing and she entered heaven.' Preaching by her graveside where she was buried beside Arthur in Highgate cemetery, Noel Palmer took the text which she had used when she was sixteen years old: 'Let me die the death of the righteous, and let my last end be like His.' 'Her life and her ministry have preached that text to us,' he said. The funeral was as quiet and unremarkable as Arthur's had been. Bramwell's children were there, and so was General Kitching of the Salvation Army, calling her by her title of La Maréchale and praying a final prayer over the grave.

Kate had always condemned hymns about heaven as selfish. 'What do I want to go to heaven for when thousands are perishing?' she asked. 'I want to get on with the work.' Nevertheless, the kingdom of Heaven suffereth violence, and the violent take it by force, and as she had so often said before, 'what joy it will be to meet them in the morning.'

250

BIBLIOGRAPHY

BEGBIE, HAROLD: *Life of William Booth* (Macmillan)

BOOTH, BRAMWELL: *These Fifty Years* (Cassell) *Echoes and Memories* (Hodder and Stoughton)

BOOTH-CLIBBORN, ARTHUR: *Blood against Blood* (Charles C. Cook)

BOOTH-CLIBBORN, ARTHUR AND CATHERINE: *For the Word of God and the Testimony of Jesus*, 1902

BOOTH-CLIBBORN, CATHERINE (THE MARÉCHALE):
A Poet of Praise (Marshall, Morgan and Scott, 1939)
They Endured (Marshall, Morgan and Scott)
Wings of Praise (Marshall, Morgan and Scott)

BOOTH-DEMAREST, VICTORIA: *God, Woman and Ministry* (Valkyrie Press Inc., 1977)

BRAMWELL-BOOTH, CATHERINE: *Bramwell Booth* (Rich and Cowan) *Catherine Booth* (Hodder and Stoughton, 1970)

BUTLER, JOSEPHINE: *The Salvation Army in Switzerland* (Dyer Bros., 1883)

COLLIER, RICHARD: *The General Next to God* (Fontana)

ERVINE, ST JOHN: *God's Soldier* (Heinemann)

GOUT, RAOUL: *Blanche Peyron* (Éditions Altis, 1939)

OTTMAN, FORD C.: *Herbert Booth* (Doubleday, 1928)

RIDLEY, JOHN G.: *The Passion for Christ* (Ambassadors for Christ, 1963)

ROSS, CLIFFORD: *The Maréchale's Tour of Australia and New Zealand*, 1938

SANDALL, ROBERT: *History of the Salvation Army* (Nelson)

STEAD, WILLIAM: *General Booth* (Isbister)

STEWART, JAMES ALEXANDER: *The General's Daughter* (Revival Literature, 1967)

STRACHAN, JAMES: *The Maréchale* (Bethany Fellowship)

WATSON, BERNARD: *Soldier Saint* (Hodder and Stoughton, 1970)

WELTY, SUSAN F.: *Look up and Hope* (Thomas Nelson, New York, 1961)

WILLIAMS, HARRY: *Booth-Tucker* (Hodder and Stoughton, 1980)

INDEX

takes a year's leave, 196; resigns his commission, 196, 198; in U.S.A., 204, 227; and history of the Army in France, 231; death, 231

Booth, Kate, birth, 1, 2; childhood and upbringing, 2–4, 8, 13; open-air speaking, 13–19; wish to go to school, 20–2; travelling evangelist, 22–4; school at Penzance, 25–6; woman officer in Army, 27

sent to France, 29–31; in Paris, 31–46, 55–73; struggles and successes, 40–5; La Maréchale, 44–5; and Arthur Clibborn, 47, 55, 66; and *En Avant*, 58–60; visit from her father, 62; and French opposition, 66, 68–72

in Geneva, 76–8; Swiss opposition, 76–8, 86–90; expelled from Geneva, 80, 82, 84; in Lausanne, 82–3, 93; in Neuchâtel, 95–9, 101; flouts Council's decrees, 105–6; arrest and imprisonment, 106–116, 135, 205; her trial, 116–24; her defence, 120–4; acquittal, 124; return to Paris, 125–8, 134; successes in France, 128–31, 134, 135, 149; and the International Congress, 137; work in Paris, 139–47, 149

engagement to Arthur Clibborn, 150–5; wedding, 154–8; in France after marriage, 158–64; birth of daughter, 165; tour of southern France, 169–70; rescue work, 173–4; fund-raising in America, 174–5; and her growing family, 175–6, 184

ordered to Holland or Germany, 177; begs to stay in France, 177; in Holland, 182, 184–6, 196–7; campaign in Brussels, 184–5, 241; visit from her father, 185; acts against International Headquarters ruling, 185; protest against new Rules and Regulations, 189; absent from Army Exhibition, 189; and Boer War, 190–1; correspon-

dence with her father, 194; new Commissioner sent to Holland and Belgium, 194; three-day interview with her father, 194–5, 217; and the Court of Inquiry, 195; her resignation, 197–8; letter to her colleagues and friends, 199–200

at Zion City, 201–4; travelling, 204–6; at St. Cloud, 205, 207–8; financial difficulties, 209–10; visit from her father, 210–11; return to England, 213; at Westcliffe, 213–17; preaching missions, 215; her father's death, 217–18; at Highbury Hill, 218, 231, 239

and the Keswick Convention, 219–21; 'the heavenly witch', 219; missions to Ireland, 223–7; in Canada and U.S.A., 227–30; at Southampton during dock strike, 230; and history of the Army in France, 231; family deaths, 231–2; successes in France, 233–4; return to Switzerland, 234–6; meetings in Britain, 236–7, 242–4; her book, *They Endured*, 237–8; in Australia and New Zealand, 239–41; in Scandinavia, 242; and Arthur's death, 244–6; Second World War, 245; bombed out of Highbury Hill, 245; at Hay Tor, 245, 248–50; Pen Mission, 245; Dublin campaign after war, 245–6; ninetieth birthday, 246, 247; request to address Army meeting refused, 246–7; Central Hall meeting, 247; *In Town Tonight*, 247; last visit to Switzerland, 248–9; death and funeral, 250

Booth, Lucy, 19, 22; married to Emmanuel Hellberg, 178; takes command in France and Switzerland, 178; mutiny of French officers, 183–4

Booth, Marian, 19

Booth, William, 28, 61, 67, 71, 72, 93, 157, 164, 171–2, 175, 182, 202, 205, 209, 210, 213, 232, 249, 250; at